THE **BEATLES**
IN SCOTLAND

THE BEATLES

IN SCOTLAND

KEN McNAB

Polygon

To the other half of the sky … this book is dedicated to
My wonderful wife Susanna and my children Jennifer and Christopher.

Polygon
is an imprint of
Birlinn Limited
West Newington House
10 Newington Road
Edinburgh
EH9 1QS

First published in 2008

www.birlinn.co.uk

ISBN13: 978 1 84697 112 9

British Library Cataloguing-in-Publication Data
A catalogue record for this book is available
from the British Library

Layout: Mark Blackadder

Printed and bound by MPG Books Ltd,
Bodmin, Cornwall, United Kingdom,

Contents

Preface

Someone recently asked me: 'Why do you like The Beatles so much?' I started to reach for an answer that has become almost stock-in-trade. The songs that changed the world, the soundtrack for a generation, the special chemistry between these four guys, the albums such as *Revolver, Sgt. Pepper, Abbey Road* that raised the bar so much higher . . .

Then I realised a simple truth. I like The Beatles so much because the music makes me happy. And it's been making me happy ever since, as a 14-year-old schoolboy in Glasgow, I first heard the 1962–66 compilation, *The Red Album.* Now I am older, so much older than yesterday, but my enthusiasm remains undimmed. The songs still make me happy. All of them.

From the raucous 1-2-3-4 intro of 'I Saw Her Standing There' to the mercurial brilliance of 'Strawberry Fields Forever' to the elegiac genius of 'Let It Be'. Growing up, there was nothing like a Beatles song to track your mood through the pitted path from adolescence to adulthood.

When my good friend Russell Leadbetter first suggested a book about The Beatles in Scotland, my instinctive reaction was to straight bat it with a 'Thanks, but no thanks,' reply. And I did. The reason? There's not enough material. And did the world need another book about The Beatles? And yet . . . a sapling of an idea had been planted. What if . . .

I knew John Lennon's cousin Stan Parkes lived in Largs and I went to see him as a first point of contact. It was purely exploratory. I expected nothing except to shake the hand that shook the hand of the late great Johnny Ace. Stan, though, was warm and welcoming and regaled me with tales of the mischievous kid who spent his summer holidays in the Scottish Highlands. Then of course there were the numerous trips north when his band became 'quite well known'. Not forgetting the car crash outside Tongue that saw him spend a week in a cottage hospital.

By the time I got back home, the sapling was beginning to take root in my mind. As well as John's links to Durness, Paul McCartney's connections to Argyll run deeper than a simple song in homage to the Mull of Kintyre.

Then there was The Silver Beetles' first tour . . . a tour that started in Alloa three long years before the first scream of Beatlemania was heard. And, of course, there were the Scottish concerts that took place when the tidal wave of Beatlemania crashed upon the rocks of popular culture. Who saw them in places like Alloa? What did they remember? Was the hysteria

Crowds outside the ABC in Edinburgh's Lothian Road, 1964.

for real or an urban myth? Were they any good?

And what about all those Scots who stood out so prominently in the circle of famous friends of John, Paul, George and Ringo – people like Donovan, Lulu, Sir Jackie Stewart, Davey Johnstone, Hamish Stuart. And has time simply airbrushed away the fact that one of the original Beatles was, in fact, a Scot? Woah! Getting ahead of yourself a bit here.

But in that hour's drive to Glasgow, I came to realise The Beatles loved Scotland and the evidence was all there. What I was unprepared for was just how astonishing that evidence would turn out to be.

This has been a labour of love, consummated by the joy in talking to so many people who have had some connection to The Beatles in Scotland. These days are past now and in the past they must remain. But I hope this book will rekindle some joyous memories for those who can truly say: 'We were there.' And for the rest of you it may open a page to an era that brought us some of the best music in modern times. Music that makes me happy.

The Beatles long ago passed the audition. I hope I've managed to do the same.

Special thanks are due to the following people in the without whom department: Stan and Jan Parkes, Russell Leadbetter, Ronnie Anderson at the *Sunday Mail* picture desk, *The Daily Record* library staff; *The Evening Times* picture desk, especially Grace; Kerry Black at the *Scotsman* picture library, Bill McLoughlin at DC Thomson, George Burton, Derek Yeaman, Fraser Watson, Donovan, Johnny Gentle, Gavin Askew, Lulu, Iain Leckie, Hamish Stuart, Pete Nash, The British Beatles Fan Club, Sir Jackie Stewart, Davey Johnstone, Richard Park, Len Murray, Linda Thomson, Al Stewart, Andy White, Barbara Dickson, the guys in *Marmalade,* the Campbeltown Pipe Band, Paul Young all the people I spoke to who saw the band back in the day, brother Ian, Bridget and Kieran, Caroline and Allan, Linda and Kieran, Jacqueline and Ronnie, Terrance and Anne-Marie, Drew and Maureen, Isobel, Gail, Keith and all the Broons, Sean Costello, Neville Moir at Polygon, designer Mark Blackadder and my agent Mark Stanton, mum and dad. And, of course, John, Paul, George and Ringo.

Ken McNab
Summer 2008

1. Durness

September, 1979. Dawn. Hong Kong harbour. The first crimson streaks of a new day break the sky with colour. No one gives the stranger gazing out over the junks and sampans a second glance. Yet there is an air of familiarity about him, a faint echo of memory. His long hair is swept back in a ponytail and his face is framed by a large bushy beard. In profile, his distinct aquiline nose looks almost aristocratic. He's wearing a long coat, a fedora and white tennis shoes. Between his fingers smoulders the ever-present Gitane, held at its familiar rakish angle.

John Lennon's eyes were fixed on the famous shipping lanes, the soft breeze washing over his face and the smell of the sea in his nostrils. Behind him, the giant peak of Mount Victoria towered above the oriental skyline. But John was 6,000 miles away from here. In a time before fame. Before money. Before the mania. Before The Beatles. In his mind's eye, John was about 11 and running through the rugged countryside of Sutherland in the far north of Scotland with his older cousin, Stan Parkes. Summer holidays were always spent at his Aunt Mater's seven-acre croft in the village of Durness, the most northerly village on this gnarled but beautiful coastline. Together, the two boys would comb the beaches looking for shells, build dykes, fish for salmon, draw the odd sketch and chat away to the local crofters.

Imagine. It's tempting to think that's what the youngster did as he felt the silver sands shift beneath his feet, followed by a blast of the searing wind as it whipped off the Atlantic. Looking round the bay, he would see rocks that had been weathered by the elements every day for millions of years, leaving the environs of Sango Bay resembling a lower jaw of rotting teeth.

Lennon once wrote a song about isolation. Durness was isolation in its purest form. The nearest train station lay 60 miles to the south. In the other direction, single-track dirt roads hugged the coastline. To the west lay Cape Wrath, as far north as you can go on the mainland. In the other direction, John O' Groats signposted the jutting edge of remote north-eastern Britain. The clear Highland air and stunning landscapes were a world removed from the smoke-belching factories of post-war Liverpool. And that feeling of unfettered freedom, the memory of those innocent summer days spent exploring the sea caves, hills, glens and Stone Age ruins never left him.

Now, in Hong Kong some 28 years later, the same longing had returned, washing over him like a ghostly reminder of more carefree times, of the fact that all his yesterdays were now carefully folded away. John said: 'I wandered around Hong Kong at dawn and it was a thrill. I was looking out over the bay when something rang a bell. It was the recognition – My God! This relaxed person is me from way back. It was rediscovering a feeling that I once had as a youngster walking the mountains of Scotland with an auntie. The heather . . . the mist. I thought – aha. This is the feeling that makes you write or paint . . . it was with me all my life! It's so overpowering that you have to tell somebody. So you put it into poetry or whatever. But that feeling . . . that's where it all began . . . And that's why I'm free of The Beatles, because I took time to discover that I was John Lennon before The Beatles and will be after The Beatles.'

Indeed, that long-submerged awakening was the first crackle of an electrical charge that ultimately lit up popular music forever and created a legend. It was also the start of a secret love affair with Scotland that continued right up until the moment a deranged fan snuffed out the life of the man who was the pioneering spirit of The Beatles and the maverick standard-bearer for a generation. In one of his final letters to Stan from his New York home, John wrote with typically mischievous word play: 'It's a braw, bricht, moonlicht nicht since I last had a word.' And, in another, he declared: 'You know I miss Scotland more than England.'

Stan told me: 'It was a typical thing for him to say. He had a tremendous affection for Scotland. These holidays in Durness were very special to him. It was a different world to the one he was used to. The area made a lasting impression. I never heard him say a bad word about Durness all his life. These were very happy times for John and I suppose that's why the memories stayed with him. And I was so glad to share them with him. We had a very special bond. He was always great fun even though he was a bit of a rascal from time to time. But I remember the other kids in the village always looked forward to seeing John because he was so much fun to be around. He was a real boy, full of energy and always looking at things differently.'

Often, when working at home on demo recordings, he would break into a broad Scottish accent, lampooning his own musical efforts. 'Ah cannae dae it, ah cannae dae it,' he chuckled in a mock Scots brogue as the first, embryonic, wistful version of 'Strawberry Fields Forever' breaks down after a few seconds.

Scotland was in John's blood and the first transfusion took place in the three-bedroom cottage at 56 Sangomore at Sango Bay. Here it was that the young Lennon ran free every summer from 1950 to 1955. But it's only when you actually visit the croft at Durness that you begin to appreciate

the effect the location must have had on young John's city sensibility. The house stands atop a windswept pinnacle, looking down like a sentinel on the rest of the village. In the distance, you can just about make out the fringes of the wondrous beaches that must have been the ideal summer playground. And a brisk five-minute walk would take him to the clifftop passageway leading down to the entrance of Smoo Cave, a natural rock formation creating a doorway into the very hillface. In front of him the mighty Atlantic seems to go on forever before, in a child's imagination, falling off the end of the world.

John's Highland holiday retreat was the perfect escape from a home life that was anything but conventional. He was raised by his mother's eldest sister, Mimi, from the age of five. His parents, Julia and Freddie, had separated. At one point, Freddie, a merchant seaman and the scourge of his young bride's family, had given the young John an ultimatum: either come with me to start a new life in New Zealand or stay with your mum. After a second's hesitation, the boy, aged just five, ran to his mother's arms. And didn't look back. Julia, though, was a free spirit and not yet ready to take on full-time responsibility for a child. So Mimi, the family matriarch and the eldest of four headstrong Stanley sisters, stepped in, and John was raised at Mendips, the couple's semi-detached bungalow in the middle-class Liverpool suburb of Woolton. John was not the working-class hero of Beatle mythology.

When he was older, parental responsibility during the school summer holidays was shared by another Stanley sister, John's Aunt Elizabeth. Known to her family as Mater, Elizabeth had remarried and her second husband was Bert Sutherland, an Edinburgh dentist whose family owned the croft in Durness. Mater's son Stan was seven years older than John.

Left. The house, with its stunning views over the North Atlantic, was John's holiday retreat for every summer between the ages of nine and fifteen.

Right. This plaque was fixed to the outside of the house during the Northern Lights Festival in 2007 to commemorate the link with the village's most famous holidaymaker.

Stan (left) and a young John stand outside a relative's home in Liverpool. Even at that age, both boys were close.

But, despite the age gap, the two cousins shared a deep friendship. And he took John under his wing during those rumbustious summer days.

Stan, now 75, recalled: 'When I first moved to Scotland from Fleetwood in Lancashire, I would go down to bring John up because his Aunt Mimi wouldn't let him go anywhere unchaperoned, but as he got a bit older, she relented and let him come on the bus. She would put him on the bus at Liverpool and that would come up through all the border towns of Scotland to Edinburgh. I'd meet him off the bus at Edinburgh bus depot and take him to my parent's home at Ormidale Terrace near Murrayfield rugby stadium in Edinburgh. He would stay there for a week or so, then off we'd go to the family croft in Sutherland at Durness.

'What a lot of people don't realise is that John went frequently to Durness, from the age of 9 until he was 15. My stepfather owned a Highland croft based in the village. It was in his family for generations and it always had to be worked as a croft even though my stepfather used it as a holiday home. It had to have sheep on it otherwise the crofting commission would take it off you.

'I used to take him up in a van or a car. We'd call in at Kirkcaldy where my stepfather's brother Angus lived and we'd pick up bits and pieces and furniture that he'd collected to go up to the croft. And I'd be driving John up and I'd get up as far as Inverness and he'd say, "Where are all these mountains? I don't see any mountains. You said there were a lot of mountains." I said, "John you haven't really hit the real Highlands yet." Anyway further on up from Lairg to Durness you're passing through various bits of the road where there are drops of 20, 30 feet either side and massive mountains overpowering you and then he went white as a sheet and said, "Oh, I see what you mean now."

'John always remembered his times at Durness. He had a fantastic memory. He loved the wilderness and the openness of the place. We went fishing and hunting and up into the hills to draw or write poetry. John really loved hillwalking, shooting and fishing, which is perhaps not the image most people would have of him. He used to catch salmon. He would have been quite a laird.'

John's annual pilgrimage was often a signal for the start of the summer holidays proper among the other kids in Durness. They were intrigued by the cheeky and irrepressible youngster from Liverpool, which must have seemed like the other side of the world. But for all his urban upbringing, John mingled well with the village children. One of them was Iris MacKay, who still runs a shop in Durness. She said: 'We just played together. We behaved just like children normally do, hit each other with seaweed and chased each other on the beach. We were always glad to see them. We didn't see that many kids from England at that time. It just added to the whole holiday feeling. They came several times over a period of a good few years. John wasn't famous then, of course. He was just another boy on his holiday.'

Lennon's links with Durness might have faded into the Highland mist had it not been for a chance encounter Stan had with the local primary school headteacher. Graham Bruce was rendered speechless when Stan told him of his famous cousin and of his connections to the place that was as far from Beatlemania as Mars. Graham listened intently as Stan regaled him with tales of his famous young cousin and a seed was sown, one that in the last few years has succeeded in earning Durness its own mark of distinction on the Scottish tourist map.

Graham recalled: 'We came to Durness in 1984. At that time, Stan and his wife Jan were still living in the village. I got to know them through the church and he told me this story about John Lennon. Well, I just laughed out loud and said you've got to be joking. You don't associate John Lennon with Scotland let alone Durness. So I became absolutely fascinated by this connection to John Lennon. I have checked a lot of books on The Beatles and that very important early influence isn't mentioned. Yet it would appear from Stan's stories that Durness had a fairly major impact on his life. You could easily picture the effect it would have on a young John Lennon coming here on holiday away from all the grime and industry of the city. The contrast must have been enormous for him.

'I felt that, as a community, we just didn't play up to this. Local people also tended to be dismissive. They would say, oh yes he came here, but they didn't seem to realise how significant this was. So it was always in the back of my mind that we should do something to recognise the fact that this very significant character had such close links with Durness.'

In 2002, work started to renovate the village hall and overhaul the gardens, which had become overgrown and overrun with weeds and dead shrubs. When Stan quietly suggested that perhaps a small memorial to John could be erected in the garden, he set a hare running in Graham's mind. He contacted the makers of BBC Scotland's long-running *The Beechgrove Garden* to gauge if they would be interested in joining forces with the village to create a horticultural tribute to Durness's most famous holidaymaker. 'But their first reaction was one of disbelief,' Graham recalled. 'They just said, "John Lennon up in Durness? He was never up there." But when we told them the story, they agreed to come up for a look and see if it was feasible.'

So it was that a BBC team went to Durness to check out Graham's tale and to see if they could be convinced about the practicality of creating a John Lennon memorial garden in one of Scotland's last untamed wildernesses. Programme producer Gwyneth Hardie recalled: 'We set out for Durness, which is extremely remote. Even from Aberdeen, it is five hours of miserable driving. It was the most astonishing landscape, it gave us goosebumps and our mouth dropped open round every bend. It is a small community yet they had managed to raise half a million pounds to build their own community hall. We met these guys and they were so welcoming and so together and just thought immediately they were going to be able to do this. We just felt we had to do this one, this is fantastic. Obviously for us the John Lennon connection was a nice hook. But it was all about the people and the place as well as John.'

Work on transforming the garden took three days in the middle of August 2002. The centrepiece was three standing stones created by local craftsman, Neil Fuller, inscribed with lyrics from 'In My Life', the classic Lennon-McCartney song from the 1965 album *Rubber Soul* said to have been inspired by John's visits to Durness. Taking centre stage at the

Stan (centre) with John's sister Julia and cousin David Birch at the memorial garden renovated in the former Beatle's name outside Durness village hall.

opening ceremony was Stan Parkes, his mind drifting back to the days when he and his wee cousin didn't have a care in the world as they ran from house to house and raced along the beach. Stan said at the time: 'John would be thrilled with this tribute and I know it would have meant more to him than any fancy statue in a hotel or whatever in Liverpool. He really loved Durness and he would have loved this.'

Beechgrove presenter Lesley Watson said: 'The work the local community put into creating the garden is amazing. Durness is a special place and to have this link with John commemorated in this way is lovely.'

The *Beechgrove Garden* programme was only screened in Scotland, but still generated a huge reaction from Beatles fans all over the country. It also proved to be the catalyst for a special event to mark the special significance of John's Highland hideaway – and the John Lennon Northern Lights Festival was born. The idea for a three-day celebration of the arts in September immediately caught fire. Among those who agreed to take part were former Runrig singer Donnie Munro and the reunited Quarrymen – John's first group – who in the autumn of their years have found a fantastic new following on the Beatles fan circuit. One of the biggest boosts came from the Queen's Master of Music, Sir Peter Maxwell Davies, who broke a 15-year performing exile to premiere a specially-written Beatles Prom with students from the Royal Academy of Music.

The festival was immediately endorsed by John's nearest and dearest including Stan, his sisters Julia Baird and Jackie and cousin David Birch.

Even Yoko Ono, who had been involved in a car accident on the occasion of their only visit to Scotland as a couple, was happy to lend her backing. In a message to the festival organisers that seemed at odds with eye-witness accounts of the time, she said: 'I have a very sweet memory of Durness, having made the trip there with John, who wished to share his childhood memory with me and had even decided at the time that he would drive the car himself to make the trip a very private one. I would most certainly love to lend my co-operation to this splendid venture to bring the world's attention to Scotland, the most beautiful and magical country, with John's name, his memory and a lovely one of mine as well.'

Stan was delighted by the success of the Northern Lights Festival: 'It has exceeded all our expectations. I wanted it to celebrate John the artist and poet, not necessarily John the pop star and I think it did that. There was a great spirit about it.'

● ● ●

As John's oldest surviving relative, Stan Parkes remains his most enduring link with Scotland. Between 1963 and 1965, The Beatles played 22 Scottish concerts, including matinee shows. And Lennon would always try to find a way to escape the mayhem to snatch a few hours with his cousin's family in Edinburgh. Even in later years, when John moved permanently to America with second wife Yoko Ono, Stan would still receive the occasional cheeky postcard from 'Jock' Lennon. Now living in Largs, Stan has every right to be called an honorary Scotsman and has done as much as anyone to talk up John's Caledonian connections as well as being the proud gatekeeper of the Lennon name on this side of the Atlantic.

Despite the geographical distance between Liverpool and Edinburgh, the two boys would see each other as often as school timetables allowed. And, in a book published last year, it was revealed how Stan played a huge part in building bridges between the young John and his mother Julia, especially at the onset of adolescence. In her own memoir of these times, John's half sister Julia said Stan would often go behind Aunt Mimi's back to spirit Lennon away for a secret rendezvous with his mum. Contact with Julia grew, a rapprochement fostered by Stan, although the task of turning the boy into a man was Mimi's. Throughout his adolescence, however, John, for all Mimi's nesting instincts, inherited his mother's restless and rebellious gene. And music, specifically a shared love of the banjo, was the cord that bound them together.

At the age of 15 John heard the radiowaves crackle with Elvis Presley's libido-charged vocals on 'Heartbreak Hotel'. Suddenly, all that pent-up rebellion, hemmed in by Mimi's well-intentioned discipline, exploded.

And from then on, music dominated John's life. He cajoled a group of schoolpals into forming their own group, The Quarrymen, named after their school, Quarry Bank. And he persuaded Mimi, against all her protests, to buy him a guitar. John was besotted and also honed his musical talents on a harmonica, striving to blow out the same raw blues he heard from black American artistes. But fate intervened once again during one of his last holiday journeys to Scotland.

Stan recalled: 'John originally had a very cheap little mouth-organ. I don't know whether he got it at Woolworths or what. Anyway he was keen on learning the mouth-organ and he would play it on the bus coming up to Scotland, probably driving everyone scatty. Anyway, the conductor had been listening to him and when he got to Edinburgh he said, "You're quite good on that mouth-organ. Would you like a real professional one with side buttons and everything?" "Oh yes!" he said. "Well there was a passenger left one on the bus months ago and it's never been played." He said, "If you come back to the bus station tomorrow, I'll give it to you." So I took John there the next morning and he was given this mouth-organ. He had it for years and in fact he played it on some of his records. Eventually he took it to America and had it in the Dakota building in New York, I believe.'

Six years later, that same mouth-organ was destined to announce The Beatles onto the world stage. The instrument was used for the distinctive bluesy blast that was the hallmark of 'Love Me Do' and 'Please Please Me', the band's first two singles.

John had total recall of his trips to Edinburgh, Scotland's capital city having made an indelible imprint on the youngster's mind. He remembered: 'Edinburgh was one of my favourite cities. The Edinburgh Festival and the Tattoo in the castle. All of the bands of the world's armies would come and march and play. I always remember feeling very emotional about it, especially at the end where they put all the lights out and there's just one guy playing the bagpipes, lit by a lone spotlight.'

Amazingly, Stan was also a witness to the day that John Lennon first met Paul McCartney. Lennon's school band, The Quarrymen, had been handed their first ever semi-professional gig at the Woolton Church fête on Saturday, 6 July 1957. Stan and his sisters had been visiting their Liverpool cousins and there was a ripple of excitement at the prospect of John's band playing in public.

Mimi, naturally, was horrified, but Julia could hardly contain her excitement. John steeled his nerves by having a couple of – illegal – light ales. Stan takes up the story: 'We were all very excited. It was a big thing for all of us that he was actually going to be playing on stage. I remember that it was a sunny day. We just wandered along until we heard him belting out this song. He sounded great, he had so much confidence even at that young age. Afterwards, we went to a backstage area and he was talking to this other boy. There was no big fanfare or anything. He just mentioned casually that this was Paul. But right away you couldn't help being impressed by Paul. He was more musical than John, especially on the guitar. But The Quarrymen was John's band. And he had to decide whether to let this young guy into the band. Paul right away noticed that John was playing the guitar strangely. He noticed instantly that John was playing banjo chords on the guitar. So he showed him some guitar chords he knew.

'At the time, we didn't think an awful lot about it. It was only later when The Beatles became so big that I could look back and say I was actually there when John met Paul for the first time. But for the family, it was just the fact he was playing on a stage for the first time that was the big thing.'

Stan naturally remained close to John as The Quarrymen slowly morphed into The Beatles with various members quitting and George Harrison and, later, Ringo Starr joining the ranks. But he had no inkling that his young cousin was in on the ground floor of a musical revolution. He said: 'We had no idea that this phenomenon would happen. John brought up his demo record of "Love Me Do" to Edinburgh and we thought, "Oh, this is great." And then "Please Please Me" went up the chart. I thought, this is going to be a bit of a success here. We've got a fine musician in the family. And then of course the concerts started and the film career started and we, as the family, were invited to these, the likes of the film premiere of *A Hard Day's Night* in Liverpool. We all went to that and the civic reception afterwards in Liverpool Town Hall. He's up on the balcony with the rest of them waving to the crowds, and of course half of Liverpool was inside the Town Hall and one of the family got lost in the crowd and John said, "Where's my family? I can't see my relatives," and we're saying, "We're over here, we're over here." "Oh," he said, "come up to the front." So we were very excited.

'We went down to the film premiere of *Help!* and to the reception at the Dorchester Hotel after. Princess Margaret was at that and she had her own private room. So it was sent through that she would like to have a dance with John Lennon and he said, "I'm not going to have a dance with Princess Margaret. I can't dance." I said, "John that's a royal command, if you don't go she'll have you locked up in the Tower of London and beheaded." "She wouldn't would she?" I said, "Yes." "Oh, I'd better go." And he did go and have a dance with Princess Margaret.'

When Beatlemania erupted into a worldwide phenomenon, Stan was simply stunned. Lennon always said that, for the four Beatles, it was like living in the eye of a hurricane. Staying grounded amid the money, adoration and the publicity would have been tough for anyone, let alone four working-class kids from Liverpool. But with the mayhem still in its infancy, John and Stan's bond remained strong. Although Stan was always quick to snuff out the flames of John's considerable ego.

'He was always very forthright. But if you stood up to him, he usually backed down. When The Beatles came up north to do gigs, John would normally stay with my mother in Ormidale Terrace in Edinburgh while the others were in hotels, until he got just too famous. Then they had a hideaway at the Roman Camp Hotel in Callander. On one occasion, however, John stayed with Jan and I at our home in Currie. The following morning after breakfast I took John down to the R.S. McColl shop for some ciggies. The girl behind the counter almost fainted when she looked up and saw who it was. The fans weren't expecting to see him where we lived, but they found out eventually.

'Jan and I once ran him up to Perth for a concert because that's where he was joining the rest of the band. The three of us had lunch at the Salutation Hotel and then John was going to meet up with Paul, George and Ringo. But when we stepped out of the Salutation Hotel, our car was covered in lipstick messages. It was wild, crazy.'

The family ties that bound Stan and John together were never broken throughout the tumultuous decade that The Beatles reigned as rock royalty. Stan said: 'He was a great letter writer and we always got postcards wherever he was in the world. In fact, in the mid seventies, he rang me up and asked me to send him a full Highland outfit including a kilt. He also asked if he could have my chanter for the bagpipes. I've never seen any pictures of him in a kilt, that would have been something. But I don't think he quite mastered the bagpipes.

'The other thing I had to send him out was a copy of the *Broons* annual. He loved things like that. John stayed close to his family. At one point, he found out from *The Times* in London that the Durness estate where he spent so many happy times was up for sale. Right away, he said he wanted to buy it. But as usual with John, he just left it too late. And it was bought by a Dutch and Belgian consortium. It's curious to think that, had that worked out, he and Paul McCartney would both have been Scottish landowners. I think John would have loved the idea of being a Highland laird, but it wasn't to be.

'In the same way, when my parents died, their home at 15 Ormidale Terrace in Edinburgh was put up for sale as part of my stepfather's estate. And John wrote me a letter saying he would have bought the house had he known. Again, he was too late. But right up to the end of his life he said he was coming home and wanted a big family reunion, possibly in Scotland. In his last letter to me just before he died, he said he always missed Scotland more than England. In that last letter he quoted a famous Scottish song that says, "It's a braw, bricht moonlicht nicht." He wrote, "Come on man, send me a postcard. Life is short." So it turned out to be very poignant.'

• • •

It was one of those curious draws from the deck of life that John Lennon should shut the door on the sixties in almost the same way he began that tumultuous decade – by being involved in a car crash in the remote Scottish Highlands. On 23 May 1960, John was abruptly woken from his golden slumbers when the van taking The Silver Beetles to Fraserburgh crashed front-on with an Austin saloon carrying two pensioners on the A96 just outside Banff. The band's van was being driven by Johnny Gentle, the Liverpool singer the band was backing on their first venture north of the border. Lennon, asleep in the front passenger seat, was all shook up but unhurt and, in the best showbiz traditions, that night's show still went on, the shunt dismissed as a consequence of life on the road.

Just over nine years later, on 1 July 1969, John's karma would not be so fortunate. A sentimental journey to take Yoko, his son Julian and his new wife's daughter Kyoko, to Durness, the Highland village where he had enjoyed so many happy summer holidays as a boy, ended in a ditch at the side of a single track road near Tongue. An ambulance arrived from Wick to ferry all four some 40 miles south to the Lawson Memorial Hospital in Golspie where they spent five days recovering from the accident. John received 17 stitches in his face, just along his jawline, while Yoko had 14 to repair a gash on her forehead.

Normally, that would be the beginning and end of the story. But John

Left. Lawson Memorial Hospital came under siege from reporters and TV crews when John and Yoko were ferried there by ambulance following their car crash just outside Tongue.

Right. The hospital entrance has remained largely unchanged forty years after the Lennons were ushered through the front door, bleeding from their crash injuries.

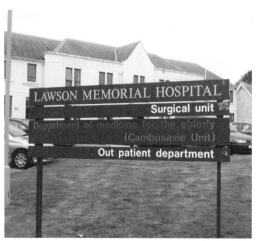

Lennon, of course, was no ordinary tourist. And this was no ordinary tale of an accidental car crash. For the best part of a week, the cottage hospital played host to a media circus that pitched its big top on the giant lawn at the front of the wards.

Every spare B&B room in Golspie and nearby Brora was quickly snapped up as TV crews and newspaper reporters flocked to the Highlands. Some flew into Inverness and then headed further north by car. Others drove the whole way from either Glasgow or Edinburgh. It was a huge story. The headlines circled the world. The maverick Beatle turned global peace campaigner, his Japanese wife of just four months and their two children – laid up in a tiny Highland hospital.

It was the last thing the Lennons wanted. If anything, John had planned the holiday to try to escape the glare of publicity that constantly shone on their lives – attention, it has to be said, they had largely encouraged. Amazingly, however, much of the circumstances surrounding this incident, the people whose lives it briefly touched and the legends it created, have disappeared from the pages of Lennon's life. The reason is simple. John and Yoko used their unexpected incarceration to haul the drawbridge up on their public activities. During their five-day stay, the couple shunned the almost hourly requests for interviews or photographs. In fact, so reclusive were they that rumours quickly grew that it was yet another weird stunt in the world according to the Lennons.

At one point a posse of pressmen sent in a joint communiqué suggesting a single interview with one of them which they could all share. John's handwritten reply? 'Get well soon lads.'

So although it was a massive media event, it generated very little newsworthy copy, much to the annoyance of news editors and foreign bureau chiefs. Indeed, a scan of the newspaper archives of Scottish publications such as the *Scotsman*, the *Herald*, the *Daily Record* and the then market leader the *Daily Express* reveal scant evidence that the Lennons were even there, such was the dearth of information.

Hospital staff may have been privately amused at the goings on. Publicly, though, they respected the couple's wish to be left alone without any special privileges. Still, it was hard for some not to acknowledge the fact they had a Beatle in their ward. By the time he was discharged from the Lawson, John had left his own distinctive mark on the staff at the hospital and one or two key members of the local community. And almost all of them have until now maintained a near 40-year silence on what was the last time John ever set foot in Scotland, a country that had forever earned a place in his heart.

First, though, it's important to shade in the background to this long-lost episode in the Lennons' lives. In the summer of 1969, John was the most famous person on the planet. Forget the fact he was a Beatle, a badge of honour that brought its own unrelenting fame. John had become a figurehead of the growing counter-culture movement which had radicalised the world's youth. There was a whiff of revolution in the air. American imperialism in Vietnam and the sight of Soviet tanks rolling into Czechoslovakia and Hungary had lit a torch of defiance among millions – and John Lennon appointed himself as the movement's *de facto* prince of peace.

The start of 1969 saw The Beatles slowly imploding before the cameras during the shooting of *Let It Be*. Arguments raged over their music and, eventually, over the appointment of New York hustler Allen Klein as the man to guide their futures. Away from Abbey Road studios, the swirling currents of John's private life had created a fountainhead of controversy. He was under fire from all sides after leaving wife Cynthia for the Japanese avant-garde artist who was, in his eyes, a mirror image non-conformist. John and Yoko soon became submerged under a single identity. The couple married on 20 March in Gibraltar, eight days after his songwriting partner Paul McCartney wed Linda Eastman.

The next day, they travelled to Amsterdam for the first of the famous bed-ins that would ultimately raise John's global profile from barmy Beatle to serious non-violence protester. For the next three months, they were never off the front pages or TV screens as they rallied the world to 'Give Peace a Chance' and end US involvement in Vietnam and other conflict hotspots. They became trapped on a self-created publicity rollercoaster that looped around them 24/7, eight days a week. And in between, they made avant-garde movies, founded their own film production company, released their second solo album, *Unfinished Music, No. 2: Life with the Lions* and splashed out £150,000 on Tittenhurst Park, an 18th-century house near Ascot. And Lennon showed the spark with Paul could still light up when they were the only Beatles to work on the recording of 'The Ballad of John and Yoko'. On the same day, he officially changed his name to John Ono Lennon, consigning his mother's patriotic choice of Winston as a middle name to the history books. As if all that wasn't enough, John announced in the middle of June that Yoko was pregnant.

Burn-out was fast approaching when a window appeared in their schedule at the end of June. So John hit upon the perfect idea for a get-away-from-it-all break to Liverpool and Scotland. Initially, he wanted to introduce Yoko to his relatives in Edinburgh, hoping naturally to win approval for their controversial union. From there he planned to head further north to Durness to rekindle the teenage love affair he had always enjoyed with the most remote village on mainland Britain. They could stop off on the way at B&Bs, just like regular tourists, he reckoned.

This was fine in principle. Except somewhere along this road of thought one of them – history disagrees over which one – suggested John drive the 700-odd miles from their home in Surrey to Sutherland. It was an almost comical decision, one that perfectly illustrated either John's charming naivety or Yoko's insistence that he behave like 'a real man', as one biographer has suggested. John had passed his driving test some four years earlier, but, despite buying a fleet of luxury cars like the psychedelic Roller and a Ferrari, he was a shocking driver. His highway skills were rusty and his eyesight, famously myopic at the best of times, made his driving even more erratic. Of course, he rarely needed to get behind the wheel since there was always an Apple flunky on hand to ferry him to all points across his own personal universe. But the minute he turned the key in the ignition, he was an accident waiting to happen. Their chauffeur Les Antony offered to drive them all the way but John and Yoko were deter-mined it would be a back-to-basics experience without any of the usual rock star trimmings.

And so it was that on 29 June, the Lennons set off on their adventure. That meant leaving behind the Roller and opting instead for a hired green and yellow Mini which had barely enough room for all four of them, plus their luggage. It also involved the biggest risk of all. Forget the fact that John couldn't possibly expect to stay incognito; the real gamble lay in driving them all the way.

The first stopover was in Liverpool to visit his Aunt Harriet and her husband Norman and touch base with old friends, but even by then the car was toiling. Unused to being behind the wheel, John often charged through the gears. They pulled into a service station where the resident mechanic took one look and told John the clutch was burned out and the gearbox wasted. Antony was duly summoned to drive up to the old hometown with John's other runaround, a white Maxi, which the next day – the last day of June – the couple commandeered for the next, cross-country, leg over the Pennines and across the border towards Edinburgh.

They arrived at the Scottish capital without mishap, eagerly looking forward to their stay in the city John knew so well. Just as eagerly antici-pated was the prospect of spending quality time as a family. First stop was Aunt Mater's house in Ormidale Terrace in Haymarket where she and Bertie were waiting to meet Yoko for the first time along with Stan. No one knew quite what to expect. Mater had always been close to John's first wife Cynthia and had natural reservations about her nephew's new paramour. Mater, like all the strong women in the Lennon family, spoke her mind and had made her feelings crystal-clear over John's divorce from Cynthia, a pretty Liverpool lass who knew her place and respected her elders. Yoko, unconventional and not conventionally pretty, and carrying baggage from

two failed marriages, was far from Mater's template of a Lancashire Stepford wife.

Naturally, she was delighted to see her famous nephew, although she could scarcely recognise him at first beneath the shock of hair covering his shoulders and framing his face. Bertie quickly made it privately clear he was unhappy at the lovers living under his roof and was already making mutterings about heading off to Durness to the croft to avoid any unpleasant showdowns. But his wife persuaded him to stay for John's sake and try to make the best of a difficult situation.

As always, Stan was on hand to provide some balm to salve any open wounds. In public, he maintained a dignified and supportive front over John's new relationship. In his private moments, though, he thought John was insane to have given up marital stability for this inscrutable woman whose main claim to fame was that she had once made a film about bare bottoms.

For John, though, Edinburgh provided a bolthole away from the ructions at Apple and the internecine warfare with the other Beatles. Heavily bearded, and with his hair at its longest, he was able to stroll round Scotland's capital largely unrecognised and free of press harassment. Even allowing for the bed-ins and peace campaigns, few people recognised Beatle John as the loveable moptop of just four years earlier. Like any other tourist, he visited the usual attractions with Yoko and the children, seizing on this rare opportunity to behave like a proper father and husband. He and Yoko popped into the Scotch House on Princes Street to kit out the kids in matching tartan outfits, with John signing the till receipt for the shop's owners.

Back at Ormidale Terrace, however, tensions were obvious. The presence of Yoko appeared to make everyone slightly uncomfortable. Even mealtimes were fraught as Yoko preferred her macrobiotic diet of sushi and shunned nearly all of Mater's meals. By the third day, she and Bertie were relieved to be hitting the high road to Durness, a diplomatic retreat that at least gave everyone a few hours' breathing space. John, desperate to show Yoko the Highland holiday destination that meant so much to him, said they would make their own way north. Stan arrived from his house in Currie to lead the way in the direction of South Queensferry, with the Lennons following behind in the Maxi. Stan however, had serious reservations over John's ability to tackle the journey, especially when main roads turned into narrow, winding, single-track farm roads beyond Inverness.

'I said to him, "What are you doing in an old Maxi like that? You've got a Rolls Royce, a chauffeur and you come up in a rubbishy old car like that. You must be mad." John was very short-sighted and not a good driver

John and Yoko, with their kids in tow, stroll past an Edinburgh onlooker outside the Royal Bank of Scotland in Shandwick Place during their 1969 visit to the city.

at the best of times. I just thought it was mad to think he could carry this off. He had this long hair and the beard, but he still thought he wouldn't be recognised. The idea was that they would stay at local B&Bs like any other holidaymaker. He just said, "I want to be ordinary." However, I warned him to be careful. I said, "Remember, John, when you go up into the Highlands, the single-track roads start after Inverness. And remember the rule of the road for the single-track road."'

John's confidence, though, had been bolstered by how far they had travelled. Stan had waited to make sure they got safely on the ferry at Queensferry for the sail across the Forth. Once on the other side, though, John was on his own again. He headed first towards the coast in the direction of Kirkcaldy to see Stan's stepfather's brother, Angus. Having fulfilled another family obligation, he then had to negotiate a route back onto the road to Inverness. Like any other tourist, John probably put his trust in a road map to find the most direct artery from the central belt to the capital of the Highlands. Most likely, he headed in the direction of Gleneagles to connect with the A9 which was then – as it is today – the road that took drivers to Inverness without having to go the coastal route to Aberdeen and round the nook of Fraserburgh.

The Lennons opted for the tourist route, a road that would have taken them through some of Scotland's most stunning scenery, with the Cairngorms forming a craggy outline against the skyline. Eventually they hit Inverness and crossed the Moray Firth to the Black Isle. Given the fact that they set off in the middle of the afternoon, they had no chance of making it to Durness in one go. Amazingly, though, they got as far as Golspie where they decided to look for a local B&B, in keeping with the ordinary-John theme of the trip. Even though it was the height of the holiday season, John and Yoko struck it lucky at the first place they tried.

The house was called Kildonan at 12 Ferry Road and its owners didn't even blink when they ushered in the longhaired Beatle, his Japanese wife, Kyoko and Julian into their home. They were shown to a snug room on the first floor where all four remained until breakfast next morning.

The Simpson's son Kevin was about seven at the time, but he paid little attention to the newcomers. Tourists were a daily occurrence in his parents' line of work, even though this particular man seemed to carry a special charisma. It was only several years later, in a passing conversation, that his father revealed John Lennon had once slept in an upstairs room. 'I was just amazed,' Kevin told me. 'To them he was just another guest. But by this time I was a big Beatles fan and John was always my favourite so to find out that Lennon had actually stayed under the same roof as me was incredible.'

The Lennons checked out early next morning. The Maxi loaded up once again, John and Yoko, after asking for directions and with a map on their knees, started out on the last leg of their marathon journey. Two hours later, the seemingly never-ending horizon of peaks and fields cleared to reveal the rugged coastline of John's childhood, a childhood that had for so long seemed so far away.

As they passed the signpost for Durness, Lennon's face must have lit up like a beacon as the memories came flooding back. He would have passed Iris McKay's shop and the caravan site on his way to his Aunt Mater's family croft at Sango Bay. The house, which seemed to stand guard over the rest of the village, was far from being a rock star's normal retreat. But for John it was a welcome signpost to a carefree past. He was delighted to walk through the front door for the first time in years and, naturally enough for a man steeped in unlikely sentiment, the memories washed over him like the breakers from the nearby Atlantic.

John wasted little time in taking Yoko, Julian and Kyoko off on a tour of the local beaches and coves and ventured down for a nostalgic peek inside the natural echo chamber that is Smoo Cave. He also followed Mater's advice to go down to the Cape Wrath Hotel to buy the villagers a drink, an occasion that is still fresh in the mind of Iris McKay, no longer the little girl he played with on the sand and in the coves.

'He came to the Cape Wrath Hotel and stood his round at the bar. There was nothing starry about him. He was quite chatty and, of course, he looked a lot different from when any of us had last seen him. It would be easy to say people were amazed to see him but for a lot of us it wasn't that much of a surprise because we all knew he had family in the area. Obviously his life had changed beyond all recognition. But I always remember the boy from Liverpool who came up here for his summer holidays.'

They then decided to follow the road north-west out of the village and headed in the direction of Loch Eriboll, driving round the Melness side of the Kyle of Tongue in the days before the road over the causeway was built. Miles and miles of stunning mountaintops formed a giant, craggy curtain on the horizon before the village of Tongue loomed into view, the first sign of civilisation they had seen since driving away from Durness.

To give the kids a break, they stopped at the local post office which also doubled as a pit-stop café. Strange as they must have looked, few people gave them a second glance. Those who did rubbed their eyes in disbelief that a Beatle was walking nonchalantly among them. One man who has good reason to recall the Lennons' visit is Norman Henderson, whose grandmother owned the post office.

Norman, who today runs the same post office, said: 'They came in for tea I think and something to eat. It created a bit of a stir at the time. Word

quickly got round, especially in such a small place, that we had a celebrity
in our midst. But it wasn't that much of a surprise to see him because the
older members of the community knew he had family in the area.

'I have a wee bit of cine film my dad took when they were here and
when they came out. It shows them signing a few autographs for the kids
that had gathered. He had very long hair and Yoko looked tiny even
among the local kids. They seemed quite happy together and chatted away
to people. He seemed very friendly and then they left after about 20
minutes or so and I think they were heading back towards Durness. It was
hard not to recognise him because his picture was usually in every paper
just about every other day but when they came in they were more or less
left alone. It was only the younger ones who eventually plucked up enough
courage to ask for an autograph. People still talk about the John Lennon
visit even today. We've had some fans coming here as well.'

By now, John's confidence behind the wheel was high, perhaps bordering on complacent. Which may explain why he forgot Stan's parting words of wisdom to remember the etiquette of driving along single-track roads in the Highlands. Squinting ahead in the distance, John glimpsed what he thought was another car trundling towards them on the Melness side of the Kyle of Tongue. Unconcerned, he drove on regardless until he realised the other driver, a German tourist, was as ignorant of the rules of the road as he was and they were both on a collision course. At the last minute, John swerved, taking the Maxi out of the other car's path but leaving it perched in the ditch at an awkward angle. John emerged with blood trickling from a gash to his face. Likewise, Yoko's forehead was bleeding. The couple had taken the full impact of the shunt. The kids in the back, although shocked, were largely unhurt although Kyoko suffered a small cut to her face.

All four staggered to the roadside and waited for help to arrive. First on the scene was a local butcher who stopped to check first of all on the injuries. He then drove to nearby Melness Farm to call for an ambulance. Unfortunately the Lennons had to wait almost an hour for an ambulance to arrive from Wick, about 60 miles away, to take the injury-hit victims to Lawson Memorial Hospital in Golspie, a further 35 miles south. By now, word had slowly spread to Tongue, the nearest village to the accident scene, that a car carrying two hippies and a couple of kids had gone off the road. So far, John's anonymity remained intact, although not for long. When he arrived, the shocked ambulance driver took one look at the victims and didn't need John to tell him his name.

Professionalism, though, quickly kicked in as he carried out a quick condition check on each of them before radioing ahead to the Lawson that four victims of a road traffic accident were on their way. None of the injuries were especially serious, despite the blood seeping from John and Yoko's facial wounds.

On arrival at the hospital, the Lennons were ushered into a side room where they were cleaned up by nurses and examined by Dr David Milne, who instantly recognised the celebrity couple in his hospital. He told me: 'I knew right away who they were and I remember the whole episode quite clearly. When they were first brought in there was quite a bit of commotion. They were quite shaken up. I thought they would be shouting for plastic surgeons and all the rest of it but there was none of that.'

A quick check revealed John had suffered a deep cut to his left cheek that would need stitches. Similarly the gash on Yoko's forehead would also require to be knitted together. Julian was the only one of the four to escape shocked but otherwise unhurt. An added complication, however, lay in the fact that Yoko was in the early stages of pregnancy, an inconvenient truth that was virtually forgotten, or simply missed by the media at the time and by Beatleologists over the years.

By now, John's senses were back on an even keel. Swimming around his head, though, was the undeniable fact that the Lennons had once again created a happening, although this time not one they had deliberately orchestrated. John was told they would have to remain in the hospital at least overnight just to ensure there were no hidden injuries. His immediate reply was to insist that he and Yoko be given beds side by side, breaking the hospital's normal policy of maintaining separate wards for men and women. Dr Milne, however, gave the unusual request the nod and they were even given a ward to themselves away from the prying eyes of other NHS patients.

In the meantime, John made a few calls to tell everyone that he might be back in the papers again so they'd better be prepared. These included informing Paul McCartney, George Harrison and Ringo Starr, through the offices of Apple, that he wouldn't be at Abbey Road studios tomorrow for the first sessions on the album that would eventually become the band's swansong. He also asked Ringo and his wife Maureen to brave the media frenzy and stand in for Yoko and him at the launch party for the Plastic Ono Band's iconic 'Give Peace a Chance' single at the Chelsea Town Hall. His other call was to Mater at the croft in Durness. At first, she was furious that John could have been so careless, especially with children in the car. Her second reaction was to ask a neighbour to drive her to the cottage hospital where, after checking on John and Yoko, she bundled a perplexed Julian into the back of a car for the return journey to Sangomore. Kyoko remained at her mother's bedside.

And then the Lennons blocked out the curtains and signalled their retreat from public life for the next five days – but not entirely from the public. They were to hold court with a number of visitors from the local community, including a minister from the ultra-conservative Free Church of Scotland.

It's easy to wonder with hindsight why the Lennons remained in the Lawson for so long for what was, in truth, a fairly minor road accident. Even allowing for Yoko's pregnancy, it seems an inordinate amount of recovery time. But then again perhaps not if we consider that the couple at that time were still recovering from a debilitating heroin addiction. It seems reasonable to speculate that their five-day incarceration could have helped them go cold turkey in a bid to purge their system of smack. For whatever reason, John and Yoko simply cocooned themselves in each other.

Inevitably, it didn't take long for word of the accident to spread. Within hours, the news wire services were sending the story all over the

The Lennons' smashed-up Austin Maxi was eventually towed to Burr's garage in Tongue and covered in a tarpaulin before being transported back to their home in Ascot.

world. The next day, the banked lawn outside the Lawson had been turned into a makeshift media centre. Newspaper reporters and cameramen and Highland freelances sensing the chance to make a fast buck jostled for space with TV crews from all over the country. But there was little hope of catching a glimpse of Beatle John and his bandaged wife. They remained incommunicado behind the hospital's whitewashed walls. Dr Milne saw his patients every day to check routinely on their progress and was impressed by John's lack of starry self-absorption.

'I had long chats with John and he just seemed like an ordinary bloke to me. We covered a wide range of subjects. We spoke at length about the life he had been leading. He told me he had been through it all from religion to drugs. He was very honest. He didn't give the impression of being a pop star, he was extremely ordinary and down to earth. One night he went down to the kitchen and said have you got any leftovers?

'I remember another night a group from his Apple organisation had flown up to Inverness and then taken a taxi from Inverness up to Golspie. They arrived at 9.30 p.m. and I went to John and said some of your mates are at the door. And he said, "I didn't ask them to come. Tell them to go away." He said, "Don't be fooled, I'm paying for all this." He seemed very intelligent to me, well-read and very well up on world events. I thought he was quite an impressive figure.'

Dr Milne practically became the Lennons' unofficial spokesman for the week, wheeled out before the cameras to give regular condition updates. In truth, though, there was very little he could tell them that would spark the call to hold the front page. Today, there would be 15-minute updates on Sky News and BBC News 24. But almost 40 years ago,

OFF THE BEATLE TRACK 1 –
BOND ON THE RUN

In the Sixties, there were no bigger cultural icons than The Beatles and James Bond. But Scots author Ian Fleming's Fettes-educated secret agent was no fan of the Fab Four . . . at least on film as played by the world's most famous living Scotsman, Sean Connery. In the 1964 movie *Goldfinger*, the second Bond outing, Connery is heard making a sarcastic comment about the musical prowess of The Beatles when he chides Jill Masterson for quaffing champagne the wrong way. He says: 'My dear, there are some things that just aren't done, such as drinking Dom Perignon '53 above the temperature of 53 degrees Fahrenheit. That's as bad as listening to The Beatles without earmuffs.'

Enough shaid then, Shir Sean.

Eventually, though, the world of Bond and The Beatles would collide. Paul McCartney's bombastic theme song for the 1973 movie *Live and Let Die* provided the perfect kick-ass start for Roger Moore's tenure as 007. The rollicking song, produced by George Martin and sandwiched between the albums *Red Rose Speedway* and *Band on the Run*, was another sign that Macca was emerging, in the eyes of the critics at least, from his post-Beatles songwriting funk.

the column inches generated by the Lennons' hospital stay amounted to little more than a trickle. A long trawl through the archives of the *Daily Record*, the *Scottish Daily Express*, the *Glasgow Herald* and the *Scotsman* reveal few headlines and prove that John succeeded in his bid to recharge his drained batteries away from the media spotlight.

Even the fact that a furious Cynthia Lennon arrived at the hospital after a turbulent flight from Glasgow to collect Julian – unaware he was with Mater at the croft – failed to ignite any serious coverage. She eventually took a taxi from the hospital to pick up Julian in Durness before heading back to Inverness for a flight back south – a round trip of some 120 miles.

In fairness, the tragic death of Rolling Stone Brian Jones from drowning in his swimming pool was enough to nudge even a hospitalised Beatle down the news schedules for the next few days. But not even that shocking event was enough to make John break his virtual vow of silence from his hospital bed. There was no public tribute from one pop icon to another nor any attempt at sympathy for the other members of the Stones, despite the close friendship John had always enjoyed with them.

Dr Milne said: 'I was actually quite impressed by the media. They had a rough time because they just had to sit out in the car park night and day. They were scared to leave in case they missed something. If their editor phoned and they couldn't answer right away they would be sacked. I used to go down at nine o' clock at night to tell them, "Look, they've gone to bed for the night, you'd be as well to go down to the pub." But they said they daren't do that. Part of their orders had been to get a photograph and apparently some painter or someone who was working at the hospital had got in and surreptitiously taken a photograph which he then tried to sell to the newspapers. And the press had all got together and said, "Look, everyone at the hospital has been so nice to us we're not going to use the photograph."'

One man who did slip through the net, however, was Free Church of Scotland minister, the Reverend David Paterson, whose church in nearby Brora provided him with a soapbox to rail against the world's worst free radicals. Like most clergymen, he had been outraged just three years earlier when Lennon suggested in a newspaper interview that The Beatles were more popular than Jesus Christ. It may have been a clumsy attempt to deconstruct and debunk modern religious teachings, but Lennon's comments nevertheless sparked a firestorm of protests across the globe, especially in America's Bible Belt.

In Scotland, the 'Wee Frees' manned the battle ramparts from their largely Highland base and denounced Lennon as Satan's spawn. And when the Rev. Paterson discovered this apostle of evil cloaked as a prince of peace was in his own backyard, the chance to reprimand him was too good to pass up.

Obviously a well-known face in the community, he had no trouble gaining access to the hospital. And his request – no, demand – for an audience with the heretic millionaire pop star was relayed to John's bedside. Minutes later the Rev. Paterson was face to face not with the Antichrist but a man of flesh and blood just like himself. And, amazingly, the two men – polar opposites in every possible way – dug out some common ground. Perhaps it was the fact both were straight talkers – the Rev. Paterson, like John, was not one to shrink from forthright views – that helped them form an unlikely bond. For two hours, the maverick musician, icon of his generation, locked horns with the Scottish Free Kirk minister.

Much of what they spoke about remained secret until the Rev.

Paterson confided the details to Derek Yeaman, a Glasgow film-maker who is hoping to make a film loosely based on the Lennon car crash and the effects it had on the local area. He hopes to use the car crash and meeting with the minister as the jumping-off point for a fictionalised story about a young woman who rebels against the church and community. Derek's exhaustive research brought him into contact with the Rev. Paterson a few years back, several years after he had retired from the church. He is now in poor health, having suffered a stroke that has left him unable to speak. But at that time he was still able to recall the untold story of the meeting of minds he had with Lennon.

Derek said: 'They talked about philosophy, Jesus, peace and war. He said to me that Lennon was obviously a really clever bloke and was always searching for something. They spoke a couple of times. It seems bizarre on the surface because they were so different but they seemed to get on well. I know he visited him a couple of times and on one occasion rushed back home to get a book Lennon was talking about that he had.'

The Rev. Paterson was one of only a handful of outsiders to pierce the Beatle bubble during the five days John was at the Lawson. For the rest of the time, he would read the papers in a secluded part of the hospital and enjoy fresh fruit scones, home-made marmalade and locally caught salmon.

He wasn't totally incommunicado, however. He sent a typically witty postcard with deliberately misspelled words from his hospital bed to The Beatles' legendary press officer, Derek Taylor. He begins by declaring, in capital letters: 'THIS IS NOT A BEGGING LETTER.' John, an inveterate postcard doodler, then goes on to write: 'I am a crippled family who need som mony to git out of Scotcland a few hundred will do.' At the bottom of the card he has signed off as 'Jack McCripple (ex seamen).' The card is addressed to 'Dirty Tayler MBE at the Apple HQ in London'. The front of the card shows a castle and John has drawn a line to one of the windows and written 'held prisner'.

But if John liked to believe he was a hostage to misfortune, his scheduled release date was coming up fast. Five days after being admitted to the Lawson Memorial Hospital bleeding, battered and bruised, John and Yoko got ready to face the world again. For the hospital, this would mean an end to the phone calls from worried fans that had almost caused the switchboard to go into meltdown. And for the staff, a sense that business would go back to normal, although in truth the Lennons' stay had interfered little with the normal running of the hospital.

Joyce Everett was one of several young nurses who often attended John and Yoko and, like her surgical colleagues, remembers only a husband and wife who had been injured in a car accident and not the

stellar couple of pop culture folklore. However, during the Lennons' recovery she was the only staff member to speak to not just one Beatle, but two. 'My outstanding memory is picking up the phone one night and it was Paul McCartney. He was my favourite Beatle, so that was nice. He was just asking how John was. It was a coincidence that I picked up the phone. But I just stayed quite cool about it and told him how he was. There was no facility in the hospital to pass Paul's call through to him or anything like that. But the message was passed on that Paul had phoned to ask how he was and I suppose he was quite pleased about that. This was at a time when they weren't supposed to be getting on so it's nice to know there was still a friendship there.

'During the time they were in the hospital they were fine. Yoko was a typically inscrutable Japanese and John was very friendly. They kept themselves to themselves and there were never any problems. They also had a ward to themselves, so that kept them out of the way of the usual running of the hospital. And it meant that the other patients weren't disturbed in any way by what was going on. I mean, they knew that someone famous was in the hospital especially since so many journalists were camped outside the main entrance. You couldn't help but notice, but there were no paparazzi with mega lenses or anything like that.'

On Sunday, 6 July, six days after they were first admitted to the Lawson and 24 hours after the Rolling Stones played a free concert in London's Hyde Park to honour the memory of Brian Jones, the Lennons gathered up their worldly belongings and prepared to re-enter the public domain.

On the morning they left, a helicopter set down on the lawn to take John, Yoko and Kyoko to Inverness airport where they would fly by private jet back down to London. Among the posse of pressmen at Inverness hoping for a snappy soundbite was Gerry McNee, now one of Scotland's foremost broadcasters and sports journalists. McNee was pictured striding across the airport tarmac right beside John and Yoko. But the encounter lasted barely a minute as the Lennons walked quickly from the chopper to the Apple-chartered Hawker Siddley that had taxied on the runway to collect its famous passengers. In fact, so quick was their getaway that McNee has little recollection of any significant remark that John made. The musician's thick beard had been partly shaved away to allow his cut to be stitched but as he made his great escape from Scotland, he covered up the scar with Yoko's hat. In the foreground, Apple executive Peter Brown can be seen holding Yoko's daughter Kyoko as they prepared to board the plane. Almost 40 years on, Gerry's memory is understandably hazy over anything that might have passed as conversation or an on-the-record remark between himself and John Lennon.

He told me: 'I got the call from the office or somebody saying they were on their way to Dalcross Airport as it was called in those days and to get down there with a photographer. He might have muttered a few words and I probably got a few paragraphs out of it but everything happened very fast. They simply came off the helicopter and straight onto the plane. One thing I do remember is that she was carrying, I think, a black plastic bag which contained bits of clothing but it also had had a salmon tail

A hard day's flight. Gerry McNee (far left), now one of Scotland's best known sports broadcasters, is among the posse of pressmen trying to get a few words with John and Yoko at Inverness's Dalcross Airport after they leave Lawson Memorial Hospital.

sticking out which was a little bizarre. We got very close to him which would never happen today but, as I say, it all passed very quickly.'

At the Lawson, Dr Milne said the couple went out of their way to thank all the staff who lined up outside the entrance to wave farewell to the most famous patients in the hospital's 120-year history. They handed out signed pictures and albums, one of which was given to Dr Milne as a token of goodwill for his discretion as much as his surgical skills. He recalled: 'I got an autographed record – I can't remember which one now – that I gave to one of my sons.'

John, wearing a large floppy black hat, shook everyone's hand and then, with one final flourish, they stepped aboard the chopper for the 15-minute flight to Inverness Airport. The waiting Press finally got their picture. One group shot still hangs in the entrance to the hospital. And they also got their parting soundbite, a mere 24 words to sum up six long days: 'If you're going to have a car crash, try to arrange for it to happen in the Highlands. The hospital there was just great.' John's comment was the last reported remark he would make on Scottish soil. As the helicopter banked south, he could not have known he would never again visit his beloved Scottish Highlands. A love affair that began when he was 9 years old would never be physically rekindled.

Derek Yeaman suspects, though, that the couple's stay, however accidental, had unexpected benefits. 'It had been a very tough and very busy period for them. It's not overstating things to say they were possibly suffering from nervous exhaustion. So, the beautiful thing about it was that it was probably the most relaxing week they ever had during those times.'

Three days later, John was back in Studio Two at Abbey Road with Yoko ensconced by his side in a double bed specially shipped in to help maintain her recovery and ease any pregnancy complications. There was, however, one final detail for the Lennons to attend to, a lasting reminder of the Highland holiday that, while not burning, certainly crashed. They had the crumpled Maxi shipped down to their mansion at Tittenhurst Park where, in true Yoko style, it was smelted down and mounted on a concrete plinth in the garden.

Several months after the accident, John's cousin Stan visited him at the house and was stunned by the sight of the twisted objet d'art. 'I couldn't believe it. I said to him, "What the hell is that old wreck lying there for?" He told me, "Yoko thinks it's a happening so she had it put on a plinth." What can you say? Mad, utterly mad.'

Baby, you can't drive my car. At Yoko's insistence the smashed-up Austin Maxi was eventually smelted down and mounted on a plinth outside the couple's home at Tittenhurst Park, Ascot.

2. The First Tour

The three teenagers gazed at the stage, their faces betraying a mixture of shock and awe, their eyes fixed on the singer milking the applause. Lined up along the front row were dozens of doe-eyed bobby-soxers, young girls swooning with delight at seeing their hero. At that precise moment, John Lennon, Paul McCartney and George Harrison were touched by a feeling of nirvana. So this is what it means to be a pop star.

Eventually, it was Lennon, his eyes squinting in the darkness and pulling on a cigarette, who broke the silence. 'Hey, that'll be us one day.' And, in his own mind, he knew it was no false boast.

A nondescript hall in a sleepy Scottish town may seem an unlikely birthplace for a major musical phenomenon. But that night in Alloa Town Hall, on Friday, 20 May 1960, provided the spark for a revolution that changed the face of pop music forever.

Earlier that day, the three youths, along with Stuart Sutcliffe and drummer Tommy Moore, had left behind the grime of Liverpool's famous Lime Street station. Ahead of them stretched nine days backing Johnny Gentle, tipped as 'The Next Big Thing', on a tour of remote Scottish

Alloa Town Hall was the venue for The Silver Beetles' first Scottish gig with fellow Liverpudlian Johnny Gentle on Friday, 20 May, 1960.

places with names like Forres, Fraserburgh, Inverness, Nairn and Peterhead.

The Hollywood Bowl it wasn't, but for The Silver Beetles, it was the first stepping stone on the road to untold riches and unprecedented fame. For two years, they had practised relentlessly, churning out covers of Elvis Presley and Buddy Holly songs, honing their own sound and playing the occasional gig at weddings and college dances. What set them apart, however, from the swarm of Liverpool bands, was the embryonic songwriting team of Lennon and McCartney. They were brash and brilliant, youthful and euphoric. And now both boys were relishing the chance to play on stage. Like proper musicians. Like professionals. By the end of this tour, Lennon, Harrison and McCartney, the ambitious musical core of the group, would be transformed from raw and unvarnished pop wannabes into three youngsters with definite stars in their eyes.

Years later, Lennon, who had bunked off his exams at art school, described that first fledgling tour of Scotland as providing the ties that bound The Beatles as a serious band. He said: 'It kind of opened our eyes. We played literally hundred of gigs before we made it, in places like the Cavern in Liverpool and Hamburg. But that first tour was the first time we had actually seen what it was like to be on the road. It was bloody hard work. There's no doubt that Scotland gave us a taste for whatever it was we were looking for. It was a turning point of sorts.'

When the steam locomotive pulled out of Liverpool that morning, en route for Glasgow Central, it left carrying The Silver Beetles. By the time the band returned home, the Silver was long gone and they were forever The Beatles, with an 'a'.

At this point, it's important to consider the pop culture landscape that had been formed as the fifties morphed into the sixties. The fifties had become a decade fuelled by teenage rebellion, symbolised by the sexual swagger of Elvis Presley. Presley's songs had slipped the chains of parental control from a generation whose unfettered independence continually bucked convention and authority. In *The Wild One*, Marlon Brando was asked, 'What are you rebelling against?' 'What have you got?' was the sneering reply, loaded with anti-establishment venom.

It was rock 'n' roll that ultimately provided the real escape route for kids born at the height of the Blitz. Every night, their ears would be tuned to late-night radio shows crackling with the latest hits from the likes of Presley, Buddy Holly, Gene Vincent, Little Richard, Jerry Lee Lewis and Chuck Berry. But by 1960, the vapour trails from rock's first trail-blazing comets were already fading; Elvis, his hair shorn and his talent curtailed, was in the army; Holly was dead, likewise Eddie Cochrane; Jerry Lee Lewis was a social outcast, in disgrace for marrying his 15-year-old cousin. In film, Brando was no longer rebelling, settling instead for a life of Hollywood glitz and movie mediocrity. Many others had fallen off the radar. In their place came a new generation of singers, more clean-cut and parent-friendly. What threat could the likes of the Everly Brothers, Cliff Richard, Tommy Steele, Bobby Vinton, Paul Anka and Jim Reeves pose?

Rock 'n' roll had arrived at its first crossroads, but for the leather-jacket-clad Silver Beetles, it was still the only show in town. And so it was that they headed to Clackmannanshire on a journey that would ultimately see them shining a light into every corner of the globe. The Beat Ballad tour had been arranged by Larry Parnes, the Simon Cowell of his day and one of Britain's foremost music moguls, as a showcase for one of his most promising artistes. Johnny Gentle, a softly-spoken 25-year-old Liverpudlian, had already been on the cusp of chart success with his first three singles. Now Parnes reckoned some decent public exposure would help propel his protégé further along the path to pop stardom.

The only problem was Gentle's lack of a backing band, an issue that could be solved by an audition of local hopefuls in Johnny's home town. Among those who turned up at the Wyvern Social Club were Gerry and his Pacemakers, Cass and the Casanovas and a clutch of other top-notch Scouse bands. The Silver Beetles were by far the most amateur of them all and hardly worth a second glance. They were dressed in tatty shirts and worn black jeans, their hair piled high. They didn't even have a drummer and had to rely on a sticksman from another group. First impressions suggested they were in the premier league of time wasters. But something in their high-energy performance alerted Parnes' basic instincts. Two weeks later, he booked them to take the high road north, entrusting their progress to Duncan McKinnon, a rough and ready Borders pig farmer who occasionally dabbled with pop show promotion to earn a few extra quid.

Together with Johnny Gentle, though, this was a giant step into the great, wide unknown for The Silver Beetles. Their fee was to be £60, split five ways and not including travelling expenses. And they would have to dig into their own pockets for accommodation. Welcome to the world of rock 'n' roll, lads.

The itinerary was as follows:

20 May: The Town Hall, March Hill, Alloa.
21 May: The Northern Meeting Ballroom, Church Street, Inverness
22 May: Day off.
23 May: Dalrymple Hall, Seaforth Street, Fraserburgh
24 May: Day off.
25 May: St Thomas Hall, Chapel Street, Keith.

26 May: The Town Hall, High Street, Forres.
27 May: The Regal Ballroom, Leopold Street, Nairn
28 May: The Rescue Hall, Prince Street, Peterhead.

Lugging their guitars onto the train, the five Silver Beetles let their minds wander. Lennon was 19, McCartney – given special dispensation by his dad to go, even though vital exams were just weeks away – was a cherub-faced 17-year-old. Sutcliffe was, like Lennon, 19, and baby-faced Harrison the youngest, having just turned 17. Tommy Moore, the latest in a line of ad-hoc drummers, was 36 and well outside the core rock 'n' roll demographic. He was taking time off from his job as a forklift driver at a local bottle works to enjoy his tilt at the big time.

As the train slowly chugged north, three of them drifted into a starry-eyed reverie. Somehow, their names seemed too ordinary for the stellar world of pop music, so why not change them? McCartney was first to announce an alternative – from now on he would adopt the stage name of Paul Ramon, a moniker that 15 years later would become the inspiration for punk hero Dee Dee Ramone. For George, Carl Harrison was the ultimate homage to Carl Perkins. Stu typically drew his inspiration from the art world and took the name of Stuart de Stael after his painting idol, the Russian abstract classicist, Nicolas de Stael.

'It was exciting changing your name,' said Paul. 'It made it all seem professional and real. It sort of proved you did a real act if you had a stage name. When we went up to Scotland to tour with Johnny Gentle, we thought we were showbiz people. And it was a Larry Parnes tour and all of his people changed their names – Wilde, Eager, Fury, Pride, all of that – so we changed ours. Not that it occurred to us that Johnny's real name wasn't Johnny Gentle. Ramon seemed to me like a sexy French name and I remember little Scottish girls asking, "Is your name really Ramon?" It made us seem like great London showbiz guys so that when we were in Fraserburgh, instead of saying – "I'm just a kid from Liverpool," – it suggested there was something more to us. It's an old trick.'

Only John and Tommy decided to keep it real. Then of course, there was the band's name, The Silver Beetles. It was almost right, but not quite.

At 6.30 p.m. the train finally crossed the River Clyde and entered the glass-covered enclosure of Central Station, some ten hours after they'd first stepped aboard. From there, the band had to haul their equipment across the city centre, past George Square, in time to board their 7.18 p.m. train to Alloa from Glasgow Queen Street Station. They arrived at Alloa Town Hall at around 8.30 p.m. They had never met Johnny Gentle or even rehearsed a note with him. And they were due to back him on stage in precisely one hour . . .

For Johnny Gentle, already relaxed and signing autographs at the Town Hall, this was not an unfamiliar pre-gig scenario. He was used to criss-crossing England with an ad-hoc group of disparate youngsters strumming familiar chords behind the latest Presley hit. So when he saw The Silver Beetles arrive out of breath that Friday evening, he knew that 60 minutes would be enough to check the song list and hammer out some loose arrangements.

He told me: 'When I was doing a new gig, I was always rehearsing with a new group which, I'm sure you'll appreciate, meant you were going into it very cold. It's such a confidence booster to go on stage knowing these boys behind you know exactly what you're going to do. But with The Beatles, I didn't know if they could do it. That was always going to be the case for the first few nights. That was always going to be a worry. So we sat down and said, "Do you know this song, do you know this one?" Until we worked out songs that we both knew. We made an act of half the songs that they knew that I knew and half the songs that I knew that they knew.'

Trouper that he was, Johnny may have been putting a brave face on things, relying on the performer's natural instinct that the show must go on, but the fact remains he was still taken aback at the first sight of his fellow Liverpudlians. 'Yes, at first I did wonder what on earth Larry Parnes had sent me. They were dressed in jeans and sweaters and were the roughest bunch of lads I had seen in my life. John and Stu were both at art college and they looked it. Their hair fell over their collars and Stu had a beard. George was serving an apprenticeship and looked neat, as did Paul who was still studying for his A- levels. John told me rather excitedly, "This is our big break."'

Of course, The Silver Beetles may have been young, but they were not complete greenhorns. Lennon, McCartney and Harrison knew this was their shot and they had already rehearsed the songs relentlessly back home. So when Johnny began singing Ricky Nelson's 'Poor Little Fool', the three Silver Beetles bent their fingers over familiar chords. Other songs included Jim Reeves' country and western tinged 'He'll Have to Go', Presley's 'I Need Your Love Tonight' and Clarence Frogman Henry's 'I Don't Know Why I Love You', a late substitute when attempts to run through Bobby Darin's 'Dream Lover' faltered. By the time the curtain went up at Alloa Town Hall, Johnny Gentle and The Silver Beetles were primed and ready – or as ready as they'd ever be.

The show attracted the usual mix of girls on the cusp of sexual maturity and local farm lads happy to heckle the bands in a swaggering show of alpha male bravado. And the message hung heavy in the air – hands off the girls, lads, they're for us.

Surprisingly, that first gig touched a lot of the right bases, considering

Gentle and The Silver Beetles had only met a few hours earlier. Johnny's smooth crooning style set the tempo and The Silver Beetles played their part to near perfection. Sure, the occasional bum note flew out like an empty beer bottle, but overall, while a little rough, it had passable potential, reckoned Johnny. Dressed identically in black shirts and jeans and two-tone tennis shoes, they hunched over their guitars, happy to let Gentle enjoy the spotlight.

Then it was their turn to take centre stage. And that was the signal for a switch back to good old rock 'n' roll. Lennon muttered a few inaudible words of introduction and seconds later all hell broke loose. Lennon's chugging rhythm guitar chords meshed with Harrison and McCartney's delicate phrases to send a power charge reverberating round the hall. And it was answered by a crescendo of screams from the girls and thunderous claps from the guys. It was a chain reaction that seemed to come from nowhere. This had not even happened in Liverpool.

Their set consisted of their own songs 'Hello Little Girl' and 'One After 909' (this was eventually to appear on *Let It Be*, a full decade later). It also featured the Everly Brothers' 'Bye Bye Love', Little Richard's 'Tutti Frutti', 'Lucille' and 'Long Tall Sally', Eddie Cochrane's 'Twenty Flight Rock' and 'Hallelujah I Love Her So', Elvis's 'Stuck on You', Buddy Holly's 'That'll Be the Day', Gene Vincent's 'Be-Bop-A-Lula' and 'Wild Cat', Ray Charles' 'What'd I Say', Chuck Berry's 'Little Queenie' and The Olympics' 'Hully Gully'.

Only Stuart seemed the odd one out, often keeping his back to the audience so no one would notice his lack of ability on bass.

For Lennon, who sang lead on almost every song, it was a road to Damascus moment. Even without his glasses, he could see the girls in the front rows swooning. Girls. Sex. When he wasn't singing, the band's leader's thoughts inevitably strayed to the prospect of a quick coupling or a frantic fumble. He was a young guy on the pull, chancing his arm with chicks he would never see again.

Later in the bar, Gentle and the band found themselves in the middle of a prepubescent scrum. A small crowd of girl fans, most armed with scraps of paper, milled around. And The Silver Beetles, especially Lennon, McCartney and Harrison, let their gaze wander over the flirty dozen. In a faraway corner, the local Teds watched enviously as those cheeky Liverpool lechers tried it on with their women. Bad enough that they were trying to score, but the fact they were from England only poured further fuel on xenophobic nationalist fires.

It was a combustible combination. And when Lennon got in a clinch with a girl called Wilma, the blue touch paper was in danger of being lit. Watching from a discreet distance was her boyfriend Tim Muir, envy welling up inside him. And he wasted no time in delivering his own hands-off message to Lennon. He recalled: 'My mum was friendly with Johnny Gentle and he invited us backstage and The Silver Beetles, as they were called, must have been just hanging about. They were all dressed in black – black jeans and black jackets. Johnny was in a sparkly white jacket. I remember Wilma's photograph being taken because I was a bit jealous at the time. She was standing cheek to cheek with Lennon and I just thought, who is this guy? What's he doing with his arm round my girl? I just wanted to thump him but I let it go.

'Then one night a couple of years later, we were sitting at the telly and a band called The Beatles came on and played "Love Me Do". Wilma thought she recognised one of them from the photograph that was taken that night in Alloa and I said, "That's John Lennon." I recognised him from that picture.'

Wilma today laughs at the memory of the moment she was snapped with John Lennon. She said: 'When The Beatles started to take off, I thought I recognised him from somewhere so I dug out the old photo and it was John. At the time I worked in Donbros Mill and one of the girls was absolutely crazy about The Beatles. I brought the photo in and it went round the mill and I never saw it again.'

Wilma wasn't the only girl in Lennon's sexual sights that night. He also cosied up to Jean Morrison, slipping his arm round her waist and drawing her close. She said: 'He just came up to me and said, "Hi, my name's John." I had this flared skirt on that was too long for me. It had "My Fair Lady" written on the bottom edge, so I couldn't cut it. So I had rolled it up at the top round my waist. John slipped his arm round me and said, "You're a chubby little thing, aren't you?" It was really the skirt but I didn't want to admit it so I just let him think I was chubby. He said he was coming back in a couple of weeks and that we should meet, but it never happened. I went on holiday and when I came back I just thought to pot with it.'

Her last memory of Lennon is watching the Austin Transit tour van fading into the distance the next day. She said: 'I remember myself and my friend May Hunter got a lift home with them in the van. John said they were going our way and I sat on his knee on the way home. It was all very innocent. It was just a cuddle and a lift home in the van. As far as I was concerned, I had just met this guy called John from Liverpool, who just happened to be in a band.'

The Silver Beetles were elated. If this was showbiz, they were in. Johnny Gentle, too, was pleased, despite the few rough musical edges. The only discordant note came from Duncan McKinnon, who was hugely unimpressed by the scruffiness of The Silver Beetles. Johnny recalled how the next day McKinnon contacted Larry Parnes to get the band thrown off the tour. 'Duncan McKinnon just didn't like them. I don't really know why. He thought they looked like buskers. He wrote to Parnes saying these lads you sent up backing Johnny aren't up to it. Parnes phoned me and asked if I should send him a new group. I said no, we were rehearsing all day today and it's getting better.

'Then we got it together and I was very pleased with them. I was very supportive of them. They had fantastic enthusiasm. They wanted to do well. The other groups I'd had backing me were a bit blasé. They thought they could make it on their own and backing Johnny Gentle was not a big deal to them. But those lads from Liverpool had never been on the big scene before. To them, I was a couple of steps up the ladder to what they'd done. So they were enthusiastic to back me and I could see that enthusiasm coming through. They were so keen to improve the act. Any little mistakes that were made were ironed out in hotel rooms with practice and practice until we got it right. And halfway through the tour they were brilliant, as good as any I'd had before and before the end of the tour they were fantastic. So much so that I gave them a spot in my act.'

The next day they rubbed the sleep from their eyes and bundled their gear into the back of the Austin transit. Ahead of them stretched 150 miles of road – north to Inverness – and seven more gigs. Huddled in the back of the van, driven by ad-hoc roadie Gerry Scott, one of McKinnon's hired hands, Lennon and McCartney pumped Johnny for the lowdown on life on the road. They traded stories and experiences as the big old van lurched along a network of pot-holed B roads on the way to the capital of the Highlands. Lennon, especially, wanted to know the inside track on the pros and pitfalls of fame.

By the time the van pulled up outside the Northern Meeting Ballroom, bonds had been forged and a rapport struck up. Three girl fans, carrying a copy of the latest teen magazine *Roxy*, were already hanging outside to ensure front-row seats for that night's show. Johnny was happy to sign his name under the cover pin-up of himself. They then turned to the band. Tommy Moore was first to sign and scrawled his name Thomas Moore. Next up was McCartney who penned the signature Paul Ramon, followed by Carl Harrison and Stuart De Stael. John kept it simple with no starry-eyed adornment, even though in *The Beatles Anthology*, McCartney insisted he did change his name to Long John to reflect Long John and the Silver Beetles.

Crucially, though, the tiny fragment of paper revealed for the first time that they were calling themselves The Beatles. And it was to re-emerge more than 45 years later as a prized artefact of early Beatles memorabilia. 'John couldn't believe that someone wanted their autographs. George said it was the first time they had ever been asked,' recalled Johnny. 'This is great,' said John. 'This is the life. Do you think we should give everything up and go full-time?'

Duncan McKinnon had also arrived to take in the gig, fresh from a session in a local pub. Juiced up, McKinnon remained sceptical about the band's ability. And his pessimism increased even further when he realised that the hall's basement was packed with people out to see Lindsay Ross and his Scottish country dance band. But the minute The Beatles charged into their solo set, the dancefloor became a heaving mass of teenyboppers. McKinnon, tapping his Wellington boot along with the music, was convinced. He then stomped off to the pub again before last orders, satisfied that all was well with the Beat Ballad tour.

The next day, a Sunday, was a chance for everyone to recharge their batteries. The five Beatles had crawled out of bed early, having had only a few hours' kip. Again, they had enjoyed the usual game of tomcatting at the previous night's show. Hungry and slightly hungover, they headed into town in search of some breakfast. But all they could find on a Scottish Sabbath was a newsagent so they made do with an amalgam of ciggies and chocolate.

Later, they meandered back to the hotel and trudged wearily up to Gentle's room, which was next door to their own. Johnny was sitting on the bed, guitar in hand, a frown creasing his brow. He takes up the story of what happened next: 'We were just jamming around with our guitars. I played John this song I'd written called "I've Just Fallen for Someone", but the middle part didn't quite tie in. I said to John, "I'm not happy with this bit, what do you think?" Apparently, he'd already written something and he played it to me saying, "This might fit." And it fitted perfectly. I was pretty amazed really. And we wrote the words for the first middle eight together.

'At first I wasn't impressed at being given a lesson in songwriting by someone who hadn't even published a song, but when I listened to what he had done, I instinctively knew it was right. He just picked up my home-made guitar, closed his eyes and sang these lines: "We know that we'll get by, just wait and see, just like the song tells us, the best things in life are free."

'Of course, the funny thing was, as Paul McCartney pointed out years later, the last line was a nick. It was word for word from "Money (That's What I Want)". But it was actually a clever nod to what was a pop standard. The Beatles even sang it on their second album. I used "I've Just Fallen for Someone" and recorded it two years later under the name of Darren Young. And later Adam Faith recorded it. The thing is John accepted it was my song. There was never any thought that I should put his name down on it. I wish I had done that. People have come up to me with that record at conventions and asked me to sign it. It's worth about £100. So it has been released but nobody knows John Lennon had a part in it and it was written in Scotland. And it was actually published and recorded before "Love Me Do", which was The Beatles' first record.'

Monday 23 May saw the Beat Ballad tour hitch its wagon for the next leg – further east to the fishing town of Fraserburgh. Already, however, just four days into the tour, a crisis was emerging through the fog of performing, pulling birds and getting pissed. The money was running out. Living expenses were fast outstripping the cash burning a hole in their pockets. Gentle recalled how he had to plead with Larry Parnes to advance them more cash, which eventually arrived by courier.

In addition, tensions occasionally surfaced over Stuart's lack of musical ability on bass (or any other instrument, for that matter). Paul especially saw his frustrations come to the boil. Yet it was John, Stu's closest pal in the band, and the only reason he kept his place, who dished out the worst treatment. Lennon's conduct towards him frequently plumbed new depths. At one Highland hotel they stayed at, a variety show had just left. There had been a dwarf in the show and John found out which bed he had slept in and said that would have to be Stu's. Impish schoolboy humour perhaps, but as Lennon said: 'That was how he learned to be with us. It was all stupid but that is what we were like.'

As they headed east, further drama was literally down the road. Their normal driver Gerry, hungover from the night before, was in no fit state to drive so Johnny took the wheel, hugging the contours of the coastal road beside the North Sea. The Beatles were crashed out in the back, with Lennon slumped asleep in the front passenger seat. At a crossroads just outside Banff, Johnny whipped the van left instead of right. From the corner of his eye, he saw the oncoming vehicle – containing a couple of pensioners – take the brunt of the smash. Lennon lurched forward under the dashboard. Behind him, Tommy Moore was wrenched from his snooze and hurled forward to crash on top of Lennon.

Johnny was first to react, checking the condition of the other car's occupants. But when he wheeled round, he saw Moore's face was a red mask of blood, crimson streaming from his mouth. They ferried the injured drummer to the nearest hospital where a check revealed he'd lost a tooth but was otherwise still in the land of the living. The shunt, however, had unnerved Moore, always a reluctant conscript to the band. Still ashen-faced from shock, Moore told the others he didn't feel up to getting behind the drums for that night's show in the Dalrymple Hall.

Lennon slowly let the words sink in, knowing they couldn't play without a drummer. Paul had always fancied himself as a drummer and could have stepped in. Johnny, however, insisted professionalism must

OFF THE BEATLE TRACK 2 –
SEE YOU JIMMY, IT'S LENIN – McCARTNEY

Jimmy Reid was a Scottish socialist firebrand, a left-wing shop union official who in 1971 became the figurehead for one of the most bitter industrial disputes ever to grip the west of Scotland. Jimmy's proud principles were imbued with the essence of the Red Clydesider and he became the fighting spirit and public face of the campaign by the Upper Clyde Shipworkers to keep their yards open and save the jobs of 8,500 men. He was not, however, a man used to receiving flowers, as he did one day when the dispute's fires raged at their fiercest and promised to spark a full-scale national strike. Not just your average bouquet, either. Rather, Jimmy had been sent a wagonload of red roses. Mystified, his fellow shop stewards gathered round to gaze at the card that accompanied the blooms. It had only one word on it – Lennon.

'It can't be Lenin,' piped up one of the lads, 'He's deid.' Priceless, but no one felt tempted to break into a chorus of 'Back in the USSR'. Alongside the card was a cheque. Jimmy recalled the episode some 30 years later. He said: 'The cheque was for five or ten grand. I can't remember the exact amount now but I do know it was a lot of money at the time.' But the former Beatle's gesture perfectly illustrated how the UCS workers' famous sit-in had caught the imagination of the whole country. And it wasn't a surprise since Lennon, encouraged by wife Yoko Ono, was in the middle of an intense political radicalisation.

Last year, Glasgow writer Brian McGeachan wrote a play based on Jimmy and was delighted to get a message of support from Yoko and a request to pass on 75th birthday wishes to the man himself. The contact came after Brian met Watergate journalist Carl Bernstein in New York and casually mentioned the Jimmy Reid project and the Lennon connection. Brian said: 'Carl said he was friends with Yoko and would put me in touch with her. I did not hold out much hope, but the meeting triggered an idea. I handed a copy of the Jimmy Reid play to her doorman at the Dakota Building before flying back to Scotland. A few months later I got an email from Yoko with her words of praise for the play and congratulating Jimmy on reaching his 75th birthday. I then incorporated these words into the play.'

come first – they needed a proper drummer. A dark rage crept over Lennon's face. Eyeballing the older man, he snarled: 'You listen to me. You're bloody playing. We need a drummer and you're it. Let's go.'

Moore probably didn't fancy the prospect of losing another tooth. Lennon already had a reputation in Liverpool for being handy with his fists when things didn't go his way. Johnny recalled: 'John's face was like thunder. He just got a grip of his arm and said, "You're playing." So Tommy played with a couple of teeth missing and dabbing at his cheek with a handkerchief.'

The dark cloud that hung over Lennon lifted the further north the band travelled. Memories of those carefree summer days spent at his aunt's croft in Durness always took him down a dreamy path of contentment. Now here he was travelling down another dreamy path, one he hoped would lead to fame. As he later sang in the song 'God' on his first solo album: 'I was the dreamweaver.' Johnny Gentle said: 'John had always considered himself to be part Scottish and loved everything about the Highlands. He'd spent nearly all his summer holidays up to his 17th birthday at the large croft with its acres of deserted hills, woods and beaches. When he had first met Stuart Sutcliffe he had been impressed with his middle name Ferguson and his birthplace of Edinburgh. Despite being absent from the country for most of his adult life, John's love of Scotland ran deep.'

Nostalgia, however, would have to take a back seat to tonight's gig at the Dalrymple Hall, the third show of the tour. Tommy Moore put a brave face on things and eased himself back behind the drum kit. And, musically, the band kicked into a higher gear. Johnny allowed himself a quiet smile of satisfaction, knowing his loyalty had paid off. He also couldn't help but notice that the screams for The Beatles were beginning to eclipse even his own ovations. Each night, the shrieks got louder, mainly from hormonal teenage girls whose eyes locked mainly on Lennon, McCartney, Harrison and Sutcliffe.

Among them was Margaret Adams, a teenager lured to the Dalrymple Hall by the prospect of seeing her hero. For the likes of Margaret, the sight of Johnny Gentle gently crooning just yards from her adoring gaze amounted to megawatt celebrity. Few pop stars of Johnny's stellar reputation ventured as far north. His backing band meant nothing.

Margaret, then 17, was given a special task for the evening and asked to look after Johnny's long-time girlfriend Marjorie. She recalled: 'I actually met them all during the day before the show. My father had a fish merchant's business in the town and had a connection with Johnny. He asked me if I would look after Marjorie. I hardly gave The Beatles a second glance, especially since I could hardly make out what they were saying because of the accents. But it was nice to be asked to look after Marjorie. It made you feel like you were an insider.'

But Margaret was unprepared for the tumult of noise that accompanied The Beatles' slot. 'It was bedlam. I couldn't quite understand it because Johnny was always the main attraction for me. After the show, The Beatles all ran out the back door and piled into my dad's Vauxhall estate car because even then the girls were chasing them. I had never seen anything like it. We then drove back to my parents' house. My mum was used to me bringing all sorts of people home so there wasn't a problem. I was the eldest daughter of nine children. Johnny and Marjorie were with us as well and I just remember my brothers staring at her. They had never seen someone with that kind of blonde hair. We had a bit of a singsong and I remember Paul McCartney singing the Jim Reeves song "Put Your Sweet Lips a Little Closer to the Phone" to my mum. My mum is still alive and she still remembers it quite clearly. John spent the night talking to my dad.

'He was quite zany. At one point I noticed that John was nowhere to be found. I found him in the front room talking to my dad who was trying to fathom out what he was talking about. At one point John sat upside down in an armchair.

'They were desperately trying to persuade Johnny to let them play more of their own music in the show. They were very ambitious. George was very quiet and hardly registered and, to be honest, I can't even remember if Stuart Sutcliffe was there. But I remember them all as very nice boys. They were all dressed in black, which was quite different because all the other groups of the time wore suits. It was a lovely night. But when I look back on the show now, I feel that I was in at the start of Beatlemania. It didn't just happen after they became famous.

'We saw it at first hand in Fraserburgh in the Dalrymple Hall. The funny thing was I wasn't very impressed by them. I was there for Johnny. He was the real star. We all thought he was gorgeous – then this other lot came on. And when The Beatles became famous, a lot of us had seen them and didn't even like them.'

Off stage, the band's financial crisis was at breaking point. Johnny's begging letter to Larry Parnes was still nestling unanswered in an in-tray. There was even a possibility they wouldn't have enough to pay for their room at the town's Station Hotel. The day after the Dalrymple Hall show, John, Paul, George and Stu cut disconsolate figures as they trudged along the beachfront. They were only halfway through the tour and skint. Ahead of them was Margaret Moffat and a pal who had been among the screaming fans from the night before. Eyeing them from a distance and perched behind a sand dune, a ripple of excitement ran through each girl.

'We recognised them right away as the band from the night before. We didn't see many strangers in Fraserburgh at that time. It was very tight-knit. They were quite a scruffy bunch. We just stood and watched them then we ran like fury down the other side of the sand dune so we could bump into them accidentally on purpose and appear very nonchalant. We got talking and we told them we had been at the show the night before. John Lennon then asked us if there was a café nearby so we said, yes, there was a café down the road and we would take them to it. That meant a walk of about a quarter of a mile, which suited us because it meant we would be walking with the band.

'We walked back along the beach to Joe's Café and discovered that they had virtually no money. There was some story about someone having absconded with the money and they were going to be thrown out of the Station Hotel because they hadn't paid their bill. John had one shilling left which is 5p in today's money and he spent it on a chilled orange for him and one for me. And that is my claim to fame. John Lennon spent his last sixpence on me.'

As the six teenagers wandered along the beachfront, a bracing North Sea wind whipping up against their faces, conversation naturally turned to the previous night's show. Lennon revealed that, in the scrum to get away safely, their black stage shirts had been torn by over-zealous female fans. And they had to wear them for the next show at St Thomas Hall, Banff, the next night. Instantly, the girls came up with a plan to save the day. Margaret said: 'We went back to my house and my friend and I stitched up the shirts, ironed them and made them some soft rolls. John Lennon was in my bedroom but it was all perfectly innocent. He actually did ask me out. But it just wasn't possible. And I never saw him again.'

As Margaret's generosity faded into Beatles' pre-history, the Beat Ballad Show tour continued to roll, even though the wheels often came perilously close to falling off. Next up was Forres, one of Scotland's oldest agricultural towns and famous for its mention in *Macbeth*. Forres became base camp for the next two shows, mainly because it lay directly between Keith and Nairn, where the band were due to play on 25 and 27 May – with the Forres gig sandwiched in between.

By now, Lennon's patience, like the cash in his pocket, had run out. Tired of waiting, he phoned Larry Parnes at his office in the heart of London's Oxford Street. Refusing to be stonewalled, Lennon stayed on the phone until finally the man known in showbiz as 'Parnes, Shillings and Pence' came on the line. Johnny Gentle remembers the teenage firebrand with the temper to match bellowing down the phone: 'Look Larry, where's the bloody money? We're broke.'

Parnes himself was taken aback at Lennon's no-nonsense bravado.

Respect for his elders didn't figure on Lennon's personal radar – especially where cash was concerned. 'We used to pay the groups £15 by post on a Thursday so they would get it on Friday or the very latest on Saturday. I always remember the second week that The Silver Beatles were working for me and I was sitting in my office on a Monday morning at about 11 o' clock and a phone call came through for me, reverse charge. "Who's on the line?" I asked my secretary. "John Lennon," I was told. "Oh well," I replied, "you had better put him on to see what he wants,"' recalled Parnes.

'John comes on the phone and says, "Larry, where's the bloody money?" "What money?," I asked. "We're broke, we're skint." John replies. I said, "But you haven't even worked the week out yet, John. In fact, you haven't even started the week." John says, "Larry, you said if we get a short week we could have a sub." So I said, "You can have a sub, how much do you want?" "Well about five pounds each." "Oh all right," I replied. "We'll send you up five pounds each." It was funny really because both weeks he worked for us he would either come on the phone on the Monday or the Tuesday or the Wednesday. He was the spokesman and he would always say the same thing – "Where's the bloody money?"'

Nevertheless, Lennon's bluster had paid off. Despite his parsimonious reputation, Parnes hated to see his artistes struggle. And he agreed to make sure Duncan McKinnon, still a tour outrider, advanced them the cash. That hurdle cleared, The Beatles and Johnny spent the night having a few – and, in George and Paul's case, illegal – beers in the small residents' lounge of their hotel.

The next morning, they all slept late but the afternoon was set aside for more rehearsals. Lennon and McCartney were keen to try out a few new songs, among them Buddy Holly's 'Words of Love', Little Richard's 'Kansas City', and to refine their own composition, 'One After 909'.

Confidence in their own abilities was coursing through their fingers. George Harrison's guitar playing had improved leaps and bounds even in the couple of nights since Alloa. And the close harmonies of Lennon and McCartney elevated them well above the herd. The only weak links were Sutcliffe's rudimentary bass playing and Moore's stubborn attitude. But the all-for-one and one-for-all belief system remained firmly in place, a musketeer mantra driven by the growing friendship between Lennon, McCartney and Harrison. And that night all that was best about The Beatles finally coalesced into a stunning rock 'n' roll supernova.

Johnny Gentle remembers a band that suddenly found their best form. 'They had already backed me more than adequately but when it came to their own set, they simply stunned the audience. Their own songs were cheered as loudly as the others, but the most successful song of the night was "Kansas City". And it remained a part of their concert repertoire for the next five years.

'Duncan McKinnon had arrived just in time for The Beatles' performance and he was shocked by what he heard. They didn't sound anything like the crummy band he'd wanted to send home just five days earlier in Alloa. I thought we had just seen the future of rock 'n' roll. I just thought they were going to make it. I had seen enough backing bands to know that these guys were different. Maybe Stuart and Tommy didn't quite fit but the other three were a rock 'n' roll triumvirate to be reckoned with. Next morning when Larry Parnes called to check on the tour, I advised him again to sign The Beatles. I said sign them up now while you can, they're gonna be big. In fact, I thought they were going down better than me. But, to his regret, he wasn't listening. He said he didn't have the time.'

On the morning of Thursday 26 May, The Beatles were still feeding off the frenzy of the night before. Adulation apart, the music had gone up another notch. And they kept up the tempo at that evening's gig at the local town hall. By now, Johnny was convinced he was in at the ground floor of something special. The band were entirely comfortable backing him. And their looseness and musicality only added to the vitality of the tour. As usual, Johnny's show-stopping moment came when he pulled up a chair and sang his ballad 'Have I Told You Lately' beneath a single spotlight. Behind him, anonymous in the dark, The Beatles strummed the now familiar chords.

When the set finished, Johnny bowed several times and then, for the first time, acknowledged the young turks who gave the show its edge. 'Ladies and gentleman . . . a big hand for The Beatles.' The five musicians stood riveted to the spot, grinning hugely, as they took their first ovation with Johnny. The moment was not lost on Lennon who said: 'I'll tell you one thing. It's better than working.'

The chain reaction generated by those young boys sparked into life again the next night at the Regal Ballroom in Nairn. When Johnny exited the stage, Lennon plucked the plectrum from his mouth and adopted his usual stance, guitar held high, his legs bent at the knees and hunched forward; McCartney took his position at the mic, his face so close to Lennon's he could feel his breath, a symbol of the harmonies that came to dominate a decade; and George Harrison was lost in his own world, his eyes fixed firmly on his red Grazione guitar. And the first few notes of 'Kansas City' triggered the noisy crescendo.

Open-mouthed with astonishment at this unexpected reaction was local musician Johnny Douglas, who was convinced he was watching a young band stamping on their own graves, so poorly did he rate their musical prowess. He recalled: 'They arrived in this old Austin 16 van. They were so poor they slept in this van. They were all nice guys and they would talk away to you. They would drink bottles of beer, all the kids were doing it. They were typical youngsters but from what I saw they seemed to be enjoying themselves. They had wee, tiny amplifiers. I was amazed they actually got any sound from them at all. They were absolute rubbish.'

But the glamour of life as embryonic pop stars quickly faded at the end of the night. Their financial situation forced them all to kip in the van that was used to traverse the Highlands. The smell of cigarette smoke curling inside the cramped interior roused all five the next morning, the last day of the tour. That night's show was to take place at the Rescue Hall in Peterhead's Prince Street. The famous fishing town lay 80 miles east so the van shuddered into life and off they went to bring the curtain down on the Beat Ballad tour. Parnes had been as good as his word and more cash had filtered through from Duncan McKinnon. This allowed them to book into a small B&B.

When they arrived at the venue, a surprise was waiting for them. McKinnon, by now delighted with the tour that had turned a handsome profit, showed his appreciation by leaving a crate of beer in their tiny dressing room. Johnny also upped his game for the last night and the responses to his showstopping finale, 'OK Alright You Win', crackled with enthusiasm. Afterwards, the beer disappeared in a frenzy of end-of-tour celebrations. A gaggle of girls milled around, innocent flirts rather than full-on groupies. This was the conclusion, but also a beginning.

The next day, Johnny and his new-found protégés rubbed the sleep from their eyes for a rendezvous at the hotel where the Beat Ballad star and his girlfriend were staying. Backs were slapped, handshakes exchanged and promises were made to do it all again soon. A couple of nights earlier, a thought had crossed Johnny's mind. Why not hire them as a permanent backing band? The idea faded as quickly as it arrived. In his heart, Johnny Gentle already knew what the world would wait three years to discover. The Beatles were on a collision course with history, having graduated from their first tour with flying colours. Not for them the thankless task of dancing to someone else's tune.

Johnny Gentle and The Beatles said their farewells with a promise to meet up in Liverpool soon. John, Paul, George, Stu and Tommy then piled into their mobile sleeping quarters for the 35-mile drive to Aberdeen's Guild Street Station and the start of the long trip south back to the 'Pool.

Many historians have tried to write off The Beatles' first tour of Scotland as a disaster. The general picture is of half-filled halls, badly-rehearsed songs and jeers for souvenirs. And that is undeniably partly true. But Paul McCartney has always valued that first tour for the way it brought the band – for the most part – together. He said: 'It was important on

helping us get our relationships right with each other.'

And 45 years on, Johnny Gentle has nothing but rose-tinged memories of those nine days in the Scottish Highlands. He told me: 'It was a huge learning step for them and Paul McCartney has said the same thing. They had never been out of Liverpool before. There were a lot of girls screaming, but they were screaming at me. But this was the first time The Beatles had ever seen a reaction like that. It was a huge stepping stone on the road to success. It's nice for me to look back now and see I was in at the ground floor of something that became very very big. That is my claim to fame now.

'I had some great times and I enjoyed it. I developed into a good entertainer. After I first heard their first singles, I wasn't surprised by how good they had become. They had come a long way. In fact, the first time I realised how successful they'd become I was in Germany. When we were in Scotland, you couldn't possibly have envisaged that kind of success for them. People like them and Elvis changed the music scene beyond all recognition. They were just ordinary lads who hoped that one day they might have a few hit records.'

'Tomorrow never knows' is a phrase that could easily have been applied to the future of the band. Who really knew what the future held for a bunch of kids tilting at windmills? Conviction, though, was the currency of the time, the feeling that one day they would make it. Especially with John Lennon, that inner fire raged fiercely. To the toppermost of the poppermost, lads.

Three years later, The Beatles were back touring in Scotland. And, by that time, the rest was hysteria . . .

3. The Scottish Beatle

Stuart Sutcliffe

Taken at face value, it amounts to a who's who of humanity, a jigsaw puzzle of pop art and the ultimate expression of hero worship. Occultist Aleister Crowley takes his place beside silver screen siren Mae West; Marlon Brando, his cold stare referencing *The Wild One*, is only a few steps away from Oscar Wilde; Marilyn Monroe is sandwiched between wartime comedian Tommy Handley and William Burroughs, celebrated author of *The Naked Lunch*; German avant-garde composer Stockhausen mingles with Carl Jung, the father of modern-day psychology, and an assortment of Indian gurus are also dotted on the canvas of *Sgt. Pepper's Lonely Hearts Club Band*. Standing in the front, bedecked in the Day-Glo colours of 1967 hippy psychedelia, are John Lennon, Ringo Starr, Paul McCartney and George Harrison.

The celebrated cover contains 62 images of the famous and the infamous in the ultimate tribute by all four to a collection of individuals whose influences had shaped their dreams and hopes. Closer inspection, however, reveals that not all the faces in the *Pepper* audience are household names. Tucked away in the third row from the back on the left-hand side is the face of a young man, his handsome features peering out just in front of celebrated Victorian artist Aubrey Beardsley. The juxtaposition is ironic; for the young man with the strangely distant look in his eyes was one of the most talented artists of his generation – and, arguably, the closest and most influential friend Lennon ever had. As a Scouser might say, they were tighter than two coats of paint.

History has foisted numerous labels on Stuart Sutcliffe: pioneer painter, fashion visionary, mediocre musician, fifth Beatle. But one has been largely airbrushed out of existence, the one that gave him his birthright – Stu was the only Beatle born in Scotland. His mother Millie went to enormous lengths to ensure he remembered exactly where he came from, even though the vast majority of his life – a life tragically cut short – was spent south of the border.

In the story of The Beatles, it was always John and Paul. Lennon and McCartney. Two sides of the same coin. One the hard-nosed cynic, the rebel convinced he had a cause to take on the world; the other the sun-kissed optimist convinced his cause was to write music that would take him

The Scottish Beatle. This haunting picture, taken in Hamburg, captures Stuart Sutcliffe's idiosyncratic style, which did so much to shape the band's own image.

out of dead-end street. Between them, the songs of Lennon and McCartney would indeed change the world. Two teenage boys hunched over acoustic guitars, fingers clutching new chords, crafting songs that altered the course of pop music forever. Theirs was a competitive relationship, born of an intense, sibling-style rivalry. The bond between them, cemented by the fact they both lost their mothers in their teenage years, ran deep.

But the truth is that, in the early story of The Beatles, it was not always John and Paul. Once upon a time it was John and Stu, two sides of the same coin. One, the hard-nosed cynic, the rebel convinced he had a cause to take on the world; the other the Ray-Ban-wearing bohemian convinced his cause was to paint pictures that would take him out of dead-end street.

The influence of the sensitive young painter on the no-holds-barred rocker has polarised opinion for more than 40 years. Without question, theirs was a hugely emotional and complicated relationship. Their backgrounds, though, could hardly have been more different. Liverpudlian cynicism festered like an open wound in Lennon. Humour, disdain, wit, rebellion and a mock-eyed view of convention were all atoms swirling inside his complex DNA. Stuart, though, was quiet, sensitive, caring, well-read and bursting with a unique talent that held experts like famed Scots artist Eduardo Paolozzi in awe.

Both were born at the height of the Second World War, 250 miles apart. As the Luftwaffe's bombs rained down on Britain in 1940, John made his entrance into the world. In a moment of patriotism, his mother Julia gave him the middle name Winston. Six months earlier, Martha Sutcliffe gave birth to her first and only son in an Edinburgh maternity hospital. Martha and her husband Charles lived for a while in London and Manchester having originally come from Wishaw and Hamilton.

Family circumstances had earlier dictated they head south following the type of religious-inspired scandal that is a cancer on the face of the west of Scotland. When Martha discovered she was pregnant, she determined that her first child would be born in Scotland. England was, she rationalised, a foreign country and she was adamant her family would never forsake their Celtic roots. So she and Charles decamped to Edinburgh.

The child was born on 23 June 1940 at the Simpson Memorial Maternity Pavilion. He was given the full name of Stuart Fergusson Victor Sutcliffe. His name was as Scottish as John's was English. Home for the first three years of Stuart's life was a tall house in an elegant, sophisticated terrace row in Edinburgh's Chalmers Street. His sister Joyce was also born there in March 1942.

Behind this picture of family contentment, though, lay a troubled past for the Sutcliffes. Charles Sutcliffe was born in Scotland in 1905, the son of Joseph and Mary Sutcliffe. He was a Yorkshire-born army major; she was a dutiful Scottish wife. Young Charles was raised in his father's religion as a High Anglican and was a pupil at Hamilton Academy. His father's involvement with the freemasons enabled him to pull in a few favours to get his son a good job with the civil service. Charles then married a local butcher's daughter and, within 10 years, was the proud father of three sons and a daughter.

Stuart's mother Martha Cronin was born only a few miles away from where the Sutcliffes lived. She was the last of nine daughters born to a retired and wealthy steel industry executive, Matthew Cronin, and his wife Agnes. Martha grew up as a Catholic in the pit village of Wishaw, not far from the giant steel furnaces of Ravenscraig that every day belched out plumes of ash and smoke. She was sent to a convent school and taught by Franciscan nuns, an early education that cemented her faith. At 18, she considered devoting her life to her church and joined a Franciscan order in Yorkshire, though she left before taking her final vows.

Back home in Lanarkshire, Martha settled into family life. Fate, however, turned Martha's world upside down when she met and fell in love with a married man. Not only was Charles Sutcliffe married, he was a mason and, religiously, from another dimension. In her memoir, *The Beatles' Shadow & His Lonely Hearts Club*, Stuart's youngest sister Pauline wrote: 'My father did divorce. The Cronins were perhaps more broad-minded but, as Roman Catholics, would not condone a marriage between their daughter and a Protestant divorcee. Father lost his civil service job and my parents their families who disowned them.'

Ostracised by their families, Martha and Charles wed in a civil ceremony and, as war clouds hovered over Europe, trekked south in search of a new start. It was, by any measure, an inauspicious start to married life for the Sutcliffes. Out of adversity, though, shone a determi-nation to make it.

Stuart's birth was the first rung on a ladder to a proper family life. Charles worked as a marine engineer at the famous John Brown shipyard in Glasgow, his skills much sought-after as Winston Churchill stepped up Britain's munitions programme. But the vagaries of war soon meant Martha and Charles were on the move again, this time back to England. With their young family in tow, the Sutcliffes moved to a council-owned bungalow in Liverpool's Huyton district. This came after Charles was drafted as an essential war worker to the city's famous Cammell Laird shipyard in Birkenhead. Scotland, of course, was forever stamped in the couple's hearts, but they would never live there again as a family.

In January 1944, Pauline's birth completed the family. Millie, by now working as a schoolteacher, doted on Stuart – so like her in stature and nature, a lovely boy with a giving personality – but never to the detriment of his two sisters. All three grew up surrounded by books and the sounds of Beethoven and Chopin and wrapped in a loving family blanket.

But, despite the English accents they heard every day, all three were quietly reminded of their Celtic connections. Special occasions were marked by Stuart and his sisters being kitted out in the family tartan. And the most important day of the year in the Sutcliffe household was New Year's Eve – Hogmanay – a celebration of all things Scottish.

Interest in the arts was hugely encouraged and Stuart soon found himself in the choir at the local church. His talent for singing was quickly spotted and promotion to head chorister rapidly followed. At school, he thrived and teachers zeroed in on Stuart's instinctive skill for drawing; he was already considering a career in canvas. He eventually left school with five O levels which gained him entry into the prestigious Liverpool School of Art at the age of just 16. Normally, students had to be 18 but Stuart's prodigious gift had already raised eyebrows.

His early work, largely impressionist in style, had drawn comparisons with the likes of the young Pablo Picasso and Salvador Dali. But his dedication to his art was tested by a serious rival. Elvis Presley, snake-hipped and sparking sex appeal like a lightning rod, had united a post-war generation of teenagers in a frenzy of rock 'n' roll. Sitting at home in Huyton, listening late at night to the crackle of Radio Luxembourg, Stuart had never heard anything like Elvis.

Across the Mersey, John Lennon, in his Aunt Mimi's home in Menlove Avenue, Woolton, switched on to the same sounds and was just as captivated. Elsewhere in Liverpool, Paul McCartney, George Harrison and Richard Starkey, like millions of kids all over the world, reached for guitars and drums, dreaming of becoming just like Elvis, dreaming of becoming the man.

Stuart moved out of the family home with his mother's blessing and rented a basement flat with a pal round the corner from the art school. These were heady, carefree days. Stuart relished life as a student; he had time to develop his art, listen to music and meet a growing band of like-minded youngsters high on the happy side life. He hooked up with the Students' Union Committee, and as his social circle expanded, struck up a friendship with a curly-haired lad called Bill Harry. Bill in turn introduced him to a new student who was the same age as Stuart. His name was John Lennon.

In the years since Stu and John first met – almost exactly a year after Lennon first shook hands with McCartney – much has been written about their relationship. What exactly was it that drew the two of them together? Which one was the teacher and which one the disciple? On the surface, they were at opposite ends of the adolescent spectrum. Lennon was a poor scholar, often skipping classes to play guitar, a quiet rage simmering inside him as a consequence of his troubled childhood, a rage that could explode at any given moment. Stuart, on the other hand, was quieter, a sensitive but popular student nurtured by his teachers and dedicated to his art. But the ties that bind could be found in the fact that both were free spirits, revelling in their teenage independence and united by a love of music.

So it was only natural that John should invite his new best pal to join his band The Quarrymen. Painting was okay but rock 'n' roll will make you a star, was the message from John. The Quarrymen's ever-shifting personnel hampered their ambitions to one day be 'bigger than Elvis', even though in 1958 gigs were few, limited to the odd local dance and wedding. Musically, they practised hard. And John and Paul had even tried their hands at writing their own songs. Anything to avoid the prospect of the nine to five.

Stuart was invited to broaden the band's evolving sound by taking up the bass. The only problem was he didn't play the bass and he was too poor to buy one. A solution presented itself when Stuart entered one of his paintings in the John Moores exhibition, a biennial event whose patron was one of the city's leading arts benefactors. Stuart's painting was accepted and eventually bought by John Moore himself for the then not insignificant sum of £65. Beatle mythology has it Stuart planked the lot on a bass guitar. The truth, though, was not so romantic. Perhaps in keeping with the Calvinistic parsimony of his Scottish background, he bought his Hofner President bass on hire purchase and kept the rest of the prize money to spend on drawing materials. He knew which side his bread was buttered on.

Nevertheless, it meant Stu was now a fully-fledged Quarryman and ready to take on the world. And his relationship with John was cemented even further. John mentored Stuart's musical education while showing John that his obscure classroom doodles, echoing the offbeat humour of the Goons and James Joyce, masked an inherent artistic ability.

The birth pangs of rock 'n' roll also signalled a fashion rebellion. Boys, especially, ditched the flannels and checked houndstooth jackets of their fathers for crotch-tight drainpipe trousers and leather jackets. Americana was in. Britannia, no longer ruling, was creaking at the seams, the sun setting on her empire. In Liverpool School of Art, no one could fail to notice Stuart. Already charismatic and good looking, he radiated a kind of James Dean persona. The transformation was complete when he adopted winkle picker shoes, piled his hair high with Vaseline and nudged a pair of dark glasses onto the bridge of his nose. Introducing Stuart

Sutcliffe, bohemian artist and would be rock 'n' roll star; the former, however, would always take precedence over the latter.

Paul and George worried that Stu's lack of musical ability would stop them earning the Big Ticket. But for John, loyalty was everything. As long as he was around, Stu was in the band. End of story. The doubts, though, never went away, eventually giving rise to petty jealousies and almost 50 years of unproven allegations and false innuendo.

Yet, for all his reputation as a ham-fisted bass player, it was Stuart who signalled the end for The Quarrymen by coming up with a distinctive new name for John's band – The Beetles. There have been claim and counter-claim over who actually came up with the name. But most of the interested parties have credited the band's name to Stuart, apparently making a pun on Buddy Holly's group The Crickets. Although it was John who modified the name by changing the second 'e' to an 'a' to reflect their 'beat' aspirations. Paul was to say: 'It was John and Stuart who thought of the name. They were art students and while George's and my parents would make us go to bed, Stuart and John could live the little dream that we all dream; to stay up all night. And it was during one of those brainstorming sessions that they thought up the name.'

George Harrison's memory was slightly clouded by the mists of time. He said: 'It is debatable where the name came from. John used to say that he invented it, but I remember Stuart being with him the night before. There was The Crickets, who backed Buddy Holly, that similarity; but Stuart was really into Marlon Brando and in the movie *The Wild One*, there is a scene where Lee Marvin says: "Johnny, we've been looking for you, the Beetles have missed you." Maybe John and Stu were both thinking about it at the time. We'll give it 50/50 to Sutcliffe/Lennon.'

Interestingly, George's comments illustrate perfectly how the lines between Beatle fact and Beatle fiction can easily blur – even among those who lived it. *The Wild One* was denied a 1958 UK cinema release because it was deemed too violent. It would be another 14 years before British big screen audiences would see it. So Stu never actually saw the famous Lee Marvin scene, although it has now become part of Fab Four folklore.

Of course, choosing a name was one thing, sticking with it another. The band went through a number of different handles, shifting from The Beetles to Johnny and The Moondogs to the Silver Beetles before settling on the name that eventually caused such a seismic shift in Western pop culture.

John and Stuart continued to make inroads on their chosen paths. The big break for The Silver Beetles came in May 1960 when they took part in an audition to back singer Billy Fury on a nationwide tour. They joined a number of local groups, including Gerry and The Pacemakers for

I've just seen a face. John Lennon insisted that Stuart Sutcliffe be included among the band's heroes for the iconic cover of Sergeant Pepper's Lonely Hearts Club Band. He appears on the far left, third row from the back.

the chance to impress London impresario Larry Parnes. On this occasion, they famously didn't pass the audition. However Parnes saw enough in The Silver Beetles to book them for a nine-day tour of Scottish dance halls backing stablemate Johnny Gentle, a fellow Scouser whose first single had already reached the outer hemispheres of the pop charts.

Again, though, inter-band jealousies pointed the finger of blame at Stuart for costing them their first tilt at the big time. Misinformed so-called experts claimed Stu kept his back to Parnes so the wily promoter wouldn't notice he was out of key, and a musical liability for The Silver Beetles. Pictures from the audition, however, told a different story.

Still, there can be no denying that Stuart was not in the same instrumental league as John, Paul or George. Friends such as Bill Harry, while dismayed that Stu was swapping his brushes for a bass guitar, have remained scathing about the picture history has painted of his musical qualities. In his book, *The John Lennon Encyclopaedia*, he said: 'Stuart was only an adequate musician, it's true, but he had presence and charisma on stage. It is also untrue that he played with his back to the audience or was instructed to turn his back when photographs were being taken. The photographs taken at the Parnes audition show Stuart facing the camera and playing his instrument.'

If meeting John Lennon was a major turning point in Stuart Sutcliffe's life, another crossroads was looming up fast. And this time the signpost was pointing to Germany. Or, more specifically, the notorious Reeperbahn of Hamburg. After their stint in Scotland, the first time Stuart had been back in his homeland since he was a child, Liverpool entrepreneur Alan Williams, who had been managing the band on an ad-hoc basis, secured them a residency at the Indra. This was a run-down beer cellar and a popular haunt for sailors, pimps, transvestites and prostitutes. In other words, it was a Reeperbahn hotspot, heaving with the sweat of sex, drugs and – with the arrival of The Beatles – gritty rock 'n' roll.

None of The Beatles, with the possible exception of George as the youngest, was exactly an innocent abroad. But Hamburg provided the key to Pandora's Box and all five – they had been joined by drummer Pete Best – soon unlocked its carnal contents. In Hamburg, The Beatles became 24-hour party people. At night, they often played for six hours non-stop, fuelled by the never-ending supply of preludins to keep them awake. Off stage, they practised relentlessly, grabbing a few hours' kip when exhaustion eventually overcame them.

At last the fact that Stuart's bass playing was the weakest link in the chain didn't seem to matter. All that the crowds who packed the Indra every night cared about was the fact that The Beatles '*mach shau*' – make a show, lads. And the louder the better.

John and Stu, in the dog days of their teenage years, felt like Caesars and Hamburg was their very own Coliseum. Word had spread about the young English group whose raucous show and on-stage charisma was a potent mix of animal magnetism and raw musical passion. In Hamburg, The Beatles unearthed the nuclear reaction that fused them as a band. They were on £15 a week – almost double what Paul's dad earned as a cotton salesman in Liverpool. They had more girl action than any of them had ever dreamt of. They were packing in crowds of fans. And they were getting better every night. There was no looking back. As far as their music was concerned, Lennon, McCartney and Harrison – Pete was always an outsider – were in perfect harmony. The bond between John and Stu was still tight but all that was about to change.

The Beatles were switched to the Kaiserkellar after the Indra was closed following complaints about the noise. The venue may have changed but the songs remained the same. In October 1960, just days before John turned 20, a young German student called Klaus Voorman heard the sounds emerging from a late-night session at the Kaiserkellar. His curiosity aroused, Voorman wandered in and was mesmerised when The Beatles began pumping out their high-octane brand of rock 'n' roll. For Klaus, it amounted to a kind of epiphany, a life-changing moment on the road to a musical Damascus. A few days later he came back, this time with his girlfriend Astrid Kirchherr and another pal Jurgen Vollmer.

Soon, their whole set of friends, dubbed the Exis after the growing Existentialist movement sweeping the Continent, were frequent visitors to The Beatles' night-long sets. The music, of course, was the main focus of attention. But the Exis, dressed in their dark rollneck sweaters and exuding bohemian chic, had their sights narrowed on one Beatle in particular. In their optical crosshairs was Stuart Sutcliffe. With his film star looks and his ever-present shades, Stu looked every inch the essence of an Exi. They rushed to the front of the stage when Stuart performed 'Love Me Tender', his one moment in the musical spotlight.

Klaus was captivated by Stuart's ethereal, almost androgynous, appearance and the effortless charisma he seemed to radiate. But he was also drawn to the young musician's love of art, a fascination that drew him naturally to the gothic architecture and renaissance paintings that hung in the Hamburg galleries.

In a rare interview from his home in Germany, Klaus, who went on to forge his own highly successful musical career as a bass player with Manfred Mann and a host of other groups, recalled the multi-faceted connection he quickly formed with Stuart: 'He was a very inspiring person. To me, he was destined to be a painter. That was his calling in life. You had to witness the way he would walk around and take in the world around him

Overleaf. Stuart at his bohemian best (far right) with John, George, Pete Best and Paul at the Indra Club in Hamburg. Only Pete is out of style with the others.

THE SCOTTSH BEATLE   59

to understand why I would say that. He was very excited about things, about life. It seemed to me that his brain was running so fast, like he was trying to put as much as he could into the few days that he had on this globe. He was very alive. He was vibrant but at the same time he was a very frail, very sensitive person. He was very subdued in a way. He was shy and very delicate.

'What did I like about him? Well, he looked great which was not the main reason but that was just a fact. He immediately jumped on anything to do with art, the movies. He was soaking it up like a sponge. And of course I got a lot of information from him so I like to think we inspired each other. We bounced off one another.'

Klaus, though, was not the only member of their circle of friends to suss out there was something about Stuart . . . Astrid, his on-off girlfriend, was smitten and it didn't take a member of Mensa to work out the attraction was a two-way street. Stuart found himself irresistibly drawn to the beautiful blonde girl with the elfin features. Klaus accepted the situation with good grace. Astrid spoke no English and Stu's German was rudimentary, but theirs was a language that needed little translation. Two months after they met, Stu and Astrid got engaged.

Stu couldn't believe his luck that he'd pulled this gorgeous German girl ahead of experienced carousers like Lennon and McCartney. In one of his many letters home, he wrote: 'The girl thought I was the most handsome of the lot. Here I was, feeling the most insipid working member of the group being told how much superior I looked – this alongside the great Romeo John Lennon and his two stalwarts Paul and George, the Casanovas of Hamburg.'

Astrid has also recalled the life-changing moment when she first clapped eyes on Stuart in the Kaiserkellar, an instant when two destinies seemed to collide. She said: 'He had his back to the audience and he completely knocked me out. He came across to our table and I was just shaking and then of course later he told me he was shaking as well. About two weeks later, I realised the only way I would get to know him was to get him on his own, away from the others. So I asked if I could take pictures of him. His face was just absolutely beautiful. He completely captivated me. He was very enthusiastic about life and the knowledge of life and that was very attractive. Of course I was dying to be alone with him. Eventually we just fell into one another's arms. Klaus was so understanding.'

Indeed, Klaus is at pains to deny the relationship was the cause of friction between himself, his new-found friend and his former lover. 'It wasn't a difficult situation. Astrid and I are really like brother and sister. I was really happy that she found somebody who she liked so much.'

But Astrid and Stuart's partnership signalled a fundamental change in the dynamic of The Beatles. John could no longer ignore the fact his friend was heading along a different path from him. Paul, sensing the shift in John's loyalties, made his move to switch through the gears of the band's patriarchal hierarchy. His eye remained on the grand prize and Stu was quite simply holding them back.

In later years, Paul admitted adolescent jealousy occasionally seeped into his relationship with Stuart. Both were vying for the attention of the undoubted leader of the gang. And McCartney admitted they all gave Stuart a hard time for his musical failings. On one occasion, it actually broke out into a fight on stage between Paul and Stuart, much to John's amusement.

In *The Beatles Anthology*, Paul tried to set the record straight. He recalled: 'Someone a few years ago said how it was my relentless ambition that pushed Stu out of the group. We did have some arguments, me and Stu, but really all I wanted was for us to be a really cracking band and Stu, being a cracking artist, held us back a little bit. If ever it came to the push, when there was someone in there watching us, I'd feel, "Oh, I hope Stu doesn't blow it." I could trust the rest of us; that was it. Stuart would tend to turn away a little so as not to be too obvious about what key he was in, in case it wasn't our key.'

The separation between Stu and the band may have been slowburning, but their Scots-born bassist still had one more contribution to make to the history of The Beatles, one that left an indelible imprint. Under Astrid's Existentialist influence, he restyled his hair, combing it forward and ditching the greasy rocker quiff. It was the precursor to the famous moptop haircut so characteristic of The Beatles' appearance when they rode the big dipper to stardom. And he swapped his black leathers for a Pierre Cardin collarless suit. The style makeover wasn't taken up by the others immediately; that would have been uncool. But over the next few months, John, Paul and George gradually binned the Brylcreem.

The Beatles returned to Liverpool in December 1960. Their stay at new club the Top Ten had ended in a police probe over an arson claim and George was deported for being underage. John stayed in Hamburg a few more days before leaving Stu behind with Astrid and taking the boat home. It was the beginning of the end for Stuart with The Beatles. He did go back to Liverpool in February 1961 and played with the band for the first quarter of the year. During one gig, Stuart received a severe beating and suffered kicks and punches to his head. The incident forgotten, Stu applied for a diploma teaching course at his alma mater the Liverpool College of Art. But he was left furious and disappointed when the application was rejected. Salvation, he felt now, lay in Hamburg with Astrid, his love for drawing pulling him back to the easel and canvas.

Stuart enrolled in the State High School of Art Instruction in Hamburg and embarked on a major body of work. He worked like a man possessed. Day and night, he slaved away in the tiny attic in Astrid's mother's house. In hindsight, you could perhaps argue that he felt his time was slipping away. Such was Stuart's talent that he was placed in a special class comprising outstanding students drawn from a number of countries. He was put under the tuition of Edinburgh-born sculptor and artist Eduardo Paolozzi, who was quick to spot Stuart's amazing potential for abstract impressionist work. In one report, he wrote: 'One of my best students. He is working very hard and with high intelligence.' But, in another, he tellingly foretold of the dark times ahead. 'Stuart is very gifted, but through medical and technical reasons, he has been unable to attend for periods, which could have been beneficial for his future development.'

Weeks later, The Beatles resumed their own love affair with Hamburg, taking top billing at the Top Ten and then the Star Club, each move demonstrating the pulling power of their performances – and their ability to generate cash for the owners. Stuart continued to sit in on the odd occasion, but it was never the same. The crunch came one night when Paul's taunts finally pushed Stu over the edge and the audience was stunned by the sight of the two Beatles grappling with each other on the stage floor. Parting was inevitable. John and Stu had a tearful heart-to-heart, but both knew it was the end of the road. Their futures lay in different directions. Slowly, Stuart disentangled himself from The Beatles and threw himself at full throttle into his art.

By the summer of 1961, however, Astrid began to notice a change in his personality. He seemed to become more withdrawn and frequently complained about blinding headaches that often left him gasping for breath. Astrid wrote home to Millie to tell her Stuart had fallen down the stairs and bumped his head, her worries all too evident between the lines of broken English.

Over the course of the next few months, Stu's condition worsened; he lost weight and was constantly sick. Doctors in Germany, largely baffled by his illness, put it down to stress and his 'artistic temperament'; hospital X-rays showed nothing out of the ordinary. He kept up a steady stream of letters to home but the distance only heightened Millie's anxiety for the boy she continued to be devoted to. She had, albeit, reluctantly, rarely interfered in his hedonistic lifestyle, but often implored him to concentrate more on his drawing. But a mother's instinct now told her something was seriously wrong.

In late August, Stuart came home. With him was Astrid, setting the scene for that awkward first meeting between the German fiancée and the doting mum for whom the memories of World War Two were still raw.

Stuart beside some of
the paintings that
eventually came to
define his style and led
to early comparisons
with Salvador Dali.

Stu's mother wanted to take over his care, fearing if he returned to Germany, she would lose him forever.

Stuart had also returned clutching the German X-rays so he could get a second opinion. But he failed to turn up for an appointment at Liverpool's Sefton General Hospital to have new X-rays taken. Who knows what they would have diagnosed?

Stuart and Astrid packed their bags in September, the frosty atmosphere between the two women refusing to thaw. Pauline stated: 'My mother and Stuart had a row about him staying to seek further medical advice and treatment, but beneath the surface was her growing resentment of Astrid. There was Stuart looking so unwell and everyone being frustrated from all sides in their attempts to help. And Stuart not helping either by telling us what he knew we wanted to hear rather than the truth about how he felt.'

By November, Stuart's life and The Beatles' career had coalesced in one of those curious quirks of fate. Liverpool record shop owner Brian Epstein ordered in copies of a record a local group had made in Hamburg. It was called 'My Bonnie' and featured Tony Sheridan backed by a Liverpool group known as The Beat Brothers. Of course, the kids in Liverpool knew the real identity of The Beat Brothers. Epstein decided to check out this local band for himself – and the rest is history. November also recorded a further decline in Stuart's health. The headaches and blackouts were getting worse – and the rest is tragedy.

In January, 1962, Stuart suffered a convulsive fit in art class and Astrid was summoned from work to ferry him home. More hospital consultations failed to find the cause of the problem. (Had Stuart's problems been diagnosed today, the chances are an effective treatment would have been put in place.) The next month, Stuart came back to Liverpool for what would be the last time. Millie was in ill-health herself, the worries over Stuart not helping. She was shocked by his emaciated appearance and the permanent black rings beneath his eyes.

He went to see The Beatles, this time playing the Cavern in Liverpool, and was amazed to see how far they had come. He was hugely proud of them but felt no regrets. He and John enjoyed talking over old times. They parted on good terms. But John never saw Stuart, the first of his life-changing gurus, again.

Stuart died on 10 April 1962. Astrid's mother felt her blood run cold when she heard a scream and noises from the attic. She found Stuart writhing in agony on the floor, gripped by another convulsion. A local doctor quickly diagnosed that Stuart had suffered a cerebral haemorrhage. Astrid navigated her way through Hamburg's lunchtime traffic to get home. He passed away in her arms in the ambulance rushing him to hospital. A post-mortem later revealed the cause of death to be a haemorrhage in the right ventricle of the brain. Stuart, The Beatles' very own art director and John Lennon's teenage lodestone, was just two months short of his 22nd birthday.

In one of those curious twists of fate, John, Paul and Pete Best flew into Hamburg the day after Stu's death as the vanguard for The Beatles' appearance at the Star Club. They were met at the airport by Astrid, her face ashen with grief. John was first to break the silence and ask where Stu was. The response was too much for any of them to take in. Astrid said: 'I arrived at the airport with Klaus. Pete, John and Paul were already there, jumping up and down and cuddling me, pleased to see me. Then I told them Stuart had died. Pete burst into tears, Paul was just holding me in his beautiful way and John just freaked out, completely freaked out, just laughing until tears came.'

Accounts of John's reaction differ. His tough-guy persona provided the ideal cloak to mask his emotions. But there is little doubt Stuart's death would have been a crushing blow. No matter what had gone down before, Stuart was one of them, a Beatle-brother-in-arms and, in John's eyes at least, always would be.

Stuart was buried in Huyton Parish Cemetery at St Gabriel's Church, yards away from the altar where he once sung as a choral boy. In her book, his sister Pauline admits Stuart's death forced her mother to rake over a lifetime of what-might-have-beens: 'Her thoughts focused on Stuart's Edinburgh birth and what might have happened if the family had never left Scotland. That was where the happy memories were, in Scotland.'

None of The Beatles attended Stu's funeral, preferring instead to follow the old maxim that the show must go on. Astrid also stayed away, citing illness, but perhaps more because she felt her presence may have made matters worse. For all parties, it was a wretched time, but time does not stand still. Six months later, under the careful stewardship of Brian Epstein, The Beatles released their first single 'Love Me Do'. In Liverpool, everyone knew their name. Soon, the world would know their name.

Stuart Sutcliffe's name rested on a cemetery headstone. Even in death, however, a legend was forming. Through the tireless endeavours of Pauline and other long-time friends like Bill Harry, Stuart's legacy to The Beatles and, more poignantly, the art world, has been brought to the attention of a wider audience. Eduardo Paolozzi's observation that Stuart was an artist of immense potential has been borne out in the work he left behind. So much so that modern experts have compared Stuart's impressionist paintings to those of Salvador Dali and Picasso. As recently as 2001, exhibitions of his paintings – he left some 250 drawings and sketches – were mounted in galleries as far apart as Tokyo, Canada and America. His canvasses can now command significant sums, such is the cult status that has built up around the tragic Beatle.

The Beatles clearly never forgot Stuart, but his involvement in the band was, in the formative years of Beatlemania at least, mentioned in hushed tones. PR handouts charting the band's beginnings made scant mention of him. Over time, though, stances softened and real feelings came to the fore. George Harrison said: 'I had a lot of fights with Stu but I really liked him and we were very friendly before he died. I suppose the reason I was fighting with him was that in the ego pecking order, he wasn't really a musician. He was in the band because John had conned him into buying a bass. He was like our art director. In a mysterious way Stuart, in conjunction with the German crowd, not just Astrid, was really responsible for that certain look we had.'

According to Yoko Ono, John's feelings for Stuart never dimmed. Proof comes in the fact that it was John who insisted that Stuart take his place alongside all his other boyhood heroes on the most iconic album cover of all time, *Sgt. Pepper's Lonely Hearts Club Band*. He was, of course, much more than just a face in the crowd. This was Lennon's very personal doff of the cap to a pal who was also a mentor. John's honesty famously veered close to masochism and he perhaps best sums up what Stuart meant to him. He said: 'I looked up to Stu. I depended on him to tell me the truth. Stu would tell me if something was good and I'd believe him.'

4. The Concerts

John Lennon described it as living in the eye of the hurricane, three and a half years when the maelstrom of Beatlemania swirled round the whole world. It was a raging storm that triggered colossal social and cultural change.

Yet, when The Beatles arrived in Scotland on 2 January 1963, no one could have forecast that the start of a new year also heralded the first tentative steps of such a global musical phenomenon. As the rest of the country was still suffering from the traditional Ne'erday hangover, The Beatles – John, Paul, George and Ringo – set off on a five-day tour of Scotland. In the next week, they would criss-cross the Highlands for shows at Elgin, Dingwall and Bridge of Allan before hitting the high road again to play Aberdeen's Beach Ballroom. All of them were outposts miles off the beaten track of pop concert stardom. Glamorous it wasn't, the band often playing to sparse audiences more interested in home-grown foot-stompers than a bunch of scrawny Scousers. There was no fanfare, even though the release of 'Please Please Me', their breakthrough second single, was incredibly only 10 days away.

Yet, five months later, The Beatles would be back in Scotland and by then the hurricane would be picking up speed by the day. Soon, it would make landfall and touch every corner of the planet.

During the Beatlemania years, between the period from January 1963 to August 1966 when they were still a touring band, the Fab Four played 22 concerts in Scotland. That may not seem like a great many – but then it has to be put into the context of the frenzied, unrelenting pace of their lives. Between January 1963 and August 1966, The Beatles recorded a mind-boggling eight number one albums and twelve number one singles. They made two films, *A Hard Day's*

Opposite. This cartoon drawing of The Beatles was penned by Scots journalist and broadcaster Fraser Elder before a concert at the Caird Hall in Dundee.

Below. *You really got a hold on me*. The historic contract signed between Albert Bonici and Brian Epstein that guaranteed The Beatles played Scottish concerts twice in 1963.

This small article and tiny advert appeared in the Aberdeen *Evening Express* ahead of the band's show at the Beach Ballroom on 6 January, 1963.

Night and *Help!* And they racked up six UK tours, two European tours, three US tours, a world tour that took them to Australia and a tour of the Philippines and Japan. By any measure, it's an astounding workload.

This chapter chronicles Scotland's own reaction to Beatlemania through these 22 concerts – sometimes featuring two performances a night – on a tour-by-tour, show-by-show basis. So take your seat on the bus for a helter-skelter ride – and a magical history tour.

JANUARY 1963
Tour itinerary
3 January: Longmore Hall, Keith (cancelled)
3 January: Two Red Shoes, Elgin.
4 January: Dingwall Town Hall, Dingwall
5 January: Bridge of Allan Museum Hall, Bridge of Allan.
6 January: Beach Ballroom, Aberdeen.

The Beatles began 1963 by shaking the dust of one era from their shoes, before embarking on another.

On 31 December 1962, the band left the sweat-drenched walls of Hamburg's Star Club behind for the last time, bringing the final curtain down on an apprenticeship that honed their musical abilities and left them as tight as a band could possibly be. Two nights later, they would be swapping the sounds of a German beer cellar, full of juiced-up sailors, pimps and transvestites, for Elgin's Two Red Shoes ballroom, playing to a small audience of largely prepubescent teenage girls and young farmers.

How they got there was largely down to the entrepreneurial courage shown by two men – Brian Epstein, The Beatles' new manager and svengali, and Albert Bonici, a silver-tongued, silver-haired second generation Scottish Italian who had established himself as Scotland's principal pop promoter. Bonici and associate Jack Fallon had used their contacts to approach Epstein in September, 1962, to book The Beatles for a routine five-day, five-gig tour of the north of Scotland in the first week of the new year. Word had already travelled north of the impact they were making in their own hinterland in the ballrooms of Merseyside and, in particular, a jazz club called the Cavern.

The deal was agreed, amid much haggling (which would have repercussions later), on 9 September, a month prior to the release of the band's first single 'Love Me Do' on Friday, 5 October, four days before Lennon's 22nd birthday.

So it was that on 2 January 1963, The Beatles flew north from London to Scotland. They had been due to land at Edinburgh Airport where faithful roadie Neil Aspinall – later to become head of The Beatles

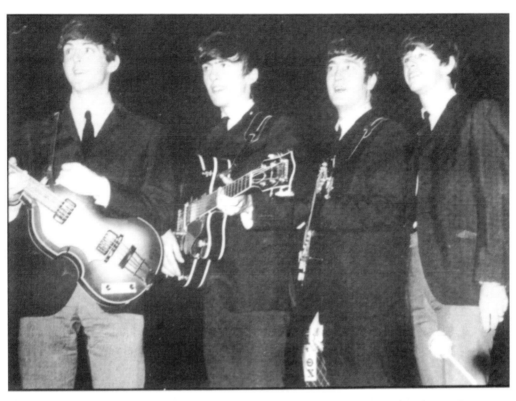

Things Start to Swing

The pop music scene rollicked and rolled through the decade with joyous, just occasionally slightly aggressive abandon. The schmaltzy, croony days of the Fifties were ousted by times a-changing; much new and original composition and presentation, a louder beat — and "louder" clothes.

In January, 1963, folk flocked to the Beach Ballroom to see the Johnny Scott Band Show featuring an odd-looking and sounding quartet from Liverpool — the Beatles, then nicknamed the "Love me do boys" after their first big hit. There were few screaming teenies for the latter; not hordes but a handful sought their autographs. Nevertheless, Aberdonians shelled out 3/- for this the "Fab Four's" first and last appearance in the city.

company Apple Corps – was waiting with the band's battered Bedford transit van, loaded with their guitars and tiny amps, to ferry them north. But Scotland was shivering in the grip of a crippling arctic winter, sub-zero temperatures carpeting the whole country in a blanket of snow and frost. The plane was diverted to Aberdeen, which suited the band but left Aspinall having to make the long journey north alone on twisty, icy roads.

The weather had already taken its toll on the concert arrangements; the first show scheduled for Keith, where the band had played two years before as The Silver Beetles, was scrapped as huge snowdrifts blocked roads, making travelling impossible. Rather than hang around for a day, John Lennon used the unexpected break to fly back down to Liverpool to see his wife Cynthia and seven-month-old son Julian. Lennon promised to be back in time for the band's first gig at the Two Red Shoes the next night. Typically, though, he was racing against the clock and only made it to the venue with a little over an hour to spare, much to the relief of his three bandmates who would have been faced with the awkwardness of having to cancel a second successive show, a move that would have undoubtedly infuriated Epstein and Bonici.

In a bid to drum up some local excitement, Bonici billed The Beatles as 'The Love Me Do Boys', their debut single having crept into the lower reaches of the pop charts just before Christmas. But the ad-hoc promotion failed to create much of a stir for the shows on that first tour. And, in stark contrast to their attitude at the height of their fame, the Scottish press ignored them.

The truth was that few people north of Hadrian's Wall had heard of The Beatles, which meant that not even the heat generated by their live performances mattered a jot if there was nobody there to see them. In some cases, those who forked out three bob for a ticket – a mere 15p in today's money – were happier propping up the bar until one of the local bands further up the bill took over. The worst audience was undoubtedly at Dingwall Town Hall where just 19 people braved the freezing cold to see them, most preferring instead to plough through the snow to see local ceilidh kings The Mellotones in nearby Strathpeffer Pavilion.

Part of the proceeds of the event would be diverted to the local fire brigade Old Folks' Appeal, a gesture that Bonici hoped would swell the crowd and guarantee The Beatles a little extra PR varnish. Organiser Brian McKenzie said: 'We were told The Beatles were coming. They must be quite good they've got a song that's almost in the charts. The thing I remember was they did seem to be quite musical and the bass player [McCartney] was left handed. There was a lot of talk beforehand about this group from Liverpool coming up with their fancy hairstyles. We thought it all sounded good but, with hindsight, folks just didn't seem to appreciate who they had. The strange thing was two or three of the band came to the hall door before the show asking where they could get cigarettes. But they had no money so I gave them what was an old-fashioned threepenny piece and off they went to buy a packet of woodbines. So just before the release of the "Please Please Me" single they were so poor they were cadging money for cheap cigarettes.'

Angus McDonald was serving behind the bar at the town hall that night. 'It's a big cavernous hall with little atmosphere. I remember they were very thin, the suits were tight and the hairstyle was unusual. They seemed to me to sing very flat. I didn't stay too long and headed up to Strathpeffer and had a job getting in. I think there were 1,200 at the dance that evening.'

The post-mortem that followed the Dingwall debacle revealed an unpalatable fact – the tour was threatening to stiff, The Beatles flatlining at the first two venues. Only when they reached Bridge of Allan and then Aberdeen's Beach Ballroom were there small signs that the patient could be resuscitated.

Gordon Hardie and Andi Lothian both acted as point men for Bonici and saw at first hand how The Beatles struggled to attract audiences, not because of a lack of musical prowess but simply because they were strangers in a largely strange land. Gordon said: 'Some people have said the tour was a disaster which was most certainly not the case. The problem was simply that not enough people had heard of them. We tried some promotion on the back of "Love Me Do" hoping it might get them more noticed. But there was never any problem with the band. By then, Epstein had cleaned them up quite a bit. They were dressed in suits, no more leather trousers or that kind of thing, and no smoking on stage. He had insisted on a professional approach at all times.

'I've heard it said they were booed at the Beach Ballroom but I never saw anything like that. That's rubbish. They got a fantastic reception at the Beach Ballroom and at Bridge of Allan. The girls who were there went wild for them. They were a young band trying to make their way in the industry and they were prepared to go to far-flung places and put in the hours. It was a lot of work. It was not an easy life for them at all. Everything was done by road and it was the height of winter. In fact, it was the worst winter for years. It took three good promotions to pay for one bad one. The Beatles were a bad promotion to begin with then it got a lot better. As I say, they were just making their way. I've kept a ledger of the Beach Ballroom show and it shows that the money we took was £45 and we paid The Beatles £43 so we made a handsome profit of exactly £2.

'The Beatles were a bunch of guys that you couldn't dislike. They were always polite. The one I talked to most was Ringo, who would stand with

OFF THE BEATLE TRACK 3 –
THE BIG YIN . . . WITH A LITTLE HELP FROM HIS FRIENDS

Billy Connolly once achieved the impossible dream – by fronting a group that contained *two* Beatles in *his* backing band. The Scots comedian had been handed a starring role in *Water*, a film produced by George Harrison's Handmade Films company. The movie centred on the fictional Caribbean British island colony of Cascara which sees its idyllic existence shattered when an abandoned oil rig starts to pump high-quality water. All of a sudden the island is at the centre of an international tug of war over its water rights, involving Downing Street, the White House, Cuba and the Cascara Liberation Front, headed by Connolly. A concert is held to determine the island's future and Connolly, starring alongside Michael Caine, ends up fronting a house band called The Rebels. A third of the way through the song – called 'Freedom', naturally enough – the house lights go up to reveal Ringo on drums and George on guitar alongside Eric Clapton and Deep Purple keyboard player Jon Lord. Connolly said: 'All of a sudden I looked round and there were all my heroes. It was extraordinary.'

Connolly struck up a warm friendship with George and his wife Olivia and visited him a couple of times at his home in Henley-on-Thames outside London. Indeed, the studio recording for the *Water* soundtrack took place at George's home studio, although Connolly was recovering from minor injuries sustained in a car crash in Devon a couple of weeks earlier. In his own biography, penned by wife Pamela Stephenson, he recalls driving up through the entrance of Friar Park. He said: 'The grounds were spectacular. Fuck, I didn't feel quite so successful around George.'

But it's not difficult to see why the Big Yin and the Beatle got on so well, especially given George's dry humour. The two men also teamed up to promote a 'Parents for Safe Food' campaign. Connolly's friendship with the Fabs also extends to Paul McCartney and Ringo Starr. He was a frequent face at Wings concerts – including at least one at the Glasgow Apollo – as well as solo gigs. And Ringo has been in the audience for a few of Billy's TV shows. In July 2002, he was given the ultimate showbiz accolade of appearing on BBC Radio 4's *Desert Island Discs*. And he included 'Across the Universe' as one of his castaway top ten songs.

me in the wings to see the changeover of various bands. George Harrison was a very easy-going lad. Lennon and McCartney tended to keep themselves to themselves. But they were always together. When they weren't on stage, you would see them hunched over their guitars working on what I now know were songs. They were virtually inseparable.

'The first time I actually saw them was at Bridge of Allan. I was standing at the back of the hall with Andi Lothian saying these guys were being tipped as the next big sensation. I shrugged my shoulders and said I don't think so. "They're far too loud." So I got that wrong. I thought they might have been a flash in the pan. I wish I could brag and say I thought they would be great, but I didn't.'

Audience numbers may have ranged from the low of Dingwall to a tour high of around 200 at Aberdeen, but for The Beatles, these Scottish concerts marked a considerable departure from their previous live shows. In Hamburg, they had been used to being on stage for up to six hours at a time. Now, under the terms of the contract Epstein had agreed with Bonici, they only needed to play for about 40 minutes. Their set list, though, remained full on rock 'n' roll and still included covers such as McCartney's tonsil-shredding version of 'Long Tall Sally' and Lennon's larynx-ripping 'Twist and Shout'. Sandwiched in between was a smattering of Lennon-McCartney originals, among them 'Love Me Do', 'I Saw Her Standing There' and 'Please Please Me', each of which would become highlights of their debut album.

And they knew how to work an audience, no matter how sparse the numbers or how paltry the financial return. For all Epstein had sanitised their on-stage appearance and antics, though, Lennon, in particular, remained a loudmouth. According to those who were at that first concert at the Two Red Shoes, he baited male members of the audiences with a string of typically smutty remarks and bawdy jibes.

•   •   •

This was Ringo Starr's first trip to Scotland as a Beatle, his only previous trips north of the border having been as a member of another Liverpool group, Rory Storm and The Hurricanes. Indeed, it was his first real Beatle bonding experience, having replaced original drummer Pete Best only a few months before. And years later, while the memories of the others dimmed with the passing of time, it was Ringo who most clearly remembered playing in the smoky dance halls in places like Elgin and Bridge of Allan.

In *The Beatles Anthology*, he said: 'Elgin was one of the strangest gigs we did. We'd got all the way to the outskirts of Scotland to find an L-shaped room – and we were playing at the wrong end. I have this vision of the audience all wearing wellies, farmers and country people. The bar was on one side and we were on the other and you could tell which side was doing the business. In those days they were still laughing at us. Then at the end we got in my car and slid all the way to the next gig.

'On that tour we were staying in one of those theatrical boarding houses. The rumour went round that before we came, they'd had a hunchback staying and we all got a bit worried that we'd be having his bed. George and John went to stay in another place but Paul and I took a chance that we wouldn't catch the hunchback.'

One retreat was the National Hotel in Dingwall's High Street, where the band enjoyed an overnight stay after arguably the lowest point of the tour. But if The Beatles were deflated by the small crowd that had turned out to see them earlier that night, Anne Gunn saw no evidence of crushed spirits. She and pal Ann McAngus were working as waitresses in the hotel that night when the four musicians trooped in, freezing from the cold but seemingly high on the happy side from that evening's performance.

Anne said: 'I remember there was about two feet of snow on the ground. There was only one other car and their van outside the National that night. They followed us in to the hotel and we just got chatting to them. I was surprised by the fact they had long hair, at least what looked like long hair at that time. We made them a cup of tea and we were blethering to them for ages in the staff room, just talking about the things young people do, music, their songs and that kind of thing. Then lo and behold the cook came through and chased them. "Get to your own side of the hotel, you scruffs," she was telling them. They did look a bit funny, I suppose, and we weren't supposed to mingle with the guests.

'Paul McCartney, I remember, was very talkative and so was Ringo Starr. They asked us if we had been to the show. I hadn't because I was out courting, I had a date. But they didn't strike us as being special in any way. They were just four boys up from England who were in a band.

'I was always slightly annoyed that so few people had turned out to see them but they didn't seem to let it bother them. They were in great spirits, laughing and joking with us. They were real characters, so much so that after talking to them I wished I had gone to see them. They seemed very good in each other's company, four young boys who loved being in a band, I thought. When I think back to it now, they did seem to have a connection with each other as if they just fitted together.

'The next morning we met up with them again and served them breakfast and then they were off on their way to the next show, which was at Bridge of Allan. They were just like any other guests but they came round the corner and said, "Goodbye, girls." I suppose they were cheeky

chappies in a way. I would have loved to have met them again later and asked if they remembered their night in the National.'

Undeterred by the less than enthusiastic response to the first two shows, the group headed south for the first time to the Victorian spa town of Bridge of Allan. This was a couple of miles north of Stirling and just a 10-minute drive from Alloa, the town where The Silver Beetles had played their first Scottish gig just three years earlier.

Bridge of Allan was essentially a rural community, mainly dependent on farming. And Saturday night was traditionally the night for most of the local lads to let off steam at the the Museum Hall dances. Responsibility for security fell to Andi Lothian, who, never having seen The Beatles perform before, had no reason to expect any bother. He said: 'I had only taken one bouncer that night because I didn't anticipate a lot of people, so therefore not a lot of trouble. About 96 people turned up and 90 of them were male. They were big, heavy-set farmers with a drink in them. It was a nightmare from start to finish. However, The Beatles went on and played their set.

'It was the first time I had heard them and I was absolutely amazed by their music. I had never heard anything like them. They had amazing charisma. I was at the back of the hall with Gordon Hardie when they announced their last number. They said this was their new record which would come out next week called "Please Please Me". This incredible sound filled the whole hall and took our minds off the punch-ups that

Four and fab. A publicity shot taken of the band for their first appearance on the Scottish Television show *Round Up*.

Ringo and Paul clown around with presenters Morag Hood and Paul Young (seated far right) during a later appearance on *Round Up*.

were going on in various corners. The Beatles never came to any harm, obviously, but it was a hairy night. I think that was the last ever pop event that happened at the Bridge of Allan Museum Hall.'

Andi also enjoyed an unexpected windfall from the evening's show. 'Afterwards, there were a lot of coins lying all over the place. I don't know whether people had been throwing money at The Beatles or each other but I picked up all the loose change on the floor at the end of the night.'

Although it ended on a high in Aberdeen, the tour had been less than a rip-roaring success. Albert Bonici's attempt to drum up some interest in The Beatles on the back of 'Love Me Do' had largely fallen flat. Newspapers and radio continued to ignore the band, highlighting the absence of any kind of publicity machine to nudge them up the ladder of success.

By the time the tour was over, the band already had their eye on their first hometown gig for months – at Liverpool's Grafton Ballroom in three days' time. Before that, though, they had to fulfil a scheduled appearance before the TV cameras at Scottish Television in Glasgow, curiously booked when there were no more shows to promote.

Worn out from pinballing the Highlands though they may have been, The Beatles always perked up at the chance to clown around whenever someone thrust a microphone under their noses. The programme, filmed before a live studio audience, was called *Round Up*, a *Blue Peter*-type show presented by teenagers for teenagers. It was already one of the most popular programmes on STV's roster and one that guaranteed healthy ratings every Tuesday.

Presenting the programme were Morag Hood and Paul Young (who went on to enjoy a career as one of Scotland's most popular TV and film actors and broadcasters). John, Paul, George and Ringo quickly struck up a rapport with Paul, then aged 19, and his co-presenter. They performed just one song on *Round Up* in the first of three appearances they would make on the programme within the next two years. Thousands of kids all over Scotland saw The Beatles beamed into their homes lip-synching 'Please Please Me', the song that would become their first number one single.

Looking back, it seems curious they mimed the song, despite having all their concert equipment in the back of Neil's van, the amps still warm from the previous night's show in Aberdeen. But the programme's sound recordist Len Southam revealed it was too difficult in these more primitive times to mix live music in the studio. And he also recalled getting an early insight into the band's bare-faced cheek.

'I was in the control booth. The Beatles were in the green room waiting to come on. A call came up over the intercom from the green room to the control booth. One of The Beatles asked if they could be paid

I want to hold your hand. Paul McCartney especially struck up a rapport with his namesake on *Round Up*.

extra as their van was having mechanical trouble. They were worried about whether it would make it back to Liverpool. I passed the request on to higher authorities. The answer came back down: "Sorry you'll get your pay, but no extra.'"

Astonishingly, The Beatles almost blew their first appearance on Scottish television thanks to John Lennon's poor timekeeping and his inability to tell the difference between Edinburgh and Glasgow. After the last tour gig in Aberdeen, he split from the rest of the band to spend the night with his Aunt Elizabeth and older cousin Stan Parkes at their house in Edinburgh. The next day Lennon spent most of his time lazing around, regaling the company with stories from their tour and talking about the future for The Beatles. As the appointed hour approached to rejoin Paul, George and Ringo for their TV show, John showed little urgency in getting his act together.

The reason for that was simple, as Stan recalled: 'We were sitting around and I said, "Don't you think you should be getting ready to go to the television studio and meeting up with the rest of the band?" He said not to worry, he had plenty of time to get into Edinburgh. But I said to him, "John, there are no TV studios in Edinburgh. The show is done in Glasgow." By this time there were only two hours before the show was due to start so it was mad panic stations to get him through to Glasgow in time. He just made it.'

Round Up was only the second TV programme The Beatles had done since coming under Brian Epstein's wing – their sole previous appearance being a short clip on a Granada teenage magazine programme. So programme presenter Paul Young is justifiably proud that the exposure provided by *Round Up* brought The Beatles to arguably their widest-ever audience at that point, just five days before EMI took the wraps off 'Please Please Me', the song that was the first link in their chain of chart-topping success.

'It is very interesting because if you look at any of the big anthologies about The Beatles, *Round Up* is never mentioned. It was quite a pivotal appearance for The Beatles then. We had three appearances from them within that first two or years of what you might call the Beatlemania period, Jan/June '63 and April '64. I think we got them because Morag Hood's brother Liam was a TV producer who knew Epstein's people.

'The first time they appeared nobody really knew who they were. "Love Me Do" had only got to about 17 in the charts. They were looking for TV exposure when they did "Please Please Me" on the first programme. When they were back up in June of 1963, just five months later, they were a lot more popular and that's when we got them in the studio for a pre-recorded show on a Friday night. This was not normal

Ringo and George in conversation with Paul Young.

Everyone keeps their eyes
fixed on the programme's
floor director.

because pre-recorded shows were unusual, but we had to fit in with their schedule or lose out.'

That second show was recorded just a few hours before the band were due to play their first gig in Glasgow, at the Odeon Cinema on 7 June in nearby Renfield Street. With the band's popularity soaring on the back of their chart-topping calling card 'Please Please Me', the number one follow-up 'From Me to You' and their first number one album, pockets of screaming teenagers had already gathered at the front entrance to the STV studios at the top of Hope Street. It was to be a familiar scenario for The Beatles over the next three years – holed up inside concert venues, TV studios and radio stations while outside legions of teenagers screamed their names in high-pitched unison.

Inside the STV studios on 7 June 1963, The Beatles performed 'From Me to You', lip-synching as they had done five months earlier. Off camera, though, John Lennon couldn't resist indulging in some Beatle banter with fellow Scouser Gerry Marsden of stablemates Gerry and The Pacemakers – and it landed him in trouble with gruff studio staff who failed to see the funny side of his antics. Paul Young recalled: 'The Beatles were on the show with Gerry and The Pacemakers. Because of our contacts with Brian Epstein's people, it was common for us to get the likes of Cilla Black, Tommy Quickly and Billy J. Kramer. At their second appearance, John Lennon was trying to make Gerry Marsden giggle and was making faces at him behind the camera. And the floor manager took Lennon aside and told him, "If you don't get a more professional attitude you'll get nowhere in this business."'

When the show finished, nipping out the front door to head down to the Odeon was an impossibility, thanks to the throng gathered at the front door. So the band was smuggled out a back entrance, and Paul drove George Harrison and Ringo Starr down Renfield Street in his recently acquired MG sports car.

Genial and laid-back, Paul Young struck a particularly warm rapport with the band who, within twelve months, would be the most famous people on the planet. All of them were just edging their feet inside the showbusiness door and enjoying their first taste of the kind celebrity fame would bring. And the friendship continued right up to The Beatles' third and final *Round Up* rendezvous on 30 April 1964, weeks after the success of their first American tour as Beatlemania gripped the globe.

Looking back, Paul remains convinced that *Round Up* was fortunate to get The Beatles for a hat-trick of appearances at a time when the whole world wanted a piece of the action. 'I think because it initially happened so early in their career and the fact it was Scotland and they had good memories of Scotland. Every time they came back they knew where they were coming to and who was going to be there. The usual question was how do Scottish audiences compare and they always said they were fabulous – but they were. My memories are all very warm. They were nothing but pleasant. It has been an interesting little slice of my life being connected to them.'

JUNE 1963

7 June: Odeon Cinema, Glasgow

The first few days of June 1963 were dominated by two events that made headlines around the world. First, Pope John XXIII died on 3 June, ending a five-year reign on the throne of St Peter. Two days later, John Profumo, Britain's War Minister, resigned in disgrace after admitting that he had lied to Parliament over his relationship with Christine Keeler, a model and topless showgirl. The Beatles, halfway through a two-month tour of provincial theatres, were preparing for their debut concert in Glasgow, the first of five shows they would eventually play in Scotland's largest city. They were part of a package tour that also included Roy Orbison, Gerry and The Pacemakers and six other warm-up acts.

When the tour kicked off at Nelson's Imperial Ballroom in Lancashire, The Beatles, despite having two number one singles under their belts, were behind the Big O in the programme pecking order and vying with fellow Liverpudlians The Pacemakers to be second in the billing. But the times they really were-a-changing. It quickly became clear to everyone that The Beatles were trumping Orbison every night. Of course, the kids screamed for Roy, the first notes of 'Only the Lonely' the trigger for an ear-splitting crescendo. But the reception for The Beatles dwarfed even that for the hugely popular American singer.

An atmosphere of healthy competition grew between the two acts. Eventually, though, the Big O graciously made way for the four youngsters who, he acknowledged, were creating a bigger storm than him. By the time their tiny amps and equipment were trundled on stage at the Odeon Cinema in Renfield Street that balmy Friday night in June, Orbison, who was one of their heroes, had been relegated to a minor key, and The Beatles were handed the job of closing the show.

By now The Beatles were centre stage in every possible way. The reversal in fortunes, however, did nothing to dilute the keen rivalry that still existed to earn the biggest cheers of the night. George Harrison, who would team up with Orbison in the 1990s for The Travelling Wilburys, said: 'He'd had so many hit songs and people could sit and listen to him all night. He didn't have to do anything, he didn't have to wiggle his legs.

In fact, he never even twitched, he was like marble. The only thing that ever moved were his lips – even when he hit those high notes he never strained. He was quite a miracle, unique.

'We soon took over as top of the bill. We had to come on after Roy. They had a trick on in those theatres where they could close some of the curtains on the stage so we could set up behind them, while the other bloke was out there doing his tunes. I can't remember where his backing group was, but Roy would be out there every night and at the end he'd be singing, "She's walking back to me, do do do do da do do do . . . " And the audience would go wild. We'd be waiting there and he'd do another big encore and we'd be thinking, "How are we going to follow this?" It was really serious stuff.'

Most Beatle commentators date the birth of Beatlemania from the band's appearance on the Royal Variety Show on 13 October 1963, when, for the first time, the sight of hundreds of swooning girls was beamed into millions of households. The fact is, though, that The Beatles had by then been playing to screaming hordes for months. Their 'overnight' success had been gaining momentum with every radio play, every TV appearance and every show. Proof of this can be found in the fact that tickets for the double-header concert at the Glasgow Odeon in June that year sold out within hours – all 6,000 of them. And no one had ever generated a ticket stampede like that before, not even Frank Sinatra at his peak. (Elvis, of course, had never bothered to play on this side of the pond.)

The popular press, usually keen to latch on to the Next Big Thing, was caught napping. Neither the *Daily Record* nor the *Daily Express* (then Scotland's best-selling daily newspaper), devoted as much as a single column inch to this new musical phenomenon sweeping the country on the day The Beatles played Glasgow for the first time. Oddly enough, it was the more douce *Glasgow Herald*, Scotland's paper of record, that covered the story. Under the headline, '6,000 Pop Fans Go Wild', the *Herald* informed its readers how the fans tried to storm the stage at the Odeon, only to be rebuffed by a thin blue line of bemused bouncers.

The report read:

'More than 6,000 hysterical fans last night tried to mob the chart-topping pop group The Beatles when they appeared at a two-house show at the Odeon, Glasgow.

'The teenagers made attempts to storm the stage when The Beatles and Roy Orbison were on, but specially-drafted attendants kept them at bay as programmes and soft drink cartons were thrown on to the stage.

'It was one of the most riotous receptions for any show since

Cliff Richard and The Shadows visited the same theatre a few months ago. After the second show, about 2,000 fans stood outside the stage door chanting: "We want The Beatles." Police dispersed them.'

Media apathy towards bands like The Beatles was wholly understandable. With very few exceptions, they were here today, gone tomorrow bubblegum – and just as disposable. Crusty newspaper editors regarded pop music as an affront to civilised values. But The Beatles represented the flip side of a new coin – girls loved them, boys wanted to be them and mums wanted to mother them. They were the first band to cross the gender barrier and vault the generation gap. Soon everyone wanted a piece of them. Slowly, Scotland's newspaper industry realised The Beatles were in the vanguard of the new cultural zeitgeist that signalled the changing of the guard from one generation to another. What's more, they soon cottoned on to the fact that coverage of The Beatles meant massive circulation. In a way the Fabs helped to invent today's celebrity-mad tabloid press.

While the press may have been caught off guard, the same could not be said of the Glasgow police. The city's Chief Constable, James Robertson, was concerned that the prospect of hundreds of swooning pop fans bringing the city centre to a standstill posed a bigger threat to public order than the thousands who crammed into Ibrox or Celtic Park every weekend. Consequently, extra officers were drafted in to control the crowds that had arrived by midday for the first of the two shows at 6 p.m. (the second one would follow about two hours later).

Among those detailed to maintain crowd control was streetwise sergeant Irene Livingstone and her colleague Jesse Milroy. And Irene was staggered by the excitement that rippled through the crowd. 'There were two shows that night, one at six and one about eight. Our job was to keep the crowd moving and not let them into West Regent Street. You wouldn't believe the number of cousins The Beatles had! They all wanted in via the back door in West Regent Street. But no one was allowed to go in there. Under no circumstances were the doors to be opened near the time of the show and absolutely no one was to be allowed in without a ticket.

'I started at 2 p.m. and the crowds had already begun to assemble even at that hour with the concert several hours away. Chief Inspector John Kirdy came down saying keep them moving. The kids were singing, "We love The Beatles, oh yes we do, we love The Beatles oh yes we do." But when they passed Jesse and myself – we were virtually at the door of the Odeon – they started singing, "We hate the polis, oh yes we do, we hate the polis, oh yes we do." The crowds just got bigger and bigger.

'I remember telling one young fellow to keep moving and he turned round to give me a mouthful because I think he thought I'd given him a shove, but when he turned round it was a police horse that had given him the dunt. So he came face to face with the horse and the look on his face was priceless.'

Although an experienced police officer, Irene had never witnessed anything of this magnitude. 'When the first lot were safely inside, you could hear the screaming and the yells. It was unbelievable. Curiosity got the better of Jesse and myself so we wandered into the Odeon to see what it was like. I met one of the girls from the St Andrews Ambulance Society, we always used to meet up at various jobs. And she was just bringing out an endless procession of bodies into the foyer. These young girls were collapsing with hysteria. This is what I imagine hell was like. It was just wall-to-wall screaming. You couldn't hear yourself think. Jesse and I went in and The Beatles were on the stage playing away but you couldn't really make out any song. We were going down a side wall when I bumped into somebody. I said, "I'm sorry," and the gentleman turned round and said, "Irene, if you stand in front of me you'll get a better view." It was Chief Constable Robertson. I was dumbfounded. I muttered, "Oh, it's alright, sir, we just popped in to see what was going on." So we very quickly turned on our heels and went back outside.

'When that first concert came out, the hysteria was incredible. They were screaming, "I want to go back in, I love Paul." I just thought in the name of heaven, out, out, out. It was a difficult situation because we wanted them to move out and they wanted to go back in.

'We had been warned beforehand that the press would be there in large numbers. There were photographers everywhere and suddenly I heard this smack behind me. I thought what the heck was that and turned round to see Jesse had applied first aid to one of the fans by smacking her across the face to calm her down. I couldn't sleep that night because I was so worried that the newspapers would be full of a picture of a police officer hitting a Beatles fan.

'The first lot left and then we had to go through the whole thing again with the second lot. Even after the second show finished, and the doors were shut for the night, they still thought The Beatles were hiding inside. They were banging the doors and we had to move them on. But they were already on their way to what was then Renfrew Airport. By the time I reported for duty at 11 p.m. that night at headquarters for a debriefing I had no voice left. With this continual calling out to keep moving, I was absolutely hoarse. And of course my male colleagues took great advantage of this and ribbed me mercilessly about being a Beatles fan and said I had been screaming along with everyone else.

'It's a memory that remains very vivid even to this day. I can still see the cinema in darkness except for the stage. You could see the silhouettes of the youngsters bouncing up and down screaming and yelling. They weren't badly behaved, it was just pure hysteria and excitement at seeing The Beatles. I never saw anything like it. They were certainly a great attraction for the youngsters. A lot of them were coming out in tears, they didn't want to leave. I was saying you can't go back, you have to go home now. I never saw anything like it again in all the years I was with the police force from the point of view of hysteria. In fact, I found it quite frightening.'

A prized souvenir programme containing autographs of all four Beatles from the mini tour of October 1963.

OCTOBER 1963

5 October: Concert Hall, Glasgow
6 October: Carlton Cinema, Kirkcaldy
7 October: Caird Hall, Dundee

One man who had already seen how far The Beatle rainbow would stretch – with a huge pot of gold at each end – was Albert Bonici, whose early contact with Brian Epstein was now reaping a healthy dividend. He was one of the first to have the vision to recognise the spark inside The Beatles and the electricity they would generate in a moribund music industry. He had staged The Beatles' first tour of Scotland at the turn of the year and had been lucky to just about break even. Days after that tour ended, however, the release of 'Please Please Me' convinced Bonici he had a goldmine on his hands if he could bring them back to Scotland to bigger and better venues.

Epstein, though, baulked at the approach, perhaps thinking Bonici was little more than a small-time huckster instead of the visionary he turned out to be. So when Albert and Andi Lothian approached the super suave Beatle boss for another slice of the pie, they were rebuffed – until the wily Bonici produced his trump card.

SOUVENIR

ALBERT A. BONICI presents

THE BEATLES

Scottish Tour 1963

GLASGOW
KIRKCALDY
DUNDEE

2/-

ALAN KING presents TOP ENTERTAINMENT at the
Carlton Theatre, Kirkcaldy

| SUNDAY, 10th NOVEMBER, 1963 6.30 and 9 p.m. | SUNDAY, 24th NOVEMBER, 1963 6.30 and 9 p.m. |

The Big Beat Show
with
DEL SHANNON
GERRY AND THE PACEMAKERS
THE FOUR MOSTS
and Full Supporting Programme
Tickets—17/6, 15/-, 12/6, 10/-, 7/6.

TOP POP 1963
with
THE SEARCHERS
MARK WYNTER
EDEN KANE
and Full Supporting Programme
Tickets—12/6, 10/-, 7/6, 5/-.

All seats can be reserved in advance for either show.
Booking Office at the Raith Ballroom, Kirkcaldy.
Open Daily 10 a.m.—5 p.m. and 7 p.m.—10 p.m.

The BEATLES in Scotland
SUNDAY, 6th OCTOBER, 1963—6.30 and 9 p.m.

PROGRAMME
1. ANDY ROSS AND HIS ORCHESTRA
   featuring Sue Taylor and Bryce Wilson

2. HOUSTON WELLS AND THE MARKSMEN

— I N T E R V A L —

3. THE CLIFTON HALL STARS
   featuring The Fortunes

4. THE BEATLES

AFTER THE SHOW —**DANCING THROUGH THE NIGHT**— AFTER THE SHOW
At the Raith Ballroom Kirkcaldy—Midnight till 4 a.m.—5/-.
TRANSPORT LEAVES THE CARLTON THEATRE AFTER THE SECOND PERFORMANCE

Dancing in Raith . . . this handbill for the show at Kirkcaldy's Carlton Theatre shows the band had two performances to squeeze in over two and a half hours.

Nestling in the small print of the initial agreement with NEMS, Epstein's company, was a clause that stipulated Bonici had first dibs on The Beatles should the band venture back north of the border in 1963. Fair enough, reckoned Epstein, who never reneged on an agreement with The Beatles during his lifetime, but the terms would have to be renegotiated because, let's face it, this band was going to be bigger than Elvis.

Bonici and Lothian travelled down to Liverpool for their face-to-face showdown with Epstein, their aim to ensure they didn't lose out on what they reckoned was a bankable asset. Lothian said: 'Epstein, after studying the contract, agreed that Albert did have the right to promote The Beatles' concerts in Scotland. He sat us down and said, "You wouldn't be here unless you know what I know . . . The Beatles are going to be enormous. Yes, you can have them back in Scotland, but the news I have for you is you won't get them for £30 a night, you won't get them for £40 a night, you won't get them for £50 a night." He said, "You can have them for £500 a night and I need to know before you leave the office."

'Albert and I were thunderstruck. Five hundred pounds 45 years ago was probably about £15,000 a night now. Brian left the office for a few minutes to allow us to talk it over. And we just said we've got to do it, they are going to be huge and we agreed to book The Beatles for £500 a night, a sum that was completely outrageous and totally unheard of at that time for any group. And that's how we were able to bring The Beatles back to Scotland later that year. It sounds mad now and it sounded mad then, but it was still a fantastic piece of business.'

The only other stipulation was that the shows be held in theatres instead of local, occasionally slightly tatty, ballrooms with their tiny stages and room for only a couple of hundred people at a throw. Bonici readily agreed, the reassuring voice in his head telling him he had the inside track on potentially the biggest band of them all.

Albert Bonici's name may be but just a footnote in the story of The Beatles but his efforts on behalf of four raw and unknown musicians cannot be overlooked. Moira Loveland's first job after leaving school was to work in the accounts department at Bonici's base at the Two Red Shoes in Elgin and she remembers the band being booked to play at the famous Highland venue.

Now Moira Malcolm, she said: 'Albert booked The Beatles long before they were famous and for that reason alone he deserves huge credit. He was a far-sighted man who saw something in them that few other people at the time did. He would often book bands maybe six months in advance and sometimes they hit it off and sometimes they didn't. It just so happens that with The Beatles he was very successful.

'Albert invited me to come and see them when they played in Glasgow, I think at the end of 1963. And all I can remember is being absolutely terrified at the sight of these young girls hanging over the balcony. I thought the place was going to fall apart. I was right at the very front and all I could think of was my goodness if that balcony goes they'll come down on top of me.'

Epstein was happy enough to keep his part of the Bonici bargain but dates for the three shows had to be squeezed into a diary that was already in danger of running out of pages. He was seriously preoccupied with the band's appearance on the revolving stage for the highly influential *Sunday Night at the London Palladium* show. This was an invitation ringed in red for Sunday, 13 October, four days after Lennon's 23rd birthday, that signalled The Beatles' ascent into the upper echelons of Britain's showbusiness league. And that would be followed by the embossed seal of approval from the country's First Family with an appearance at the Royal Variety Performance before the Queen on Monday, 4 November.

So the mini-tour of Scotland was ring-fenced for the start of October, just three days after Paul and Ringo returned from a break in Greece and Lennon from a similar battery recharger in Paris. George Harrison had returned from visiting his sister Louise in America and had barely time to unpack his suitcase before he was back on the road with the band.

The first stop was Glasgow, their second visit to what was then still the second city of the Empire and one which shared so many similarities with their own home hub of Liverpool. On the Saturday morning of the show, they all piled into Neil's trusty Bedford for the long road trip north. 'We always loved coming to Glasgow,' said Lennon. 'I said it many times. We were always being asked which was the best place to play and I always said Glasgow. Maybe because they didn't have anything else to do up there but scream.'

Initially, Bonici had angled for a return to the Odeon where the first gig in June had gone down so well but the Renfield Street cinema already had a booking for 5 October and so was unavailable. Scouring alternative venues, Bonici settled on the city's old concert hall. Opened in 1877, the grand old dame of Glasgow's vaudeville era was a shabby shadow of its former self, having in its time played host to the likes of Harry Lauder and Laurel and Hardy. But by 1963 its grandeur had faded, the greasepaint

Overleaf. This lucky fan gets up close and personal with John, Paul, George and Ringo in Dundee.

Hanging around. Taken before their first gig at the Caird Hall, this picture illustrates perfectly The Beatles' zany sense of humour.

having long since peeled away, leaving the old lady a wrinkled, clapped-out wreck. And when The Beatles started singing, they almost brought the house down – literally.

Gordon Hardie said: 'I remember there were acres of muddy ground around it. It must have been a time when a motorway was being built or something. This building was not in the best of condition. The passageways had buckets to collect the rain and some of the water was dripping through the roof. It was really a terrible, miserable night but I do recall that as the MC announced the names, "John, Paul . . . " the screaming and the clapping was off the scale, I had never heard anything like it. I was in the wings close to the speakers and amplifiers and I could hear nothing and I'm sure the audience couldn't hear a thing the whole time they were on.

'During "Twist and Shout", the youngsters were all jumping up and down and the balcony began to flex and the plaster began to fall. There was a big crack right across and it was potentially very dangerous. There was a senior police officer beside me and he realised I had something to do with the show and he turned to me and said, "You must stop this," and I just sort of smiled. "Do you want to stop it?" He said, "How long have they got to go?" I said another 10 minutes and I could see that he was counting every minute and praying that the place wouldn't fall down about our ears. And I can tell you it was a very long 10 minutes.'

Along with Hardie, Andi Lothian was also riding shotgun as Bonici's eyes and ears for the tour. As was the case for the first Glasgow show four months earlier in June, demand had exceeded ticket numbers and the mania, rather than abating, had swelled like some kind of social tsunami. Andi's key responsibility each night lay in ensuring security was watertight, even if the Glasgow Concert Hall was not. No one was expecting trouble, only trauma. But Lothian's normally well-oiled stewarding machine went awry when his bouncers went AWOL.

As the clocked ticked down on the curtain going up, Andy decided on a quick head count among the bouncers to make sure everyone was in place. Arriving at the front of the house, however, he got the shock of his life. 'When The Beatles were due to go I looked round and they weren't there. All the bouncers, all 40 of them, had decided they needed a refreshment and had all disappeared to the nearest pub. At this point I didn't know where they were. All I could do was to round up the St John's ambulancemen, the St Andrew's ambulancemen, the caretakers and go round the hall and pick 18 of the biggest guys I could lay my hands on and said would you help me out and come to the front. I promised them they would get a better view of The Beatles, but we had to keep those kids back. So for the first 15 minutes The Beatles were on, this motley crew was the

Overleaf. A rare picture of the Fabs on stage at the Caird Hall as a string of bouncers line the front of the stage.

thin blue line between The Beatles perhaps not surviving their success. In the event, 40 drunken bouncers came back and we were saved but it was a hairy moment.'

Lothian's thin blue line inside the hall was backed up by another thin blue line outside the venue in Argyle Street. According to the next day's *Daily Record*, 200 extra police had been drafted in to cope with the number of fans who laid siege to the hall with or without tickets and all leave was cancelled. Fifty female fans were treated in hospital for exhaustion and hysteria.

After being smuggled out a side door of the theatre, The Beatles were driven the five-minute journey back to the city's Central Hotel where they had booked three suites. But the plan quickly backfired as hundreds of fans gathered outside the main entrance in Hope Street and police had to erect barriers to keep the fans in check. The old hotel in the centre of the city had played host to many stars, including Frank Sinatra, but no one had any inkling that the guests who had been booked in months earlier under the unassuming names of John Lennon, Paul McCartney, George Harrison and Richard Starkey would be the catalyst for the unprecedented scenes on their doorstep.

The next morning, having slept typically late, in what was fast becoming a routine on the road, the band set their compass north-east for Kirkcaldy. Behind them, though, they left a concert hall in an even worse state than it had been when they took the stage. Several seats had been damaged by over-exuberant fans, a number of whom had been arrested for breach of the peace offences. The damage ran into several hundred pounds, with the tab being picked up by the prickly City Fathers. Disgruntled by this outrageous example of teenage behaviour, Glasgow Corporation banned subsequent pop groups from appearing at Glasgow Concert Hall. Ironically, the first victims of this local authority diktat were The Beatles' Liverpool chums Gerry and The Pacemakers who were forced to switch their upcoming Glasgow show to Paisley.

Coverage of the band's 'riotious' behaviour propelled The Beatles onto the front page of the city's *Evening Times*. Under the headline 'Beatles Fans Tore Up The Hall', it reported:

'So much damage was done by spectators at The Beatles jazz (sic) group concert in Glasgow Concert Hall on Saturday that it is unlikely the corporation will again let the hall to similar groups.'

'The screaming of spectators, some of whom danced on the seats, caused plaster work at the side of the balcony to come loose. After hearing of the scenes, the property sub-committee of the corporation decided to cancel another jazz (sic) group, Gerry and The Pacemakers.

GLW. MOBILE No. 4
AT KIRKCALDY

Glasgow's Central Hotel comes under siege from hundreds of fans after word leaks out that they are staying there.

'City treasurer Richard Buchanan said: "This kind of behaviour will not be tolerated. There was so much shouting and screaming that the group could not be heard. The balcony was actually felt to be shaking with all the pandemonium that was going on."'

Not surprisingly, Beatle fans leapt into print in defence of their heroes. One wrote to the same paper: 'You should be happy The Beatles came to Glasgow.' And another said: 'The Beatles were great. Surely you don't expect the fans to sit in silence?'

By now, Beatlemania was moving like a giant tornado across Scotland's central belt, sweeping up new converts at every turn. Next up was Kirkcaldy's Carlton. The musty old theatre, with its art deco interior, had played host to dozens of new acts. But nothing prepared residents of the town for the hysteria that accompanied The Beatles' back-to-back shows there. Amazingly, this was their 165th live date of the year – and that doesn't take into account the fact many shows included two houses.

Yet it was a quirk of fate that brought them to Kirkcaldy at all. Brian Epstein's demand that the band only play bigger venues meant the concert had originally been pencilled in for the Kinema Ballroom in Dunfermline. So a few phone calls were required to switch venues to the larger Carlton Cinema 15 miles to the east in Kirkcaldy, although local folklore has it that Sally, the opera-loving wife of the Kinema's owner, Cecil Hunter, just didn't fancy the look of 'those Liverpool lads' when she saw them on television. And she had a word in his ear that they might just be bad for business . . . and he should pass on them.

The two sold-out shows attracting 3,000 fans provided further proof that Scotland had succumbed to the Fab Four. On this tour at least, the last bastion to crumble would be the Tayside city of jam, jute and journalism. As a proud native of Dundee, Andi Lothian had special reason for seeing The Beatles play the city's showpiece venue, the Caird Hall which stands guard over City Square. Just four weeks earlier, Lothian, whose father Andy was one of Dundee's best-known jazz musicians, had masterminded the sale of tickets for the concert from his city-centre office.

Speculation that The Beatles were coming to Dundee had been swirling for weeks. So when the official announcement finally came, the dam of expectation among the city's teenagers broke in a torrent of fever-pitched excitement. Lothian said: 'I was selling the tickets from my little office in Dundee. And the tickets were due to go on sale at 9 o' clock in the morning. I was sleeping at half past two in the morning and the phone rang. 'And the voice said, "Is that Andi Lothian?" And in my best theatrical voice I kind of stumbled, "This is he." "Well, Andi Lothian, you get your arse down to your office. This is the Dundee police here. There's about 500 people outside your office demanding tickets for The Beatles and nobody can get to sleep. You get down to your office now and start selling these tickets." I was at my office with my secretary at 3 a.m. It was about a month before the event but I realised then how sensational this was going to be.'

Like the previous two nights, both houses at the Caird Hall went down a storm. News had already filtered through from Glasgow about the damage done to the Concert Hall, so Dundee was happy to engage in a bout of inter-city one-upmanship. The next day the city's *Evening Telegraph* put the story of the concert on page one along with a ringing endorsement from the city fathers praising the behaviour of the fans. Andi Lothian was quoted having a gentle dig at his west of Scotland counterparts: 'The kids were marvellous and exploded the myth that they are vandals at such shows. They've also proved they are much better behaved than their Glasgow counterparts.'

The *Telegraph*'s review of the Caird Hall hoedown matched the mood of the fans who screamed and sang lustily at each of the two shows. Filed without a byline, it read:

'After their dynamic performance at the Caird Hall last night, no one can say The Beatles are just another bunch of pop idols. They are entertainers.

'From the moment they took the stage to the moment they left – 30 marvellous minutes – they transported their audience to another world. They wasted no time in getting the audience "in the mood" and swung right in to the first number.

'Heads, complete with Beatle cuts, were shaking, hands were clapping and feet were stamping. Girls were swooning and shouting, boys were snapping their fingers in time to the rhythm. The seats became trampolines, with thousands of figures bouncing up and down.

'When The Beatles began to sing "I Saw Her Standing There", I realised just how good they were. The record of the same name was fabulous – but then it's easy to make a great sound on a record with all those echo chambers and devices to make even a plain voice sound dynamic. Last night they had no such devices. Just microphones. Yet the sound was just as good – even better – than their records.

'And last night they had their personalities to add life to the numbers. No matter how good a group is, their personalities can't really come across the same way on a record. It was The Beatles themselves who held us spellbound for that golden half-hour . . .'

As the last chugging guitar chord and three-part harmonies of 'Twist and Shout' died away, The Beatles were already sprinting for the exit, and the cars that would ferry them to the safety of Perth's Salutation Hotel. The date was Monday, 7 October, almost nine months to the day they first launched into the same song at the Two Red Shoes Ballroom in Elgin. So much water had flowed under The Beatles' bridge since then that their Highland fling would seem a small lifetime away.

Before their next visit to Scotland – in six months' time – life for John, Paul, George and Ringo would change out of all recognition. By then, their run of number one singles would have stretched to four, filming for their first big screen outing – *A Hard Day's Night* – had been completed and slated for a Christmas, 1964 release – and the four Mersey moptops had conquered America.

APRIL 1964

29 April: ABC Cinema, Edinburgh
30 April: Odeon Cinema, Glasgow

George Harrison reckoned 1964 was the year in which The Beatles lived a week for every day that passed by in a blur. In February, they had jetted off from Heathrow for their first visit to America, a country still traumatised by the assassination of JFK just three short months before. It was a two-week stay during which they were slated to appear on *The Ed Sullivan Show*, a platform that had kick-started many a show business career, including that of Elvis Presley some eight years earlier.

Among the entourage was Scottish photographer Harry Benson; it was the trip that would not only redefine The Beatles' career but also his own. He said: 'There was a real feeling of expectation. I just had this feeling that they would bowl America over. There had never been anything like them for charisma and music.'

The American trip was swiftly followed by the start of filming for their first venture into the world of celluloid with *A Hard Day's Night*. And sandwiched in between, of course, was the constant demand for new songs from record company EMI and a conveyor belt of requests from newspapers, TV and radio stations the world over.

The Beatles were, by now, a global phenomenon and quite easily the four best-known people on the planet. Most of their spare time was taken up in the studio, crafting songs for *A Hard Day's Night*, their third album. Fighting deadlines to complete the album in time for the film's release later in the year, all talk of a UK tour had been put off until the autumn. So these two shows in Edinburgh and Glasgow stand out in splendid

Newspapers began to realise that Beatles ticket contests were surefire boosts in the drive to increase circulation.

isolation on the treadmill that had by now become The Beatles' lives. They took place just five days after filming had wrapped on *A Hard Day's Night* and before the start of a world tour that would take them to Australia for the first time.

Fans in Edinburgh had camped out all night when tickets went on sale three weeks before the scheduled date of 29 April. Across country, however, Glasgow's corporation chiefs were in no mood to follow this example. They insisted that fans apply to a first-come-first-served postal ballot for the show at the Odeon Cinema. Consequently, a deluge of letters descended on the Renfield Street venue and all 6,000 tickets were allocated even before they had been printed.

The most notable feature of this brief jaunt to the north was that it marked the first of only two appearances The Beatles made in Scotland's capital city, representing something of a homecoming for John Lennon. His older cousin Stan Parkes still lived in Edinburgh as did John's beloved Aunt Elizabeth, his late mother's sister – known to the whole family as Mater. As boys, John and Stan had shared a remarkable bond that would last a lifetime. So John made sure that his 'Scottish' family would be given VIP tickets when The Beatles played Edinburgh for the first time.

Earlier that day, the band's two-engined plane had touched down two hours late in pouring rain at Edinburgh's Turnhouse Airport. After the obligatory photo call at the top of the plane's steps for the Scottish press – now fully aware of the circulation jackpot The Beatles represented – they headed off in two black cars on the four-mile journey to Edinburgh city centre for the first of two same-day shows at the ABC. When they got there, they were met by the sight of a cordoned-off Lothian Road with hundreds of screaming girls snaking their way round the cinema, the queue seeming to last for miles.

The first sight of the band was the signal for mass pandemonium to erupt. Amazingly, all the side doors were locked so stewards had to clear a path at the front of the cinema and then rush the band inside. Of course, all this was nothing new to the band who maintained considerable grace under pressure. All that was required to restore their cool was a pack of ciggies and, in George Harrison's case, a bar of chocolate (usually Fry's chocolate creams).

Rather than kicking their heels for a couple of hours, the band were happy to take part in a couple of interviews, one of them with Moira Furmage for Edinburgh Hospital Radio. Moira found the band in typically playful and mischievous mood. 'I went to interview them in the old Regal cinema. We just chatted away and they would make cheeky remarks at various things but it was all done in fun.' Lennon, in particular, was on typically acerbic form, referring to Moira at the start as 'Mein Führer'.

Blown away. The Beatles are greeted with high winds and a young fan presenting them with tiny Scottish dolls at Edinburgh's Turnhouse Airport.

McCartney, as ever, provided The Beatles' PR sheen. Asked for his verdict on Scottish fans, Paul replied: 'We've been up to Scotland before, you know, and the audiences are really marvellous, knockout, wonderful. The only thing that frightens us is when you get a Jelly Baby or a penny flat in the middle of your nose. You suddenly think, "Hello, hello, hello." But it's not frightening, it's a great feeling.'

After the show, the band hightailed it some 50 miles north-west. Base camp was the Roman Camp Hotel in Callander in the heart of Rob Roy country. Private and secluded, it seemed the ideal sanctuary to escape the madness even if only for a few precious hours. After arriving just after 11p.m., Lennon, Harrison and Starr sipped on a couple of malts and picked at a buffet before heading for their kip. Paul McCartney, though, the adrenalin of performing earlier still coursing through his body, was ready to party. He and Derek Taylor, Brian Epstein's PR man, were said to have headed out into a cottage in the grounds owned by a local West Indian George Caruth with two hotel waitresses. And they were reported to have danced the rest of the night away to a selection of Beatles records.

Despite the cloak-and-dagger business of ensuring secrecy for The Beatles' stay at the Roman Camp, word inevitably leaked out. By lunchtime, several dozen local schoolkids had skived off classes to mill around the hotel hoping to get a glimpse of The Beatles. An hour later, the number had swelled to siege-like proportions. The kids were only dispersed when teachers arrived to shepherd them back to school.

None of the band emerged from their slumbers before 2 p.m. Breakfast became lunch as staff served up porridge and home-made bannocks. As they shook off the previous night's torpor, they were visited by a BBC Scotland camera crew, shooting a short interview for transmission that evening on the news magazine show *Six Ten*.

Then it was back on the old familiar treadmill as the Beatle bandwagon swung west to Glasgae, as Paul always called one of his favourite touring cities. The Odeon had, by now, emerged as the only place in town suitable to host a Beatles concert. In the hours leading to curtain up, the band renewed acquaintances with Paul Young and Morag Hood, whom they had met on their last appearance on Scottish Television's *Round Up*. This time, without a single or album to promote, it was a strictly non-singing, non-dancing visitation. It had been precisely a year since their last appearance, but it was clear that here were four young heads mushroom-grown in the hothouse of Beatlemania.

Paul, though, reckoned they were as grounded as they had been when he last saw them. 'They had been to America and that signalled a massive change in their fan base. But they were delighted to be on *Round Up*. I think they always remembered that we had given them a break when no

Lyons Maid

ICE CREAM
ICED LOLL
DAIRY ICE

one really knew them. They didn't sing the last time they were on but they were in great spirits – as usual.'

Indeed they were. Although the guitars were en route to the Odeon, John, Paul, George and Ringo were happy to apply their clown make-up to ham it up before the cameras for the pre-taped programme. (It would be transmitted six days later on May 5.) They took part in *Round Up*'s popular 'Personality Parade' and gave lengthy interviews to the show's two hosts; first John and Paul chatted to Morag then George and Ringo brought Paul up to date with the colour of the sky in their world. The four Beatles and two interviewers then got together in the closing minutes to chat about group topics and generally lark about and act the fool. At one point George even attempted to strangle John.

The date of this second show at the Odeon, April 30, had been dubbed B-Day in Glasgow. In stark contrast to their visit seven months earlier, there was a creeping acknowledgement of The Beatles' power among Scottish newspapers. The *Daily Record*, the *Express* and the *Evening Times* all ran contests to win tickets for the Glasgow gig, hoping to hook young readers with Beatle bait. Normally, these competitions attract fewer than a hundred entries. Copy boys, though, were seen taking delivery of mail sacks bulging with thousands of postcards.

The Glasgow shows were always seen as the highlight of the Scottish tours, especially by the band itself. And, on this occasion, the fans rose to the challenge to out-scream and out-sing their east of Scotland counterparts.

OCTOBER 1964

19 October: ABC Cinema, Edinburgh
20 October: Caird Hall, Dundee
21 October: Odeon Cinema, Glasgow

On the morning of 19 October, 24-year-old *Daily Record* photographer Eric Craig packed all his cameras neatly into his bag before slinging them in the back of his car and shifting into first gear. Uppermost in his mind was that day's job, a photocall with The Beatles at the Four Seasons Hotel at St Fillans in Perthshire; then onwards to Edinburgh for the band's two shows at the ABC Cinema. It was a good assignment for Eric given the fact he was a young, hip guy, something that should help give him an in with the world's biggest pop stars. After all, he was the same age as John Lennon and Ringo Starr and just a couple of years older than McCartney and Harrison. There might even be the chance to have a couple of drinks with them at some point.

John Lennon gets a close look at Edinburgh Lord Provost Duncan Weatherstone's symbol of office.

Forty-five miles east, 19-year-old Bill Barclay was rubbing the sleep out of his eyes and waking up to the realisation that he, too, had a date with the Fab Four. Weeks earlier, he had answered a job application for stewards at the Lothian Road cinema. He was a big, brawny lad, 'handy' in his own words. Plus, it gave him the chance to make a few quid, see some of the biggest stars in the world and impress his mates – not to mention the chicks.

The tour had kicked off on 9 October, Lennon's 24th birthday, curbing any plans John might have had to party hard. However, his disappointment may have been diminished by the fact that this tour would earn The Beatles the then astronomical sum of £850 for two houses each date.

OFF THE BEATLE TRACK 4 –
POWER TO THE PEOPLE

Locals in the sprawling Glasgow housing scheme of Castlemilk were stunned to see a giant poster of John and Yoko's famous peace slogan 'War Is Over – If You Want It' draped on a giant billboard in December 1983. Community chiefs had approached John Lennon's widow to use the poster to spearhead a health campaign and information about local southside community groups, not thinking they had a hope in hell of getting a reply. The poster, based around the couple's worldwide Christmas hit from 1972, once lit up billboards in Times Square, London, Paris and Moscow – with love from John and Yoko, naturally. But it was rare for Yoko to give permission for it to be used free in this fashion, the only proviso being that the poster should mention that the copyright was owned by Yoko Ono Lennon. Along with her blessing, Yoko also sent this message of support: 'Carry the clearest vision of a peaceful world you can imagine. Let's do it with a spirit of fun and joy, not with anger, not with fear.' The poster, on a site donated by billboard firm Maiden, was unveiled by local three-year-old Abbie McCluckie. Healthy Castlemilk project co-ordinator Frank Creighton told the *Sunday Herald*: 'People said you'll never hear from her but I contacted Yoko through a fans' website and then wrote and emailed saying this was what we'd like to do. The message was created to draw people's attention to the war in Vietnam but it is as relevant now as it was then.'

This latest quickstep round the British Isles had been arranged by Brian Epstein at the start of the year. That, though, was before anyone could factor in the huge impact America would have on The Beatles or the lure the mighty dollar would have on Epstein's plans. So a second American tour was shoehorned into the already exhausting schedule, which included finishing off their fourth album, *Beatles for Sale*, a title loaded with irony and not a little world-weariness.

The screams from the last American show, at New York's Paramount Theatre on 20 September, were still ringing in their ears when the Fabs touched down at London's Heathrow Airport. The next day they were back in the studio, polishing off songs for *Beatles for Sale*, and by 9 October they were back on the road.

Somehow Scotland always seemed like the outer reaches of the empire, a country that wrapped the band in a warm bear hug of a welcome and yet gave them some space. The band loved their base at the Four Seasons, the stunning views across Loch Earn a world away from the claustrophobic confines of hotel rooms in the middle of hot and heaving cities and towns. All that clean air, rising up like a Highland spring, filtered out the toxins of Beatlemania from exhausted nervous systems.

The day after they wowed Edinburgh, Lennon, McCartney and Harrison were, unusually for them, up at midday and heading down towards the loch-side. Of course, a media scrum had already gathered as well as a throng of local youngsters stunned at the sight of these gods coming down from Mount Olympus to walk among mere mortals. John, Paul and George fancied stretching their sea legs, so small motor boats were quickly commandeered to allow them to go for a spin on the loch. As they waited, Lennon serenaded everyone with a jokey rendition of 'The Bonnie Banks o' Loch . . . Earn', the other two quickly joining in. George and John teamed up in one boat with McCartney in another and both delighted in trying to outdo the other as they weaved across the surface. Then of course there was the old game of soak the press as Lennon, who always fancied himself as a bit of a sailor, skimmed past the shore, sending plumes of freezing water into the faces of the assembled hacks.

Meanwhile, the hotel's sole telephone operator was under siege from calls from all over the world, reportedly at a rate of 50 every minute. The local paper, the *Strathearn Herald*, revealed how local folk revelled in having four such VIPs in their midst, while ensuring at the same time that public curiosity didn't vault over the line into public intrusion. Part of its report on Saturday, 24 October read as follows: 'Police had to be called to disperse several car loads of teenagers and students who had followed the group back from Dundee on Tuesday night . . . On Wednesday morning the only Beatle to appear in public was Paul McCartney. The other three

Picture yourself in a boat on a river. The band loved taking a small motor launch for a spin on Loch Earn during their stay at the Four Seasons Hotel, St Fillans.

preferred the peaceful seclusion of their chalets to the quiet bustle of the dining-room . . . The Beatles like this part of the countryside and found the peace and quiet of St. Fillans a pleasant change. Paul wistfully wished he had a cottage there but realised it was out of the question. The Beatles need a lot of sleep on their tours and the quiet of St. Fillans is the place to get it.'

Having covered The Beatles shows at Edinburgh and Glasgow earlier in the year, *Daily Record* photographer Eric Craig was lucky to have seen them at work, rest and play. 'We were in contact with Brian Epstein and he allowed certain photo calls at St Fillans. So we got them rowing boats on Loch Earn. It was terrific. We had great times with them. We went back to St Fillans a couple of nights and had a few beers with them. They were absolutely smashing guys, great fun, great laugh. The concerts themselves were absolutely fantastic to cover. The youngsters went absolutely over the top with them. The hysteria was tremendous and so was the atmosphere. I had covered a couple of concerts for the *Record*, but I had never seen anything on this scale. It was mind-boggling.'

As the minutes ticked by to the first of the two houses at the ABC, Bill Barclay had already reported for duty. Occasionally, Bill would turn up not knowing which star he would be shielding from the mayhem erupting in the front-row seats. Today, though, 19 October, everyone and their auntie knew the identity of the band making their second appearance in Auld Reekie inside six months. All police leave had been cancelled to ensure public order was maintained. Inside the venue, however, policing was the responsibility of hired hands like Bill.

'When The Beatles were coming, the management picked four guys out of the lot of us and I happened to be one of them to be with them all day. They needed a security guy all the time they were there to make sure nothing happened to them. So my job was to stick with George Harrison,' said Bill, who would later make his own mark on the showbusiness circuit as one of Scotland's leading comics and character actors, appearing in the likes of *Taggart*, *Rab C Nesbitt* and even Martin Scorcese's acclaimed *Gangs of New York*.

'I was handy. I played football. I was a bouncer for a while as well. Then it was just the thrill of the thing because The Beatles were enormous. I was a huge fan, everybody was, boy or girl it didn't matter. We were all Beatles fans.

'I went up to the ABC in the afternoon. It was rumoured The Beatles were going to arrive on the roof by helicopter. There were thousands of kids in Lothian Road so we thought there was no chance of them arriving by road. They would have been lynched. Then they were going to come through a back door but if truth be told we hadn't a clue how they would

arrive. We were all standing in the foyer and we heard this enormous scream go up. I mean, they had been screaming all day but this was even louder than before. Then we looked up and saw John Lennon's face pressed up against the glass at the front door. The doors were locked. We couldn't even see how they arrived, all we could see was his face pressed against the door getting mauled to bits. So we dived out and managed to get them all in, but Brian Epstein was left locked outside. So we had to open the doors again to get him in.

'We just hung about with them all afternoon. They spent some of the time playing with their guitars and playing cards. I remember one particular time because I was looking after George Harrison. I asked him if he wanted a drink or anything and he said a glass of milk. So I got him a glass of milk and all the photographers went mad clicking away just because he was drinking milk, something as stupid as that.

'The press were as bad as the punters outside. You had to get all the reporters back, let the photographers take their pictures then get them back to make way for the reporters. The press conference was just as manic as anything that was going on outside. And it was amazing how many women at that time suddenly worked for newspapers . . .

'Harrison used to eat these Fry's chocolate creams. He had dozens of these and I was actually taking the wrappers off them and later selling them to punters. You know the drill, "This is George's sweetie wrapper." We managed to get some autographs but in the end we were signing autographs ourselves and selling them. The kids were buzzing so much they never knew the difference.'

As the clock ticked closer to curtain up, all the stewards were directed to their designated crowd control areas. Some were placed at the exit doors and some formed a line along the front of the stage. It may have been raised some 20 feet from the floor but that was no obstacle to fans getting as close as possible to their idols. Bill's standpoint was in the stage wings, a vantage point that gave him a VIP view of the band, the best seat in the house.

As he took his place he heard compère Charlie Sim, one of Scotland's best-known showbiz personalities, ramp up the frenzy by deliberately baiting the fans. 'He kept them waiting for as long as possible. I was standing behind the curtain and I could hear Charlie out front saying, "Give us a B, give us an E." And all you felt was all these jelly babies hitting the curtains. The whole curtain was shaking under a hail of jelly babies. I was backstage all the time and had a great view because you were virtually right next to them. It was incredible at that time because they were so big. It would be difficult to think of anybody bigger. So I actually heard them pretty well. It would be worse in the audience with all the screaming.

The bouncer at the ABC, Edinburgh, keeps his eyes fixed firmly on . . . the audience.

'I was a big fan. Everybody envied you. Imagine landing a job like that and walking about with them for the whole day? They never left the theatre. It would have been a security nightmare. We got paid in sweeties. I think it was about £1 a night, but we made a few bob in other things so that was always good. The whole thing was unforgettable, really.'

Unforgettable was also the assessment reached by the *Edinburgh Evening News*'s music and theatre critic John Gibson who rounded upon the merchants of doom who suggested the hurricane of Beatlemania had finally puffed itself out. In a review of both shows, he wrote: 'Beatlemania on the wane? Don't you believe it. They are maybe being pushed a bit by some dishevelled people called The Rolling Stones but, as far as Edinburgh goes they are still THE GREATEST and STILL FAB. There wasn't the slightest hint of a slip from the absolute pinnacle in pop entertainment.'

The second night took the band back to the Caird Hall where the show had almost a 'By Royal Appointment' feel to it. Earlier in the day, The Beatles had politely turned down an invitation from Margaret, Countess of Strathmore, to pop into Glamis Castle for a spot of afternoon tea. But the Countess was determined to have her five minutes in the limelight with the band and duly blagged a ticket for that night's show. Undaunted, she pulled up outside the hall in her chauffeur-driven Rolls at 6 p.m., edging past a scrum of fans, and was ushered backstage to meet music's own royal family in their dressing room.

That, of course, meant another stiff-necked photocall with the kind of establishment figure The Beatles generally loathed. In fact, the countess didn't even know which Beatle was which as she confused John Lennon with George Harrison. For Lennon especially, this bowing and scraping to blue-blooded Beatle fans was the ultimate sell-out. As usual, though, Paul McCartney smoothed over the cracks with a couple of facile comments and queries. 'How big is your castle? Is it bigger than Buckingham Palace?' he asked.

Shortly afterwards, compere Bob Bain's voice was drowned out as he tried to introduce the band that, of course, needed no introduction. Almost immediately, scores of ambulancemen and Red Cross workers swung into action to pick out the casualties. According to the *Dundee Courier*, 50 kids were ferried out in the first five minutes, most of them sobbing ecstatically or in a state of collapse. Bouncers, many of them muscle-bound Taysiders hand-picked from local wrestling clubs, patrolled the aisles and formed a defiant line of defence across the front of the stage.

It had been just over a year since The Beatles' last visit to Dundee and, if anything, the hysteria this time around was even worse. One reporter

said: 'I was here last year and it was nothing like this, although at the time I thought that was as loud as it would get. You got the impression The Beatles, with the exception of Paul McCartney, were going through the motions. They must have known that, musically, these kind of concerts were killing them. They couldn't have got any satisfaction from singing every night knowing no one could hear them. They could have played the National Anthem and no one would have noticed.'

'Long Tall Sally' had replaced 'Twist And Shout' as the show-stopping finale and then they were gone, the curtain coming down on what would be The Beatles' last appearance in Dundee. Nearly all the fans filed out delirious at The Beatles' performance. However, one sour note was struck by the band's newest fan, the pop-loving Countess of Strathmore, who complained afterwards to the *Courier and Advertiser* that the fans' shrieking fans had ruined her evening. 'I couldn't hear one word of their songs. The audience was appalling and completely bad mannered to make so much noise. Most of the time I had my fingers pressed over my ears to keep out the awful noise. But I love The Beatles. I think they are fab – that's the word, isn't it? I must buy one of their records.'

Quite, ma'am!

This Scottish leg came virtually in the middle of an amazing 32-day unbroken grind of live shows around Britain. And, although obviously no one knew it at the time, they would only do this on home soil one more time. It was already becoming impossible to keep the momentum going. Their fourth album, *Beatles for Sale*, would be released that December in time for the lucrative Christmas market. As usual, it followed its predecessors to the summit of the charts, but half of the album consisted of covers, the band reaching back into even their Hamburg concert days to resurrect enough songs to make a long-player.

The relentless touring was beginning to take its toll on the band's musical creativity. Recording sessions were now squeezed in between live shows, many of them still being churned out before two houses each night. As a result, the doom merchants were queuing up to write the band off, especially in the face of raw, crackerjack groups like The Rolling Stones and The Who that were emerging in their slipstream.

But if fan reaction was anything to go by, reports of their demise were exaggerated. In Glasgow, as with all the other Scottish dates, tickets for the Odeon show had sold out within hours. And, from the vantage point of all four Beatles on stage, there was no let-up in the adulation whipped up by the band's fourth appearance in the city. One witness said the noise was like standing beside a jet as it thundered down the runway.

This time, trouble flared outside the cinema. Some fans took their frustration at being unable to see the band out on parked cars and the

windows of shops in Renfield Street, acts of wanton vandalism that were met head-on by Glasgow's no-nonsense police. There is no doubt the authorities feared they might have a major riot on their hands and several dozen people were arrested. The *Glasgow Herald* reported:

'Despite the efforts of scores of police, thousands of screaming admirers of The Beatles got out of hand in Glasgow last night. Plate glass windows were smashed in Renfield Street and a car was overturned in West George Street.

'The teenage crowd, chanting and shouting for their idols, were sent scurrying along the streets by mounted policemen. It was after the first performance, when the thousands outside were joined by the 3,000 enthusiasts who watched the show, that the trouble started. Seven were charged with breach of the peace.

'Hundreds of girls who did not have tickets marched outside the theatre carrying placards and setting eardrums throbbing with their screaming, chanting and singing. Ambulancemen and nurses on duty in the foyer and in the streets treated hundreds of girls suffering from hysteria. At one stage West Regent Street had the appearance of a field hospital with dozens of girls propped up on the pavement being attended by nurses. More serious cases were taken to Glasgow Royal Infirmary.

'A car in West George Street was overturned when the crowd was herded there by mounted policemen. Petrol spilled across the street and a fire appliance was called out to hose down the roadside.'

Such evidence suggested Beatlemania still had a long, long way to run. Set against this, though, was the undoubted reality that the fun was slowly being choked out of playing live, singing the same songs every night, dodging the barrage of jelly babies at every gig from Denver to Dundee. Trapped like performing rats in a wheel, John, Paul, George and Ringo were beginning to face up to an unavoidable dilemma: pull back on the tours or suffer the inevitable burn-out that could destroy each of them, mentally and physically. George once said: 'The fans came and gave their money and gave their screams but we gave our nervous systems.'

Never again would The Beatles submit themselves to a year like 1964. And their Scottish fans would have only one last chance to see them perform before the band would bow and walk off the stage for the last time – never to return.

Stage struck. The ABC stage is littered with Jelly Babies and other missiles as the band plays on.

DECEMBER 1965
3 December: Odeon Cinema, Glasgow

That last chance came in the final month of 1965, four and a half years since the raw, young (Silver) Beetles embarked on their first tour of Scotland. So much had changed. Edinburgh-born Stuart Sutcliffe, John's best buddy, had left the band to pursue his love of art in Hamburg only to die tragically of a brain haemorrhage in April, 1962. Tommy Moore had quit his short-lived stint as the band's skinsman, the drum seat now permanently occupied by Richard Starkey, aka Ringo Starr.

Oh, and the band was now bigger than Elvis. Without question.

Yet, 1965 would be a snapshot year of The Beatles in transition. The unrelenting adulation and constant demands from a world still hooked on Beatlemania was in danger of suffocating their musical creativity. Not even the fact they played before a world record 55,000 shrieking fans at New York's Shea Stadium could make up for this. More and more, they were stepping away from the spotlight of live shows and retreating to the studio. Indeed, the year could be sliced into three parts. The first six months were spent filming their second celluloid outing *Help!* along with the album of the same name. The next three months were spent gigging in America's Midwest. And the last three months saw the band holed up in Abbey Road recording a milestone album, *Rubber Soul*, the record that invented folk rock and signposted the path popular music would take for the next 18 months.

In their minds, they already had the germ of an idea to stop touring. For Lennon, Harrison and Starr, the game was up. Only McCartney still needed the buzz of the stage. Never one to pull his punches, Lennon said on the eve of the tour: 'I reckon we could send out four waxwork dummies of ourselves and that would satisfy the crowds. Beatles concerts are nothing to do with music any more. They're just bloody tribal rites.'

So it took Brian Epstein all his powers of persuasion to convince The Beatles to drag their sorry tails onto the treadmill one more time, beginning in Glasgow at the start of December 1965. The only consolation was that at least the songs would be fresh; a set list was drawn up which ruled out any songs from their first three albums, binned forever in favour of their most recent hit singles and album tracks from *Beatles for Sale*, *Help!* and *Rubber Soul*. On this tour, the screams would drown out debut live performances of 'I Feel Fine', 'She's a Woman', 'If I Needed Someone', 'Act Naturally', 'Nowhere Man', 'Baby's in Black', 'Help!', 'We Can Work it Out', 'Yesterday', 'Day Tripper' and curtain-closer 'I'm Down'.

Rehearsals, though, had been perfunctory for this ten-day jaunt. Indeed, they had only run through the songs once, an impromptu busk at

Neil Aspinall's flat; such was the importance they attached to the forth-coming shows.

Amazingly, for all their global superstardom, The Beatles set out by road for Glasgow on Friday, 3 December. By the time they reached the border, however, they could have been forgiven for wishing they had chosen to let the plane take the strain. Just outside Berwick, a stunned George Harrison felt the Austin Princess, driven as usual by their regular chauffeur Alf Bicknell, shudder. Unknown to the quiet Beatle, his beloved Gretsch Countryman guitar was bouncing up and down the A1. And that was the last George saw of it – seconds before a huge truck ran over the top of the precious £300 instrument, causing it to splinter into a thousand pieces.

Alf recalled: 'I went back to this great big articulated lorry and the driver said to me, "I think you've dropped a banjo back down the road." I couldn't believe it. So I went back to my car and Neil Aspinall and I just stood there looking, we both couldn't believe it. We just stood there, staring at the back of my car, noticing that the straps were broken. There were two guitars there, but now there was only one. I remember thinking, "I can get a lift home." I thought that was it. I said to Neil, "You'd better tell them." He said, "No you tell 'em." So I went round to the car and said, "I think we've lost a guitar." In the darkness, a voice comes out, "Well if you can find it you'll get a bonus." This was John. I was always frightened of John more than anybody else, so I said to him, "Well, what's the bonus then?" He replied: "You can have your job back!"

'So anyway, we got back in the car and we got to the end of this 12-mile stretch of motorway to turn round to come back. We are coming back on the other side in the fast lane and I'm going along as slow as I can and if anyone came I had to move over to let them pass and then go back out into the fast lane. But I couldn't see a thing, nothing. It was raining and it was dark. I told them – "I want to go home now." So we got right to the other end where we started from and we started to come back but there was nothing. The roads were clear as anything. Then we started to find little bits of wood and then a guitar string. We ended up with a little piece of the guitar each. Anyway, there was no more said about it and I was quite pleased. But I was very sorry it happened, believe me.'

Carrying on to Glasgow, George, pointing to his new-found interest in Hinduism, put the unfortunate incident down to 'instant karma', content in the knowledge he had a spare guitar in the back. His memory of the event differed somewhat from that of the band's driver. He said: 'Fourteen of our guitars were strapped to the roof of the Austin and the only one lost was my Gretsch. It fell onto the road and into the path of oncoming traffic. About thirteen lorries went over it before our chauffeur could get near it.

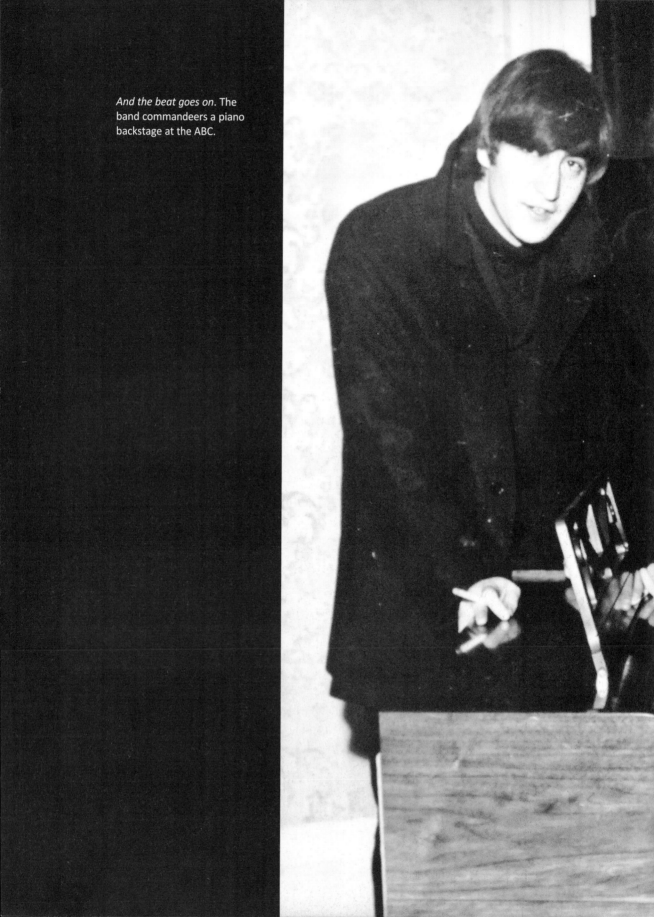

And the beat goes on. The band commandeers a piano backstage at the ABC.

Then, one of the lorries stopped and the driver came up with the dangling remains of it and said, "Oi! Is this banjo anyfink to do wiv you?" Some people would say I shouldn't worry because I could buy as many replacement guitars as I wanted but you know how it is, I kind of got attached to it.'

• • •

One hundred miles up the road, brothers John and Peter Douglas were readying themselves for a familiar onslaught at the Odeon in Renfield Street. Both worked in the projection room at the cinema on the days it screened the latest movie releases. But when the venue played hosts to pop concerts, both men could be found balancing the sound from the stage for the cinema's PA system, a difficult job at Beatles concerts when the band was playing into the teeth of a high-pitched hurricane.

John Douglas had been on duty for the band's debut at the Odeon in June 1963 and had seen at first hand the incredible effect on the fans and the struggle the musicians had to make their songs audible above the din. Now here he was again for what would be the last time the Odeon would welcome the Fab Four to Scotland. 'The projection staff during these shows were far from redundant; they manned the spotlight. They had six in the Odeon. But because I had a particular interest in sound, I did the sound for those shows,' recalled John. 'The artistes didn't bring along their own sound equipment like they do these days. But the Beatles got so frustrated at not being able to hear themselves playing. They were singing their songs and no one was really listening. Occasionally, they even sang very odd words to their own songs. No one in the theatre would hear that but I could pick it up very easily directly on the recording.'

Warming up the crowd for this last hurrah in Glasgow – although no one knew it at the time – was the usual complement of support acts. One of the acts was The Moody Blues, an up and coming Brummie band that featured a certain Denny Laine on vocals. Paul was to file away his positive impressions of Denny in a mental drawer that would be reopened seven years later to take flight in a band called Wings.

For The Beatles, the spotlight shining on the stage was fading. Within seven months, at Candlestick Park, San Francisco, The Fabs would take their final concert bow, bringing the curtain down finally on the phenomenon that was Beatlemania. A phenomenon that, arguably, began to take root at tiny Alloa Town Hall on Friday, 20 May 1960, when John Lennon, Paul McCartney and George Harrison took their first faltering steps on the long and winding touring road to becoming the biggest band of all time.

MON – FRI
8AM TO 6PM
SATURDAY
8AM TO 1PM

5. The Fans

ALLOA TOWN HALL, ALLOA, CLACKMANNANSHIRE
Friday, 20 May 1960

Mary Craig

Mary Craig's concentration was fixed on the threads in front of her, her fingers weaving through the various stitching patterns. But her eye was already drifting towards the clock on the wall in the sewing room at Peteman and Baldwins, one of the biggest employers in the Clackmannanshire textile town of Alloa in central Scotland. Indeed, like all the other teenagers in the mill, she was willing the hour hand towards the point that would signal the end of the shift – and start the stampede towards the weekend.

It was Friday, 20 May 1960, and for 17-year-old Mary it just another day at the factory. Uppermost, in her mind, though, was the local dance being held that evening in Alloa Town Hall, the sprawling 19th-century building that was the main magnet for the town's youngsters. Already, her hair was a mass of curlers, a crowning glory piled high in anticipation of it being set just right when the singer or band booked for that night's show launched into the first song.

Tonight, opportunity knocked for Johnny Gentle and his backing band The Silver Beetles. It might just as well as have been Rikki and The Red Stripes for all the strange-sounding names registered with Mary. Right now, she was more concerned about what to wear, a favourite black dress being the likely choice. Of course, several bands would be on the bill, including a 25-year-old singer from Glasgow who was already garnering interest from record company bigwigs. Alex Harvey's distinctive gravel-coated vocals and virtuoso guitar playing had already set him apart from a clutch of contemporary musicians striving to get their foot on the bottom rung of the ladder of success.

Johnny Gentle was a good few rungs further

LATE NIGHT
DANCE

BEAT BALLAD SHOW
Presenting
Star of TV and Decca Recording Fame—
JOHNNY GENTLE and HIS GROUP,
Supported by Scotland's Own Tommy Steele—
ALEX. HARVEY and HIS BEAT BAND,
With Ballad Singer—Bobby Rankine.

To Entertain and Play For

DANCING

in the

TOWN HALL, ALLOA,

on

FRIDAY, 20th MAY,
9.30 — 1.30.
ADMISSION—Before 10 p.m., 4/-; after 10 p.m., 5/-.

Buses After Dance to the HILLFOOTS DISTRICT.

NEXT FRIDAY, 27th MAY — JOHNNY DOUGLAS and HIS NEW BEAT COMBO with Happy Jackie Benson and Andy Cook of S.T.V.

up the showbiz ladder than Alex, having already recorded a single which had crept into the lower reaches of the UK charts. Johnny, more a crooner than a rock 'n' roller, was part of the Larry Parnes stable of pop wannabes, a roster that also included some of Britain's biggest up-and-coming singers. By virtue of the fact he had already recorded a single that had received significant radio airplay, Johnny was top of the bill at Alloa. The name of his backing band was The Silver Beetles, who two weeks earlier had been given the nod by Parnes to join Johnny on his first tour of Scotland, taking in places such as Alloa, Inverness, Fraserburgh, Keith, Forres, Nairn and Peterhead.

Neither Johnny Gentle nor The Silver Beetles meant anything to Mary Craig nor her friends Margaret Cullen and Wilma Muir, all of whom she would meet up with later to go to the dance. Mary recalled: 'We had never heard of Johnny Gentle or the Silver Beetles. In fact, I can't even remember there being any mention of The Silver Beetles. We didn't care about which bands were on. For us, it was just a big night out. We were more interested in the local talent. It was no different than any other Friday night.'

But for The Silver Beetles it *was* different. This eight-day tour of Scotland – the first time they had set foot outside of their native city – was proof that the band, along with temporary drummer Tommy Moore, was at last going places. George had quit a short-lived apprenticeship as an electrician; Paul had persuaded his dad that a week away would not see him turn his back on vital school exams; while John and Stuart had bunked off their courses at Liverpool Art College, stopping only long enough to 'borrow' the famous establishment's PA amplifiers.

By the time the train carrying The Silver Beetles pulled into Glasgow's Central Station, Mary was already back at home, giddy as a schoolgirl in anticipation of her night out. Eventually, she shouted out goodbyes to her parents and headed out in the balmy May evening to meet up with her pals. She said: 'I remember I was wearing my black dress, which was a favourite. I spent ages getting ready because this was our big night out. All the girls lived for Friday nights in the town hall. We didn't know what to expect this particular night. We were only interested in having a laugh and a good time. Obviously you wanted to hear good music but it wasn't the be all and end all for us.'

As Mary applied the last piece of make-up, The Silver Beetles were already on the 7.18 p.m. train from Glasgow to Stirling which would stop off at Alloa. And then the fun would really begin, for none of them had even met Johnny Gentle, let alone played so much as one single musical note with him. By John Lennon's reckoning, they would have less than an hour to get their act together – or face humiliation and embarrassment a

THE SCOTS WHO UPSTAGED THE BEATLES AT THE CAVERN

Scots folk duo Robin Hall and Jimmie McGregor once took on The Beatles in their own heartland of Liverpool's Cavern – and relegated the Fab Four to support act *twice* on the same day. In the early sixties, Robin and Jimmie were leading pioneers of the growing folk music movement. They were propelled to sudden fame by TV and their starring appearances on the BBC's *Tonight* programme, which made them familiar faces in the homes of millions of people. On 12 December 1962, they topped the bill at the Cavern at lunchtime and in the evening, leaving local favourites The Beatles to play second fiddle just two months before the release of 'Please Please Me'. The Fabs were tuning up for their final gigs in Hamburg and their tour of Scotland in January, 1963. That accolade earned Hall and McGregor their own place in the rebuilt Cavern's wall of fame 35 years later. They became the only Scots to have their names etched in the stonework for posterity, an acknowledgement of the day they topped The Beatles twice in a single day. Cavern spokesman Dave Young said at the time: 'It was remarkable. These two young Scots, who had been together for less than two years and never released a single – only albums – beat The Beatles into second billing at two gigs in a row. They deserve their names on the wall of fame.' After hearing of the tribute, Edinburgh-born Jimmie said: 'We are chuffed to bits. Us? On the Cavern Wall of Fame? Amazing.'

long way from home, not to mention the prospect of being turfed off the tour before it had even started.

When they finally arrived at Alloa Town Hall, having lugged all their gear from the station, the mood was a nervous mixture of elation and apprehension. Any traces of anxiety, though, quickly melted as they approached the old hall and clapped eyes on Johnny standing outside a side room signing autographs for a clutch of local girls. Among them was Mary and her chums, delighted to have caught the eye of the main attraction. All of a sudden, a local newspaper photographer emerged from the shadows to fire off a couple of snaps in quick succession of Johnny and the girls. And it wasn't long before George Harrison was getting in on the act as well, draping his arm around Mary's shoulders as another couple of shots were fired off.

Mary said: 'I remember getting my picture taken with George. He was very good looking, they all were I suppose, but George was very cute. He was about the same age as us so that probably helped a bit. But we were just happy to be talking to the band. We asked them what they were called and they said The Silver Beetles. It was a real thrill because to us they were proper musicians. There was a wee bit of flirting but nothing out of the ordinary.'

Mary then left Johnny Gentle and The Silver Beetles to work out their act, unaware this was the first time they had met. When she next clapped eyes on them an hour later, Johnny Gentle was quickly into his stride delivering the tunes that were by now a staple part of his act. Mary paid little attention to the backing band. 'We were more interested in Johnny Gentle. He was very professional and all the girls loved him. There was a bit of screaming going on but it was nothing to do with The Beatles. The girls would scream for Johnny because he was the number one attraction and the top of the bill. I thought Johnny Gentle was really good but at that age you think everyone's good. I've since found out, of course, that he had never met The Beatles before but you would not have known that from the way they played. From what I can remember, they sounded great. If there were any mistakes, I can't remember them.

'What I do remember is that Johnny did his set and then he introduced The Silver Beetles and asked us to give them a big welcome. And almost from the minute they started, the place was in an uproar. There was a lot more screaming. People might tell you there wasn't any screaming but I can assure you there was. We screamed ourselves hoarse. They were a lot more rock 'n' roll sounding than Johnny Gentle, it was more powerful. Johnny sang a lot of ballads but The Beatles played rock 'n' roll. There was a great atmosphere but then again there always was at the town hall.

'I don't think they played for very long but they certainly caused a stir. But once it was all over, they just disappeared in the night and we never gave them another thought. There was always another band on the next week so you quickly forgot about the one that was on the week before. It was only when we heard them a couple of years later on the radio that we realised that was the same band we heard at the town hall. The strange thing was I was never a fan. I am still friendly with the girls who were there that night so it's a subject that still crops up in conversation – "Do you remember the night we saw The Beatles?" I say to my granddaughter I saw The Beatles but she just gives me a funny look as if to say, "Aye, that'll be right."'

As the last guitar chord died away, The Beatles headed off into the night to conduct a post-mortem into the first concert they ever played on Scottish soil. Next stop was Inverness's Northern Meeting Ballroom and any bumps in the evening's performance could be ironed out along the way.

The Beatles never came back to Alloa, the venue at which they kicked off their first tour north of the border and the first time any of them had witnessed the effect they could have an audience. Mary, on the other hand, has stayed there all her life with no regrets. Well, except the odd one perhaps. 'Look at what I could have had if I had stayed with George Harrison,' laughs Mary now, almost 50 years after the event. But Mary has another good reason to remember the night: 'I wasn't supposed to be at the dance, I told my parents I was going to a friend's house. But I was found out when I appeared on the front page of the local paper with George Harrison! Actually, they weren't too bad about it but I had to clean all the rooms in the house before I could go out the next week.'

DALRYMPLE HALL, FRASERBURGH
Monday, 23 May 1960

Margaret Moffat/Margaret Adams

The two teenagers stood probably only a few metres apart, neither knowing the other and both unaware of the lifelong connection this evening would bring about as they kept their eyes firmly fixed on the band. All around them, high-pitched screams erupted from the darkness in accompaniment to the high-voltage rock 'n' roll. Dominating the front of the stage, raised about six feet above the audience, were John Lennon, Paul McCartney and George Harrison, each of them dressed in black shirts and jeans, their guitars held high above their waists. To one side, the bass player Stuart Sutcliffe seemed strangely detached while the older-looking drummer Tommy Moore frequently dabbed what appeared to be blood away from the side of his mouth. For 40 minutes, the shrieks ebbed and flowed through a performance that was part youthful energy and part rough-edged ambition, bum notes lost in the bedlam.

The hall was packed. Buses from Peterhead and Banff ferried kids the 25 miles to the Broch, as Fraserburgh is popularly known. The band had a captive audience of kids who lived for rock 'n' roll. Normally, their only outlet would be crackly broadcasts on Radio Luxembourg. But this was a real band.

And at the end of their set The Silver Beetles got a taste of a future yet to unfold as some girls tore at their shirts and grabbed their hair. Was this the first sign of the hysteria that would ultimately spread all over the world? Unlikely as it may seem, especially since 'She Loves You', 'Day Tripper' and 'I Want to Hold Your Hand' were still more than three years away, that's the firm view held by Margaret Adams and Margaret Moffat, the two youngsters who saw at first hand the effect the band's music had on their audience.

'They were fantastic, just superb,' said Margaret Moffat. 'They just seemed to give off this raw kind of energy. I sang in a band when I was 16 and the guys all had on suits and ties. The Beatles were just raw. They wore black shirts, black trousers, they were wild and they were different. I wasn't taken aback by their appearance. I thought it was great. Anything to do with rock 'n' roll at that time was great for us. The thing I remember most was just the power of the music. Oh, and Paul McCartney had the most gorgeous eyes I had ever seen.'

In contrast, Margaret Adams was not struck by the band's music – but the sight of local girls going mad for them remains imprinted on her memory. She had already met The Beatles earlier in the day because her father, a well-known local fishing merchant, had a connection with Johnny Gentle who, of course, was the man receiving top billing at the show and the only reason Margaret was going to the Monday night show. She said: 'The one thing that sticks in my mind about the show was the sight of them running down the stairs at the end and then piling into my dad's car. I remember John Lennon's shirt was torn so I think that could have been the start of Beatlemania really. Maybe not the fully-fledged craze that came later but something definitely happened that night. Some of the girls tried to mob them at the end. Having said that, I really don't know why they went down so well.'

Almost 50 years on, fate has drawn the two Margarets into a firm friendship that didn't exist the night they saw The Beatles. Today, they are pillars of the Fraserburgh community and leading lights in the town's drama group. And that band of amateur thespians often meet in the same hall where both women still believe they saw the first electrical sparks of a pop phenomenon that lit up the world. Margaret Adams said: 'We didn't know each other then. I suppose it is bizarre that we both saw The Beatles on the same night. It's amazing to think we were there. All my life it's something you can roll out as a conversation piece at parties. It's a bit surreal. The Dalrymple Hall feels like our hall. It has hardly changed since that night. The décor is the same and the lights are the same. If Paul McCartney was to walk back in today and if he remembered what it was like, he would find that nothing had changed. I suppose it is still strange for me to have such a strong connection to the hall even today. And it's nice for Margaret and I to have such a nice shared memory.'

ST THOMAS HALL, KEITH
Wednesday, 25 May 1960

Leslie Bisset

Wednesday evenings at the St Thomas Hall in Keith were rock 'n' roll nights. For the local teenagers in the sleepy Highland market town between Aberdeen and Elgin this was their chance to let off steam. Handbills put up a few days earlier advertised the fact that chart singing star Johnny Gentle would be appearing. Closer inspection of the tiny black print revealed that Rikki Barnes' All Stars would also be taking the stage on Wednesday, May 25. There was no mention of Gentle's backing band The Silver Beetles – or The Beatles as they were now calling themselves. And even if there had been, it would not have generated a single ripple of interest, especially not with Leslie Bissett, an 18-year-old worker with British Rail.

Leslie's was a familiar face at St Thomas's Hall, especially during the week when it became the focal point for teenagers to mill around and listen to live music. He had already seen the Rikki Barnes band cranking out their saxophone-driven rock 'n' roll a couple of times and he was eager to make sure he was there when they returned. Leslie, though, was in a minority of Rikki Barnes fans in Keith. That night he turned up early as usual for the show to find little more than three dozen people in the hall. And not even the lure of 'chart star' Johnny Gentle had managed to generate much excitement at the front door.

'Rikki Barnes had played there before and gone down well,' recalled Leslie. 'They were magic but on this particular night there was hardly anyone there. I don't know why. Maybe it was the weather or something. I wasn't that bothered by the turnout to be honest. I liked the band, they played my kind of rock 'n' roll.'

But Rikki Barnes and his All Stars had to give way at the top of the bill to the Liverpool singer whose debut single 'Wendy' was already on the radio and creeping into the bottom reaches of the national pop charts. The evening had been billed as the Beat Ballad Show, heralding the fact that the main attraction was miles away from footstomping, pumped up dance music. So when Johnny began his act perched on a chair, Leslie's enthusiasm went through the floor.

'He was too much of a crooner type for me. I preferred the rock 'n' roll,' he said. 'Wednesday night was a sort of jive night and it was the usual scenario of the boys on one side of the hall and the girls on the other. But when the music started you just made a mad dash across the floor to the other side of the hall and got stuck in with the dancing. Johnny Gentle just

OFF THE BEATLE TRACK 6 –
A PORTRAIT OF JOHN

Celebrated Scots artist Peter Howson caused a stir in 2007 when he painted a sequence of pictures of John Lennon looking more like an Old Testament prophet than a rock 'n' roll star. Glasgow-based Howson created 32 images of Lennon at various stages of his adult life. But the centre-piece of the collection captured a heavily bearded Lennon looking more like John the Baptist than Beatle John. Howson, who has also painted controversial images of Madonna, rated the drawings as among his finest work. He said: 'I could feel John's spirit right next to me – it was kind of weird. He kept egging me on until he was pleased with it. It is probably the finest portrait I have ever done. At first I didn't want to do it. I see parallels with my life and John's. We both knew how to press the self-destruct button. I have depicted him expressing his spiritual qualities – a bit of a Saint John if you like. He looks like a biblical prophet because that's how I see him.'

sat on a chair singing ballads and that wasn't really for me I'm afraid. It was a bit cabaret.'

Yet his curiosity was mildly pricked by Johnny's backing band, four kids largely the same age as he was and a drummer who looked out of place and considerably older. And when Johnny exited stage left and intro-duced 'The Beatles' the tempo kicked up a gear as the sugary-sweet ballads made way for high-energy rock 'n' roll.

Leslie would have been unaware of it, but the band had been working hard on shoehorning new songs into their act. That night was the first public airing of a song written by The Beatles' two charismatic frontmen. 'One After 909' would eventually end up on the last album The Beatles released, 1970's *Let It Be*. Hardly a classic, admittedly, but the band felt the song still carried enough punch, sandwiched between Buddy Holly's 'Words of Love' and Little Richard's 'Kansas City', to get people off their rear ends. They were wrong. According to Leslie, the show – the fourth date of their Scottish tour – was a monumental flop. And he reckons that in the battle of the bands between Rikki Barnes and The Fabs, there was only one winner – and they weren't from Liverpool.

'They weren't very impressive, from what I can recall. John Lennon sang three songs standing on one leg and played side-on to the audience and Stuart Sutcliffe mostly kept his back to the audience. George Harrison was wearing a silver locket which was unheard of for the time. They were dressed in black jeans with green stitching and shirts with silver collars. They just didn't cause much of a stir and I must admit I didn't like them. Frankly, I could hardly understand them. It was mostly cover songs because that is what all the young bands did. I certainly didn't see anything that suggested they were going to be something special. I think there was some polite applause but no one went crazy for them. I couldn't tell you what songs they played because they just didn't register with me on the night. When they finished, I just assumed that was the last I would hear of them.'

Yet, in his own book chronicling The Beatles' pre-fame tour of Scotland, Johnny Gentle reckoned Keith was a turning point in the band's career. His view could not contrast more starkly with Leslie's eye-witness account. Johnny recalled: 'The Beatles had backed [me] more than adequately that night but when their own turn came later they simply stunned the audience.' He felt he had 'witnessed the future of rock 'n' roll that night in the tiny Scottish market town.'

REGAL BALLROOM, NAIRN
Friday, 27 May 1960

Scott MacPherson

Their name never appeared on any promotional posters so for the kids in the Scottish fishing port of Nairn, The Silver Beetles were completely anonymous. Not so Johnny Gentle, the undeniable star of the show this Friday night at the town's Regal Ballroom. Johnny was the magnet that would draw out several hundred teenagers to the former cinema in Leopold Street, its vaudeville seats having been ripped out to create space for weekend revellers to stomp themselves into a dance hall daze.

His backing group attracted not a ripple of pre-show interest. None of the regulars who trooped along to the ballroom had ever heard of The Silver Beetles. The previous night, John, Paul, George, Stu and drummer Tommy Moore had backed Johnny in the town hall at nearby Forres, but apparently talk of that show had not reached Nairn. Almost a week earlier, Johnny's Beat Ballad tour had clicked into a higher gear at the Northern Meeting Ballroom in Inverness, some 15 miles away, the second staging post of this northern jaunt.

However, Friday nights at the Regal always guaranteed a big crowd, especially because, as far as the local teenagers were concerned, it was the only place in town. Among those who took the familiar trail to the Regal at the top of the brae that night was 18-year-old Scott MacPherson. The truth is, he would have been going there whether Johnny Gentle was playing or not.

He said: 'Everyone went to the Regal. There was always some kind of dance and a band on. That particular night was not much different than any other as far as I can remember. We had heard of Johnny Gentle. He had a record in the charts and you heard him occasionally on the radio. He wasn't what you would have called a star but because he was on the radio and sometimes in the paper, people obviously knew a bit more about him. He was like Marty Wilde or someone like that. He was a bit of a crooner and the girls liked him. As for his backing band, none of us had ever heard of The Silver Beetles. When we found out what they were called, it just sounded daft, to be honest. They were only the backing band so no one paid them much attention.'

Earlier that day, the band had strolled along the town's beautiful sea-front, walking in and out of the dunes that formed sandy hillocks on the long stretch of beach. Mingling with the fresh sea air was a mood of optimism as Lennon, McCartney and Harrison especially kicked over the traces of the past week, ruminating that the highs had far outweighed the lows. Sure, they were broke. So broke that the previous night they had done a runner from the Royal Hotel in Forres. And hungry. And cold. But six gigs in eight days had seen the band improve by leaps and bounds and opened the door to . . . possibilities. Each night had been a challenge to win over new audiences, to see whether their reach could exceed their grasp. And they had found a genuine ally in fellow Liverpudlian Johnny Gentle, who was already considering making The Silver Beetles his permanent backing band.

That evening, the hall was pulsing with a low-fi hum of excitement when Johnny gently opened with his first song, a cover of American balladeer Jim Reeves' 'Have I Told You Lately'. For the next 45 minutes, Johnny remained note-perfect on songs such as Ricky Nelson's 'Poor Little Fool' and 'Mary Lou', Clarence Frogman Henry's hit 'I Don't Know Why I Love You', Presley's 'I Need Your Love Tonight' and the tub-thumping curtain closer Peggy Lee's 'Okay, You Win', with its popular audience-participation, trading-responses moment.

By the time The Silver Beetles were preparing for their turn in the spotlight, the hum had been replaced by a throbbing pulse of teenage *joie de vivre*. George Harrison recalled peering out through the curtain only to be met by a sea of smoke and a wave of heat and yellow light. Lining the front of the stage was a crowd of girls dressed in a mixture of twin sets or

Overleaf. *Twist and shout.* Fans at the Odeon dance in the aisles even before their heroes hit the stage.

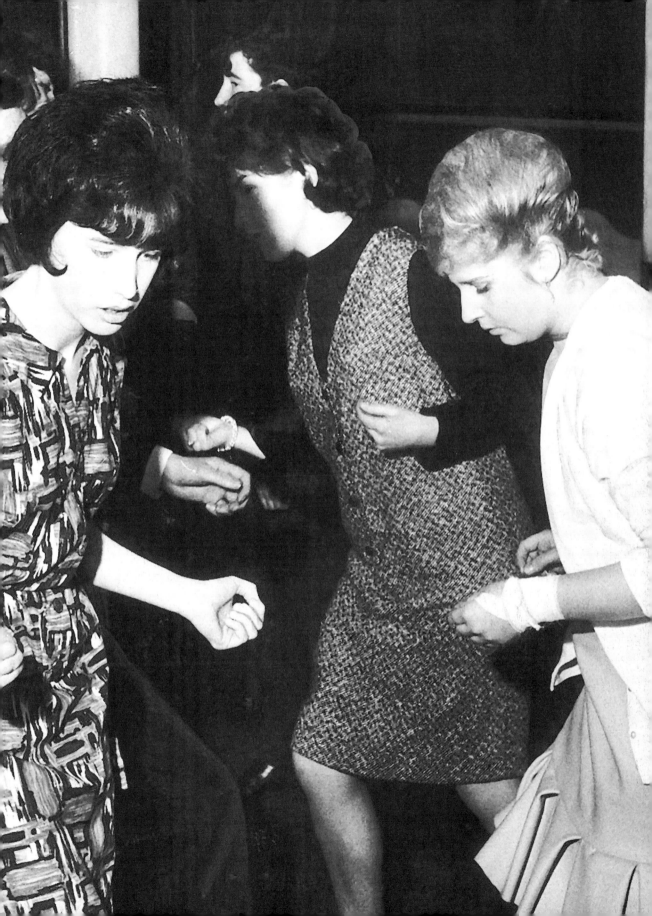

polka dot flared skirts with high-collared blouses and stilettos. Their hair was back combed and lacquered and the smell of cheap perfume hung heavy in the air.

As the last of the cheers melted away, Johnny came back on and, for the second last time, introduced the five-man band – he never mentioned them by name until the end of his set – that had been layering the chords and high harmonies behind his vocals. Grabbing the microphone, he announced: 'Boys and girls – for you – all the way from my hometown Liverpool . . . The Beatles.'

At this point, though, accounts of the evening diverge. Johnny reckoned The Beatles' performance outstripped their previous efforts. But for locals like Scott MacPherson, their set was a mind-numbing waste of time. Scott, now 65, still cannot find a good word to say about the group that would, in just four short years, become the biggest musical force on the planet. 'They were crap,' is his honest, if succinct, summing up of The Silver Beetles. 'Musically they were terrible, and they were scruffy as well. The only reason I remember them is because I couldn't believe how they eventually turned out. The band I saw was a joke. Hardly anyone paid

OFF THE BEATLE TRACK 7 –
SEAT OF YEARNING IN EDINBURGH

Visitors to Edinburgh's Princes Street Gardens are often surprised to see a small, wooden bench commemorating John Lennon's links to Scotland's capital city. Mainly because few tourists are aware of how much of a part Auld Reekie played in John's early teenage years. For a start, his older cousin Stan Parkes, John's first role model, lived there and John was often sent north to spend part of his school holidays in Edinburgh. The two boys went to the cinema and watched the city's speedway team in action. The bench was installed a few years ago and commissioned by the now-defunct Edinburgh Beatles Appreciation Society. Stan said: 'John loved Edinburgh Castle, especially the Military Tattoo. We used to go to the old Roxy in Gorgie Road, which was his favourite cinema. All you hear about with John these days is New York and Yoko, but John loved Edinburgh just as much as New York. I would like to see a proper memorial in Edinburgh to keep that connection alive.'

them any attention. I certainly don't remember any screaming or anything like that. Some people might have clapped just to be polite but I just remember they were rubbish. Compared to a lot of the bands who came to the Regal in those days, they were one of the worst I saw.'

This is how Johnny Gentle remembered the Nairn show in his memoir: 'As they came off stage, I patted each Beatle on the back . . . The Beatles must have been ecstatic as they went out through the hall's rear fire doors to the car park only to be greeted by lungfuls of air and a dozen or so local lovelies. I think they're going to be getting used to that – they were bloody great tonight.'

THE TWO RED SHOES, ELGIN
Thursday, 3 January, 1963

Eithne Kneale & Ralph McKay

He had the gut instincts of a Mississippi gambler and a heart of gold. Albert Bonici was always prepared to put his money where his mouth was. The man who, in the early sixties, was Scotland's foremost music promoter, was a risk taker, a high roller who was prepared to lose a little to gain a lot. So far, his judgement had rarely let Bonici down. And when word reached him that a promising Liverpool band called The Beatles were on the brink of a major breakthrough his entrepreneurial antennae automatically twitched into life.

Contact with the band's manager, Brian Epstein, quickly followed and so it was that, three days into 1963, The Beatles kicked off a pivotal Scottish tour at the Two Red Shoes, the famous Elgin ballroom that Bonici owned and the venue that was the nerve-centre of his business empire.

The Two Red Shoes, with its L-shaped dancefloor, was mainly a magnet for jazz groups reminiscent of Glenn Miller's big band sound of the 1940s. But when Bonici first heard the harmonica that heralded the opening chords of 'Love Me Do', The Beatles' debut single, he quickly recognised that the face of Britain's music scene was changing.

'Albert was always very quick to catch onto something he thought would be the next big thing,' said Moira Loveland, who worked in the office at The Two Red Shoes. 'He was always ready to take a chance on young talent. When we first heard he had booked a band called The Beatles no one blinked an eye. The name meant nothing. Even though "Love Me Do" was on the radio, it wasn't something that meant a great deal to folk in the office. As far as we were concerned they were just another band. It was a bit unusual they were from England but Albert often went out on a limb. He often took chances and for the most part they paid off.'

Yet Bonici could have been forgiven for wondering if this was one gamble that had 'loser' stamped all over it. The tour had already got off to the worst possible start when the opening show in Keith's Longmore Hall had to be scrapped, victim of the worst winter seen in the Highlands for decades. And, as he sat in the downstairs café at the Two Red Shoes, Bonici saw little sign that his ad-hoc promotion for a band billed in the *Northern Scot* as The 'Love Me Do Boys' had been enough to tempt out any more than the usual crowd.

That crowd, an 80-strong mix of farmers and country types, were more interested in local favourites the Alex Sutherland Jazz Band, fronted by 16-year-old Eithne Kneale, than a bunch of long-haired Scousers. Pop music was still considered several rungs down the ladder of social acceptability. In truth, The Beatles' appearance at the Two Red Shoes was a vital staging post in their career. In 2007 the *Scotsman* listed it in the top ten most important Scottish gigs of all time, placing it at number 2 with only Oasis's seminal gig at Glasgow's King Tut's Wah Wah Hut edging in at the top slot.

Just four days earlier, they had been on more familiar ground in Hamburg's Star Club, the last of 13 nights in the notorious Reeperbahn sweat-box and the climax of some 800 hours playing to German audiences. Typically it was a full house, the crowd pumped up to see a band that was now top of the bill rather than the makeweights they started out as. Lively and responsive, they were just the kind of people The Beatles loved playing to. No one probably realised it at the time, but that last German show – on Hogmanay 1962 – brought the curtain down on The Beatles' apprenticeship as musical wannabes. A new year signalled perhaps not a new beginning but certainly a new era. Already in the can at Abbey Road studios was a recording of 'Please Please Me', their Lennon and McCartney-penned second single that would be released in just nine days' time. Now things were getting serious.

But in Elgin, The Beatles were, to all intents and purposes, in enemy territory. Winning over audiences, even audiences weaned on the likes of jazz, was not new; the Cavern in their home city, after all, had been predominately a jazz club before The Beatles signalled a changing of the guard by turning it into an outlet for high-energy rock 'n' roll. But despite their best efforts, The Beatles could not prevail on this occasion. The band played in between two sets by Alex Sutherland's group and their appearance on stage was the signal for most folk to drift casually towards the bar. It was a losing battle that, years later, was recalled by Ringo Starr as one of their strangest gigs.

The less-than-rapturous reception would have blunted the morale of many performers. But any evidence of sagging spirits was not detected by Eithne, the young schoolgirl whose singing ability made her the focal vocal point of Alex Sutherland's band. She remembers coming face to face with The Beatles in the café as they waited to take to the stage at their appointed hour.

She recalled: 'We would go from the ballroom down the steps to the café and that is where I first saw them. They were just sitting together chatting with Albert Bonici. Of course he stood up and introduced me and we shook hands. And the first impression I had was what a scruffy lot they were. This was during the interval and they sort of tried to chat me up but I was so young I didn't know what to say. They were just so hairy, unusually dressed and a bit less than hygienic, I suppose you could say.

'The café was like an American diner with those tables where you slide along the bench. The Beatles all stood up and I went in the back so that meant, of course, I couldn't get out. So they could joke about not letting me get out and trying to embarrass me. It was all harmless fun, really, and just the kind of thing young lads did. I was a bit snooty with them, I suppose. I thought they were a little bit beneath me, to be honest. After all, I jokingly thought I was the star here. They were just riff-raff.

'John Lennon was cheekier than the rest. He was quite scary, actually. He was a good few years older than me and you could tell he was worldly wise. You have to remember this was after the Cavern and after they had been to Hamburg so they had experienced quite a lot of life already. Most of the talking was done by John and Paul. You could tell right away they were the mainstays of the band even at that time. They were all covered with beards, not long ones, but just with a growth of stubble. In those days that was just not on. All the pop stars of the time seemed perfectly groomed but they just seemed scruffy to me. They were wearing leather jackets and even went on stage wearing the same clothes as they did sitting in the café, which was quite shocking to me. It certainly wasn't the done thing.

'The Two Red Shoes then was really all about jazz. We had Kenny Ball and Acker Bilk so pop music was never the main attraction. It was so unusual to have a guitar line-up at the Two Red Shoes. Guitar music was just not our thing at the time. But Albert obviously saw something in The Beatles. Perhaps he saw that things in the music industry were changing because he was very much a visionary in that respect. The Beatles didn't really go down all that well that night, to be honest.'

Within weeks, though, The Beatles' bandwagon was rapidly gathering speed. 'Please Please Me' stormed to the top of the charts, concerts sold out and, by the end of 1963, the Fab Four had become the biggest musical phenomenon in Britain since Elvis. Like millions of other star-struck teenagers Eithne quickly fell under their spell, the irony of her own brief encounter with The Beatles not lost.

'It's amazing to think looking back that it was just a week later that "Please Please Me" came out. I had no inkling at all of what was to follow. How could you? We were in the sticks at the time and maybe The Beatles were ahead of their time. It is not like nowadays when everything spreads so quickly. It wasn't until much later on that I realised maybe I should have been a bit nicer to them.'

Eithne put her own singing career, which included stints with an all-girl band called The Copycats, on the back burner when she married and had four children. Today she occasionally turns the clock back to sing the odd tune, in some cases her love of jazz having been supplanted by the songs made by those four scruffy Scousers who tried to get up close and personal in the Two Red Shoes.

'Oh yes, I am a big fan. The last CD I bought was the *Love* album and it is just fantastic. They didn't go down well at all in Elgin but I'm sure it wouldn't have bothered them. We couldn't have expected them to become the worldwide popular hit they would become. There were a lot of bands after that like The Merseybeats, Gerry and The Pacemakers and Brian Poole and The Tremeloes, but none of them had the sustainability of The Beatles. I think really John and Paul's songwriting marked The Beatles out as something different and something special. That was what did it for them. You never get fed up hearing the songs. I know them all inside out. I could probably sing every one to you.'

Home for the holidays from a first year course at Aberdeen University, 18-year-old Ralph McKay and a group of pals were on the lookout for anything that would break the monotony of the inevitable wind down that always followed the Hogmanay high. 'We were just looking for somewhere to go and have a few pints and listen to music. So we thought we would go and check them out. The initial impression was just the volume they made. Compared to what we had been listening to at the Two Red Shoes, this was like a wall of noise. Alex Sutherland was a jazz band with a brass section, that kind of stuff. Then these guys came on and it seemed like extreme volume in a fairly small dance hall. Three guitars and a set of drums played at maximum volume. It was a shock to the system in a way.

'The general reaction was that people didn't know what to make of this, it was so different to what we were used to hearing. What is going on here, who the heck are these guys? Things took a while to reach the North-east of Scotland in those days. What might have gone down big time in Liverpool was a long way from Elgin.

'They certainly had a handle on their music and on the set they were performing. They were sure of themselves. It wasn't a case of four rookies looking at each other and wondering what to do next. They played covers like Buddy Holly songs, but it wasn't as if they replicated the same sound, they had their own twist on it. We would recognise it as a Buddy Holly song, but it was far from a straight imitation.'

Ralph emigrated to Winnipeg in Canada in 1968 but still keeps in

OFF THE BEATLE TRACK 8 –
DUCHESS OF KIRKCALDY AND SIR MATT

Scottish references in Beatles' songs are extremely rare but there again so are any signposts that point the way to their home city Liverpool, with the famous exceptions of Penny Lane and Strawberry Fields Forever. So it's a pleasant delight to discover the name of a famous Scottish town nestling in one of the band's finest songs – and one that has such a strong link to their past.

John Lennon's stylish nursery rhyme 'Cry Baby Cry' from the White Album includes the line 'The Duchess of Kirkcaldy always smiling and arriving late for tea'.

The song is a slice of typical Lennon-in-Wonderland-type whimsy, but John's nod to the town in Fife is inter-esting for two reasons. First, he used to stop there with his cousin Stan Parkes to visit Stan's stepfather's brother Angus en route to their holidays in Durness so he could have remembered it from those trips. Later, though, The Beatles played at the town's Carlton Cinema in late 1963 so it may be that's what came to mind as he wrote the song.

The only other Beatles song to contain a specific Scottish connection was 'Dig It' from *Let It Be*, a long-running rap that was more a string of sub-conscious words than a proper song. It nevertheless includes the name of Sir Matt Busby, the legendary manager of Manchester United which in itself is curious because none of the Beatles showed much interest in football, despite coming from a city that, like Glasgow, was largely divided upon football lines between two great clubs, Liverpool and Everton. Busby, though, had been in the news because he had just announced his retirement as manager after 24 years with the Old Trafford club so that was perhaps the reason for his inclusion on a song that was more a throwaway and was, in fact, credited to all four members of the band. It was rightly left on the shelf when Paul McCartney masterminded the release of *Let it Be . . . Naked* a few years ago.

touch with pals who were with him the night he checked out the 'Love Me Do Boys'. 'If you're asking me if I saw anything particularly special that night, I would have to say no. There was nothing to suggest they were on the cusp of greatness. Was it a surprise when they achieved some level of success? Absolutely. When they were number one we kind of shook our heads. I mean, I'm a huge fan now, but it took me a while to listen to their music and say, yeah they really are something special. But that night, when we all walked out of the Two Red Shoes, I had no reason to think I would ever hear about them again.'

Today, the Two Red Shoes remains on Elgin's cultural map as the base for a theatre company. Any memory of the Fab Four playing there at the outset of the year that heralded Beatlemania remains fogged in the Highland mist. That sad fact is a source of some irritation to former Elgin schoolteacher Stan Williams who has become one of the foremost experts on the pre-Fab Four. Stan, who actually attended the same primary school as John Lennon, reckons local civic fathers should consider mounting a plaque outside the Two Red Shoes to mark Elgin's connection to The Beatles. He said: 'Albert Bonici would have liked that. Such a gesture would not only celebrate a significant occasion but also commemorate a remarkable local entrepreneur who left the town such an enviable musical legacy.'

DINGWALL TOWN HALL
Friday, 4 January 1963

Margaret Paterson

More than 1,000 teenagers, demob happy for the weekend, were shoehorned into the dance hall. It was a Friday night and the place was heaving. On stage, the band were going down a storm. The venue was Strathpeffer Pavilion in the sleepy Highland town of Dingwall. Far from being the local dive, the Strath had a magnetism and charm that drew people from miles around. The band was The Mellotones, a four-piece combo belting out a mixture of bobby-soxer doo-wop and rootsy rock 'n' roll. The feelgood vibes of New Year celebrations still hung in the air.

Somewhere among the sea of bodies, four musicians from Liverpool watched the kids go wild . . . and cursed their luck. Just an hour earlier, John Lennon, Paul McCartney, George Harrison and Ringo Starr had been on stage themselves just two miles down the road at Dingwall Town Hall. The Beatles had been ready to rock the town, but the town hadn't been ready to rock with them.

Unlike The Mellotones, there was no rapturous applause for the four Scousers, no packed dancefloor and no sense of this being where it's at. When John Lennon, legs slightly parted and his guitar hung menacingly at his side, looked myopically out from centre stage, he saw just 19 people looking back. Not exactly his vision of the toppermost of the poppermost. Still, a show was a show and The Beatles, their act honed from hundreds of gigs in Liverpool and Hamburg's notorious Reeperbahn, stuck manfully to their game plan.

In just five days, their second single would be released by their record company EMI. Five days. Yet, tonight, The Beatles couldn't even compete with the local foot-stompers at the Strath. And there would be precious little sympathy from the motley crew that made up this husk of an audience at the town hall. Quite simply, this was the night The Beatles died on stage before the showbiz equivalent of two men and a dog. It was no great surprise, since their billing meant zilch to kids largely cut off from the current pop grapevine, kids for whom ceilidhs were more the norm than Cliff Richard.

Watching from near the front of the stage was Margaret Paterson, who was waiting patiently for her date to show up. He never came. Unknown to her, Tommy Paterson had high-tailed it to the Strath to see a 'real' band. Margaret, though, stuck to the original arrangements and saw The Beatles on a night that has become part of Dingwall folklore.

She said: 'It was just after New Year and I had just met my late husband Tommy on Christmas Eve. So this was our first proper date together and he didn't turn up. I thought he had stood me up, but he had actually come along and there was hardly anybody there. So he told a pal that when Meg comes along, tell her I have gone up to the Strath because The Mellotones were on there. They were a very big and popular local band at the time. But the guy forgot to tell me. So I went to the Town Hall and the most I counted in the audience was 19. I only stayed because I thought Tommy was going to turn up.

'None of us had heard anything about The Beatles. We knew they were from Liverpool and there was talk of them having a record out. But that was about all we knew. They were just another band at the Town Hall. I think they were surprised at how few people were there. They just said, "Where is everybody? What is wrong with this place? It's like a ghost town." And I just said there was a big band playing at Strathpeffer and everyone had gone there.

'They were very pleasant and as I was leaving I said to them that I was going up to the Strath to meet the chap I was supposed to meet at the Town Hall. And I said you should come up there because they're a great band. Two of them came on the bus with me, but I can't even remember which ones. The other two went in their van. I met Tommy at the Strath and when you're smooching you don't really notice what else is going on around you, so I never met them again.'

The Beatles may have bombed in Dingwall, but Margaret has never forgotten the frisson she felt for the Fab Four. She recalled: 'Because there was hardly anyone there, I just started sitting on the stage and chatting to them. They were really charming. Had I not been on this date, I would have quite fancied them. They were all very nice-looking and very nice boys. Paul McCartney had the most gorgeous eyes I had ever seen. Ringo was full of devilment. But Paul was the nicest looking. The music was good. It had a great beat and I was sorry and embarrassed that there were not more people there to see them. One or two people that I knew were leaving because it wasn't a good crowd.'

Dotted round the side of the stage were dozens of publicity posters showing The Beatles in their Pierre Cardin collarless jackets. One of them, Margaret cannot remember who, asked her if she wanted one and then offered to get the band to sign it. She said: 'I had it for a long time but it just disappeared eventually. At the time, you never think that these things will become valuable, but it would have been worth a small fortune.

OFF THE BEATLE TRACK 9 –
BACKING IN THE USSR

Struan Stevenson, a long-serving Scottish member of the European Parliament, is an unlikely hero to Beatles fans in the former Soviet satellite state of Kazakhstan. Fab Four followers in the country began a campaign for a Beatles memorial to be built in the country's capital city Almaty. But the plan looked to be foundering because approval could not be sought from The Beatles' hierarchy. When Ballantrae-born Struan, who has campaigned in the Euro Parliament for the victims of the Soviet nuclear testing programme in Kazakhstan heard about the dilemma, he volunteered to act as a middle-man to try and break the impasse. He said: 'I talked with Paul McCartney and personally let him know about the monument and he was very excited. Paul in turn discussed it with Ringo and Olivia Harrison and Yoko Ono who gave the project their blessing.' As a result, a five tonne, two metre sculpture of John, Paul, George and Ringo now stands outside Almaty's main music hall, thanks in no small part to the efforts of a veteran Scottish politician.

'After that night I forgot about them completely until they went into the charts. And then I couldn't believe it. I went and looked out the poster they had signed. And then it all came back to me that they were the same band. All of a sudden they were everywhere, on the radio, television and all the papers. But I have always cherished the memory. There was less than 20 people there that night – and I was one of them. It's a great memory.'

Dan McKenzie, of local band The Drumbeats remembers his band playing a set alongside the Fabs at Dingwall. He recalled: 'Only 19 people out of the whole population of Ross-shire turned up to see and hear The Beatles. While we were having a break at the back of the hall, the man that booked them turned round and said: "What do you think of that shower there?" I said, "They're very loud and they're very young – they're keen." "Keen," he says. "They're a shower of rubbish. I'll never book them again as long as I live."'

MUSEUM HALL, BRIDGE OF ALLAN
Saturday, 5 January 1963

Neil Cunningham

Neil Cunningham was with a clutch of friends who braved the Arctic cold of a Scottish winter's night on Saturday, 5 January 1963, to venture out to the Museum Hall in the Stirlingshire farming town of Bridge of Allan. As usual, it was the only place for youngsters to hang out on a weekend. Most Saturdays a band would be playing in the old hall. Some billboards around the town talked about a Saturday night show by a band called The 'Love Me Do Boys'. But Neil recalled the name of the band as The Beatles and this is his recollection of the show by a band that was only weeks away from becoming a household name.

'That night in January was bitter. We two met outside the Museum Hall early. What was important was to get to the middle of the front of the balcony before anyone else. As the time grew near for the music to start, the hall began to fill. Upstairs, there were just a few couples, I remember about 20 or so young people, scattered around the seating, huddled in pairs. The main hall lights were lit and the coloured footlights illuminated the stage curtain.

'Downstairs a crowd eventually gathered, about a hundred or so I suppose. The curtains parted as this new group began to play. There were four of them – the most striking thing about them was their hairstyle. The music was sharp and loud and the group played Ray Charles songs to begin with. The sound was thin and slightly harsh but I noticed that, in their own way, they all played fairly well.

'About ten minutes or so into the session, the crowd downstairs became restless. From the remarks that floated up from the floor of the hall I gathered that the punters were not too charmed with the act and someone began calling out that everyone should leave and go to the Stardust Club in Dunblane. The crowd disappeared within the next 20 minutes or so and eventually all that was left was the upstairs few, probably too lazy to leave but I think they were all were too engrossed in each other to care.

'The group took a break. When they returned to the stage, the bass player called to the couples upstairs to come down beside the stage and dance. They would, he said, play some of the stuff they had written recently. They played the numbers "Love Me Do", "Please Please Me", and "I Saw Her Standing There". They were jaunty songs, different, and all right to jive along to. The evening turned out to be quite a pleasant one and I've often thought since that the crowd that went off into the freezing cold to wait for buses and taxis to Dunblane were a bit daft, especially as events turned out.

'There were reports later in various books saying The Beatles were booed off stage but that is most definitely not how I remember the night. What I do I remember is coming out after the event and seeing a mid-grey coloured Austin A40 with the name, "The Beatles", in black tape on the rear wings and a trailer to carry the gear, parked at the side of the hall.'

BEACH BALLROOM, ABERDEEN
Sunday, 6 January 1963

Malcolm Strachan

The northern lights of old Aberdeen were scarcely visible in the night sky as Malcolm Strachan and his two pals braved the bitter cold to head to the city's Beach Ballroom six days into the new year of 1963. Once inside, though, they could blot out the chill and warm to the sounds of whatever band was on stage at The Beach. Tonight, a Sunday, the band was called The Beatles, four guys from Liverpool whose first single 'Love Me Do' had already made a tiny encroachment on the lower rungs of the pop ladder.

'I quite liked "Love Me Do" and then I had seen a small clip of them on a Granada television programme, so I was quite intrigued to see them. They sounded very different to what a lot of the other groups were doing,' recalled Malcolm. The 15-year-old schoolboy had been going to the Beach since he was 12. Music was undoubtedly his first love and he even played in a local band called The Playboys. Concerts at the Beach provided an important education, a peek through the keyhole into a more professional musical world.

The three youngsters stumped up the admission money of three shillings (15p today) and made their way inside. The hall, though, was virtually deserted. The dancefloor was covered in tarpaulins because the Beach didn't have a dance licence and the audience was expected to behave with a certain decorum. Bemused, the three youngsters made a beeline for the cafeteria. 'And that was when we saw the four of them huddled together in a corner talking among themselves, John, Paul, George and Ringo. Of course, it sounds amazing when you say the names like that now, but all we knew then was that they were the band that would be playing at the Beach that night.

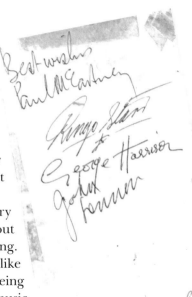

'So we just went up and said hello. They were very approachable and we chatted to them for ages about music, bands, how the rest of the tour had been going. They were great to talk to. They were smoking like chimneys. I had never seen so many cigarettes. And, being in a band, they were really keen to know what sort of music we played and what sort of songs the audience would like that night. I got the impression they had a big repertoire of songs rather than just a set list.

'Paul was already a bit of a PR type, he was the spokesman and did most of the talking. And John's wit was razor sharp. I asked him what it was like in the Star Club in Hamburg and, quick as a flash, he said it was like a converted gas chamber. It took me a few minutes to realise he was pulling my leg.'

Eventually, The Beatles, already wearing their suits with the velvet collars and Cuban-heeled boots, collected their guitars and made their way towards the stage. They would be playing two sets, alternating with local outfit Johnny Scott and his Big Band, not to mention the regular Sunday night quiz. By now, the hall was beginning to fill up but it was a long way short of being even half-full.

'There weren't that many people there, I remember that. And the other thing, of course, was that because the hall had no dance licence, you couldn't really let yourself go. There was a strict dress code and everybody was expected to sit down and be well-behaved – no jumping up and down. Any shenanigans and you were out.'

But from the opening chords of their first song, Malcolm was transfixed. 'They were fantastic. I just thought I had never heard a sound like them. What I loved most was the vocal ability, the three-part harmonies. And I was intrigued by Paul McCartney being a left-handed bass player and his Hofner guitar was just so unusual. And they could switch effortlessly from Chuck Berry stuff and Crickets covers, to early Tamla Motown to showtunes like 'Till There Was You' and 'Besame Mucho'. We had been used to bands like Joe Brown and the Bruvvers, Johnny Kidd and the Pirates or Mike Berry and the Outlaws, bands that always had a frontman, but The Beatles were a group in every sense of the word. They had a real spark.

'They sang "Love Me Do" and also "Please Please Me" which they said was going to be their next single, coming out in a couple of weeks' time, so please buy it. It was quite funny seeing the different styles between them and the Johnny Scott Band, who were employed by Aberdeen Corporation and played every Sunday. In fact, I think at one point they asked if they could share the Johnny Scott drum kit but were turned down.

'It's true there weren't that many people there, but it was a Sunday night and no one had really heard of The Beatles. But they went down very well. There was no screaming, but there was plenty of polite applause. I have heard it said – and I've also read in books and newspapers – that they were booed off stage and people were throwing coins at them. Well, I was there and I can tell you that is absolute rubbish. It is no more than an urban myth. They got a better reception in the Beach Ballroom, they said, than other places they had played in Scotland.

'I could see that they were talented, no doubt about that, although I don't suppose any of us knew how big they would become. But they were really inspiring, especially for someone like me who was already playing in a band. My abiding memory is just how lucky I was to have been there.'

And today, Malcolm has a lasting legacy of the night he saw The Beatles in his home city. Slightly star-struck, he had earlier asked the band if they would scribble their signatures on a Parlophone Records postcard, a memento he reckons is now worth between £1,500 and £2,000. 'I've never been tempted to sell. The funny thing is my mother kept it. If it had been down to me, I might have thrown it out years ago. But it's a nice thing to have and I'm still as big a fan today.'

ODEON, GLASGOW
Friday, 7 June 1963

Linda Petiffer/Thompson

She was not quite 17, but the scene unfolding before her eyes was indeed way beyond compare. Linda Pettifer saw The Beatles standing there right in front of her singing the songs that had already begun to form the soundtrack to her teenage years. It started with that raucous Paul McCartney 'one-two-three-fooouuurrrr' intro to 'I Saw Her Standing There', the opening track of *Please Please Me*, their first album.

Rising inside her right now, though, was a wave of anger mixed with frustration and confusion. Yes, she could see the band onstage at Glasgow's Odeon Cinema. But the sounds were lost in a cacophony of screams that all but drowned out the songs she had longed to hear played live. As she struggled to make sense of her emotions, the youngster from the south side of Glasgow was suddenly aware of a mental light bulb being switched on and it burned bright with ambition, hope and excitement. She said: 'It was my epiphany with music. Watching them onstage that night, I suddenly saw the light. It was like power and glory coming together in one universal big bang.'

Like countless others of her generation, Linda Pettifer had The Beatles to thank for inspiring her to pick up a guitar, find a set of chords and turn them into a song. But while others may have fallen by the wayside, Linda's talent shone through. The songs of Lennon and McCartney – as well as those of Carole King and Gerry Goffin – were the prime motivation to make her own mark on the music industry, especially the burgeoning folk movement that would enlist the likes of Sandy Denny, Nick Drake, Richard Thompson, John Renbourn as well as Scottish traditionalists such as Hamish Imlach and Archie Fisher to its ranks.

Of course, Linda long ago waved farewell to her maiden moniker but as Linda Thompson – the name she still retains from her marriage to Richard, the acclaimed guitar virtuoso behind Fairport Convention – she is warmly acknowledged as one of the foremost figures in Britain's folk-rock scene. But, as she readily confesses, life could have veered along a different path had she missed out on the chance of seeing John, Paul, George and Ringo on stage that night in June, 1963.

'I was already interested in music and folky things. And I had been a fan of The Beatles since "Please Please Me". I thought they were amazing. So of course it was natural to take your devotion a step further and that was to see them in concert. I was so looking forward to it. I went with a friend called Lindy. We were hugely excited, this was a big event in our

Paul McCartney is mobbed by fans while taking refuge in a Glasgow hotel after his car broke down on the outskirts of the city in 1967.

lives. There were other bands on the bill but we weren't much interested in them, we were only there to see The Beatles. You could feel the sense of hysteria building up. And when they came on stage it was just bedlam. And I was very annoyed because I wanted to hear the music. Some people will tell you that you only went to a Beatles concert to see them, not to hear them. But in my case, I wanted to listen. I could just feel myself getting more and more annoyed.

'No one could hear them, they couldn't hear themselves and that of course was the reason they eventually gave up touring because no one was listening and the performance deteriorated. There was no creativity and I remember just being furious, but it was still amazing. You understood the Nuremberg Rally if you went to a Beatles concert. It was mass hysteria. From an anthropological point of view it was an amazing study of human behaviour. And if Ringo or Paul said all of you go now to Loch Lomond and throw yourselves in they would have done it. It was interesting to see that kind of power, which fortunately nobody has. I wasn't a screamer and I was so annoyed. It was hopeless, I couldn't hear a damn thing. Even now you would need to show me a setlist to tell me what they played. All the kids just came to scream.

'Some of those songs would have made a great live album but no one could have recorded it from the desk because the screaming was just too loud. I had the opportunity to see them again, but I didn't take it because it was just utter madness. I wouldn't say it was a disappointment because it definitely helped me make up my mind that I wanted to make music of my own, but even now I just wish I could have heard them singing live properly in a proper concert.'

Actually, Linda was one of the luckier ones among the 3,000-odd kids who crammed into the old art deco cinema in Glasgow's Renfield Street. For some five months earlier, in January 1963, she was among around 50 kids who made up the audience for Scottish Television's popular teen music show *Round Up*. The show was presented by aspiring actor Paul Young and Morag Hood, one of Linda's chums from drama school, whose brother Liam was also the programme's producer.

The day before transmission, Morag badgered Linda to come along and listen to this hot new band that she said was going to be the Next Big Thing. 'I remember Morag telling me all this and I was going yeah, yeah, yeah. She said they were from Liverpool, as if that was meant to impress me in some way,' laughed Linda. 'I still needed some persuading and then she said, "Oh, they're gorgeous," and that was the clincher for me. And I have to tell you it was amazing. They were in the studio a few feet away from us singing "Please Please Me". It was a mind-blowing experience. The song was just great and they sounded fantastic.

'We were told this was their first TV appearance and they had just come off the back of a tour of the Highlands, so looking back it seems even more of a thrill for me that this was a pivotal moment for the band. It made me think I had discovered something new and fresh, which is what they were. Up until that time I had been listening to genius music like Buddy Holly and a whole host of other people. But this was something very, very different. They were beautifully crafted songs and beautifully sung.

'Up until that time pop songs had been very forgettable, although obviously not Buddy Holly or Elvis. And the likes of The Everly Brothers had great songs, but The Beatles were just amazing. Then we found out they had written these songs themselves and that was hugely impressive. That was very unusual in those days. Carole King wrote for people but she didn't sing in those days, likewise Gerry Goffin. It was the time of Tin Pan Alley songwriters. So not only was this music incredibly sung with unbelievable harmonies, and beautifully crafted, but The Beatles – or Lennon and McCartney – had actually written them. Nowadays everybody writes everything but in those days this was very leftfield. Also there was a feeling that these songs would be around for a long time, they had a very enduring quality about them. It was definitely a life-changing moment.'

Despite her Scottish upbringing, Linda was actually born in London, although her mother, the daughter of a vaudevillian entertainer, was born north of the border. When Linda was six, the family moved to Glasgow's south side where her father opened a TV repair shop. By the early sixties, she was a star pupil at Queen's Park Secondary. Away from the classroom, she dreamt of writing her own songs rooted in traditional music rather than rock 'n' roll.

Under the spell of Dylan's *The Times They are a-Changing*, she gravitated further towards folk music while at the same time maintaining her love of the Fab Four as they continued to conquer the world. She began appearing in local coffee bars in Glasgow, juggling her musical dreams with the practical needs of a proper education.

In 1966 she was drawn back to the city of her birth to study modern languages at London University. But the pull of songwriting and music was too strong and she dropped out after four months. Soon, she was moving in the same circles as fellow folkies Sandy Denny and Richard Thompson, the mainstays of the band that would later, of course, mushroom into Fairport Convention, the band she would also play a huge part in.

In a career that has suffered the obligatory showbiz highs and lows, Linda Thompson's musical output – both with Fairport Convention and as a solo performer – has rightly earned her a top-table place in the British folk hall of fame. And although her career never scaled the dizzy heights of The Beatles – she never wanted it to – she has never forgotten the debt she owes to four guys from Liverpool who proved it wasn't an impossible dream.

'When I was at school, you were either a Beatles fan or a Stones fan. I liked them both, actually, but I never let on. It was an interesting juxtaposition because the Stones had these weird American accents and The Beatles had these Liverpudlian accents and I loved the fact that the Beatles to me, even though their influences were obviously American, kept their accents. And that Englishness and their irreverence I really liked. They were the first people in the pop world who weren't putting on American accents. They remained very much true to themselves. And their mastery of songwriting was evident at a very early age.

'It was a long time after I first saw them on *Round Up* that I began to write songs myself. The minute you start trying to be a songwriter you think you're either a genius or you're not, and I'm not. But when you heard the songs of Lennon and McCartney you instantly thought they were geniuses. You knew they were streets ahead of everyone else. I mean you could put a Lennon McCartney song on and a Cole Porter song after it – and he was a great songwriter – and you wouldn't say The Beatles song was inferior. They wrote some amazing, amazing songs, dark songs, light songs, rock songs, funny

OFF THE BEATLE TRACK 10 –
A HIGHLAND HOME IN THE HAMPTONS

John Lennon fell in love with a house in the exclusive Hamptons area of New York and was prepared to shell out a fortune to buy it – because it was decorated like a Scottish home. Much of the house was covered in tartan carpets, apparently a big plus where John was concerned. The incident came to light in an email to me from John's former lover May Pang who revealed how they had been house-hunting in upstate New York during his separation from Yoko Ono. May told me: 'John didn't speak about Scotland to me but at one point in our relationship, in fact just before we broke up, we were contemplating buying this house out in the Hamptons. It was an imitation Scottish house and John just fell in love with it. We went to view it and he was just amazed at the tartan carpets. And then I realized how sentimental he was about Scotland and how much it meant to him. It was on a cliff and looked out to the water. It was lovely. He loved the water very much.'

songs. Their whole collection is like an encyclopaedia of western music.

'In terms of my own career, they gave me the belief that a working class person could go out and do this and maybe write something. They didn't influence me – more's the pity – in writing million dollar songs but they gave me the self-belief. I still have a great affection for The Beatles. They never age for me, they are timeless. And they are as special to me now as they were then.'

CONCERT HALL, GLASGOW
Saturday, 5 October 1963

Robert Robertson

With his collarless Esquire suit and his Cuban-heeled boots, Robert Robertson looked every inch the part, and, as he bounced along Glasgow's Sauchiehall Street that Saturday night, he had every reason to feel good. In his mind's eye, he was Beatle Rob, the fictional singer in a fantasy band. Tonight, though, he was going to see the real deal, and it was important to dress to impress.

'We all wanted to look like The Beatles. I had all the gear. It cost a few bob but you had to have that look. You had to have the collarless suits, the shirts and the pointy boots with the big heels and the trousers with the split in the sides. And the Crombie jackets. It wasn't just fashion. It was a badge of honour. None of the bands or singers that came before had this kind of effect on the youngsters. It wasn't just the music – which was fantastic – it was also what they wore and the way they spoke. Of course, all the guys wanted to be a Beatle. I wanted to be John Lennon. I loved his whole attitude. He was a rebel even then. Being a Beatles fan was like a way of life. I loved them then and I love them now.'

This was the second time The Beatles had played in Glasgow in the last five months. In June, they had appeared as part of a package tour which included, among a number of other acts, Roy Orbison. At the start of that tour, the Big O was the showstopping finale. By the time the tour bandwagon hit Glasgow's Odeon Cinema, however, The Beatles had taken over at the top of the bill.

When they returned to Glasgow in October, there was no doubting their place as the main draw. This time, though, they would be playing at the city's dusty old Concert Hall, a vaudeville relic well past its prime, as part of a hat-trick of Scottish gigs. 'I don't think it was in great nick,' recalled Robert. 'It was owned by the old Glasgow Corporation and I think there had been a few concerts staged there but nothing on the scale of

The Beatles. The Corporation people had no idea about The Beatles or how popular they were.'

That, though, was the furthest thing from Robert's mind as he and three other pals joined the huge swell of fans making their way to the venue. 'I was just amazed to get the chance to see them. Everyone wanted to go, all your pals at work, everyone. But there was no way I would have parted with my ticket. I had got "Please Please Me" when it came out and they just sounded so different. You have to remember that the people in the charts at that time were the likes of Slim Whitman, Roy Rogers and Dean Martin. Then The Beatles came along and changed everything.

'On the night of the concert, Sauchiehall Street was just awash with fans. There was no way they all had tickets. It seemed like half of the kids in Glasgow were there. But everyone was in good spirits.'

Once inside, Robert and his pals waited patiently as the support acts showcased their routines. Polite applause, however, soon gave way to raise-the-roof rapture when the curtain eventually went up on the top-of-the-bill band. 'The whole place just erupted. I was shouting and screaming along with everyone else, not in a girlie way you understand,' he laughed. 'More in a sort of manly way. But it was totally wild. Everyone was standing on their seats and I remember the Corporation stewards with their little uniforms trying to get people to sit down. But they were absolutely wasting their time. It was definitely a struggle to hear the songs although you could still make them out. In many ways, though, you weren't there to hear the songs. You were there to actually see The Beatles in the flesh. And it was just fantastic. The whole place was jumping. The noise was deafening. We didn't know what had hit us. It was like a jet taking off.

'They played "Please Please Me", "From Me to You" and "She Loves You" – at least these are the ones that stick in my memory, along with "Twist And Shout". They were only on for half an hour but what a half-hour. It was sensational. Lennon was the main man, from what I can remember. He did most of the talking. I mean he was about the same age as me and there he was up on that stage belting out these great songs. It didn't matter that you couldn't hear the songs properly. No one cared less. The fact of the matter was I saw The Beatles and I'll never forget it.'

The gig became one of the last pop shows to be held at the Concert Hall. And the aftermath was dominated by reports of fans rioting and hundreds of pounds worth of damage being done to seats. Robert, though, has no memory of youngsters going over the top. 'What I can tell you is that Glasgow Corporation was completely unprepared for a Beatles show. Maybe there was a bit of damage but the stewarding was a joke – all these wee guys in their corporation uniforms against hundreds of kids at fever pitch. They just kept telling us to sit down as if that was going to stop us.

'I was on such a high at the end I don't think I came back to earth for about a week. And, of course, there were lots of girls at the concert so it was a great way to meet them and chat them up. I only wish I had kept my ticket and my programme. They would be worth a good bit now.'

CARLTON CINEMA, KIRKCALDY
Sunday, 6 October 1963

Barbara Dickson

'Ticket to Ride' may not be top Scottish singing star Barbara Dickson's favourite Beatles song, but the title has a special resonance for her. In 1963, Barbara was one of thousands of British teenagers caught up in the bedlam of Beatlemania. She had been hooked from the moment she heard John Lennon's wheezy harmonica heralding the start of 'Please Please Me'. And the follow-up single, 'From Me to You', cocooned her even more inside her Beatle bubble.

When the Dunfermline youngster realised her heroes were due to play two concerts on the same day at the Carlton Cinema in nearby Kirkcaldy, the only thing on her mind was to see them in the flesh. The drawback was getting a ticket. A determined Barbara got on her bike – quite literally – and set off on the long and winding road that stretched 15 miles between the two Fife towns. But when she got to the concert venue, the wheels quickly came off her plan.

Barbara said: 'I decided to cycle all the way to Kirkcaldy from Dunfermline to the Carlton to get a ticket. It was a bit of a nightmare because it was all the twisty wee back roads, but I thought it would be worth it. But when I got to the Carlton, I was told it was postal applications only. So you can imagine how I felt, somewhat crushed I think. So I had to cycle all the way back to Dunfermline without my precious ticket.'

As it happened, Barbara did manage to secure a precious ticket. The concert was to take place just days before The Beatles played the London Palladium, bringing the first real wave of Beatlemania into millions of homes through television. Recalled Barbara: 'All I can remember is this wall to wall screaming. You can't begin today to tell people what it was like. Funnily enough, I don't think I was a screamer. At least that's what I tell people. It was one of the first concerts I saw so I think I probably just sat there goggle-eyed. To be honest, it was over in a flash. I would even struggle to remember which songs they played. But what I can say is that it was hugely exciting. It's a lovely memory to have, especially since I am still a huge fan to this day.'

Richard Park

The last word of the MC's introduction died in a cacophony of ear-splitting screams: 'And here they are, the Bea . . . ' As the lights faded, more than 1,500 teenagers suddenly morphed into a single, screaming mass at Kirkcaldy's Carlton Cinema. Standing there transfixed was 15-year-old schoolboy Richard Park, his eyes squinting in the darkness for a glimpse of his heroes.

Forget any idea of actually being able to hear The Beatles. The music was already in danger of being drowned out by the hysteria rising from the aisles. But none of that mattered to Richard. His eyes were firmly fixed on the four figures on the high-rise stage, the front sealed off by a line of stewards.

He was already a seasoned concert fan, having seen a number of bands play his home town en route to their very own fame academy. Some made it; others crashed by the wayside. None, however, penetrated his soul like The Beatles. Now here he was, in the same room as John Lennon, Paul McCartney, Ringo Starr and George Harrison. It was a moment he had dreamt of, having bought the first two albums, *Please Please Me* and *With The Beatles*, as well as all the 45rpm singles. Unknown to him at that time, it would be the only time he would see The Beatles perform on stage. But it would not be the last occasion he would be in the same room as them. Years later, Richard would be able to bathe in the friendship of at least three Beatles as well as John Lennon's son Julian.

These are the kind of doors that swing open when a career takes you on a path to becoming one of Britain's most distinguished and influential figures in the world of radio, television and media. For now, though, young Richard was happy just to pinch himself, knowing that it wasn't, in fact, a dream. He really was at a Beatles concert.

Looking back on the momentous events of that afternoon in October, 1963, the former Kirkcaldy High pupil admitted it was a life-changing event. He told me: 'It was a major occasion for those of us of a certain age. I don't think my parents thought there was anything good about this until the end of that year when The Beatles appeared at the London Palladium and the Royal Variety Show, that kind of thing. That gave them a sort of seal of approval from the older generation. That's the way their appeal crossed over.

'It wasn't my first concert because I had seen plenty of bands in the Raith Ballroom, but they were my ultimate heroes so to see them was like a dream. It was the most exciting thing that had ever happened to me. What I do remember is you couldn't hear anything, absolutely nothing, that was the problem. The screaming was at a level I had never experienced. It was at a much louder noise than anything that came afterwards like David Cassidy, the Bay City Rollers, George Michael, stuff like that. But the thing for me was actually to be able to see them.

'I went with three other friends. The crowd I hung about with never talked about anything else other than The Beatles. It was music, fashion and style. People might not believe it but Kirkcaldy was one of the trendiest places ever. The enthusiasm of the people was fantastic.

'My God we were on such a high after the concert. We used to have beach parties and things. I think we went down to, of all trendy places,

OFF THE BEATLE TRACK 11 –
DUNDEE'S UNIQUE PHOTO ARCHIVE

A treasure trove of some 400 lost Beatles photographs was unearthed at Dundee University ten years ago. They were donated to the city's principal seat of learning by the family of renowned Hungarian photographer Michael Peto, whose stepson had been a student there. The remarkably intimate pictures, taken when the world was still monochrome, capture The Beatles during the making of their second film *Help!* on Salisbury Plain and also show them relaxing off camera at the nearby Antrobus Arms Hotel in Amesbury. One candid snap shows an unshaven Paul McCartney, cigarette hanging from his mouth, with his hands resting on an open piano, highlighting perhaps his relentless drive to finish off another song. Another poignant picture shows Ringo at home with first wife Maureen, her hair piled high in a fashion-conscious beehive.

The Peto portfolio's existence was known only to a select few at Dundee University. Over time, though, their significance had been forgotten. And it wasn't until an audit took place in the late 1990s that staff realised Peto had been given unprecedented access to the group as they changed from loveable moptops to serious artistes. Patricia Whalley, the university's archivist who worked on the massive collection, said: 'We don't know why Peto was there, but he must have been trusted because we see The Beatles as young boys, their hair unkempt, not moptops at all. But how he managed that kind of access we haven't been able to find out.' The collection has now been published in a limited edition book called *Now These Days Are Gone*. Last year, the pictures were put on display at Liverpool's National Conservation Centre as part of an exhibition of the same name.

Seafield Beach to talk about the show and come back down to earth. I don't think we were aware at the time how mega it all was. The Beatles have stood the test of time better than any other band. I always think people's greatest musical memories are between the ages of 14 and 16. Real love memories, the ones you feel real emotion for. And that was certainly the case with The Beatles and myself.'

Music had already lit the fire of ambition that burned within Richard. So it was no surprise that it should play such an important role in a roller-coaster career that has seen him climb the ladder of success to reach the pinnacle of Britain's radio industry. After leaving school, he began work on the *Fife Free Press* before that deep-rooted love of music lured him into broadcasting. He joined the pirate station Radio Scotland which broadcast from an old ship called the *Comet* off the coast of Dunbar. And it was here that he introduced audiences to a new wave of artistes such as The Small Faces, Desmond Dekker, The Four Tops and Tom Jones.

His broadcasting talent eventually caught the ear of Radio One, where he stayed until the mid-seventies. Richard then joined Scotland's newest commercial station, the fledgling Radio Clyde in Glasgow. After garnering a clutch of top radio awards, he was lured back to London in 1987 to

OFF THE BEATLE TRACK 12 –
LAMENT FOR LINDA

Linda McCartney's enduring love for her precious nook of Scotland was underscored with a very special musical performance at the memorial service that took place for her in June 1998 at the London church of St Martin-in-the-Fields. Paul personally asked John McGeachy, pipe major of the Campbeltown Pipe Band, to fill the church with the sound of Scotland, as guests, including George Harrison and Ringo Starr, filed in for the poignant service. And his emotion-charged rendition of 'Mull of Kintyre', the song that had been a hit for Wings 20 years earlier, only heightened the emotion of what was intended as a massive celebration of Linda's life. It was the perfect reminder of the days she and Paul had spent at the farm in Argyll and of the special place Scotland had in her heart. McCartney's special fondness for the Campbeltown pipes also emerged when daughter Stella married husband Alasdair Willis on Bute in August, 2003. The man giving a good old 'blaw' on this occasion as Stella walked down the aisle at Mount Stuart stately home was Lorne Cousin, whose father Alastair is Paul's long-time vet in Campbeltown.

become programme controller for Capital Radio. Today, he runs his own highly successful media consultancy. And, in recent years, he has moved effortlessly from behind the microphone to take up a role as the acid-tongued judge on BBC1's *Fame Academy* show for wannabe pop stars.

Richard Park today remains a champion of music new and old, but he admits The Beatles retain a tight grip on his heart and his memories of the Raith Ballroom and the Regal Cinema. 'After all these years I am still a huge fan. My enthusiasm for The Beatles and the music of that era is undimmed.'

CAIRD HALL, DUNDEE
Monday, 7 October 1963
Wednesday, 21 October 1964

Brian Mechan

Brian Mechan was an 18-year-old trainee hairdresser who joined about 2,000 other music-mad teenagers to see The Beatles play Dundee's Caird Hall in October of 1963. This was the first of two visits the Fabs would make to the city of jam, jute and journalism during the band's touring years. And Brian saw them on both occasions, the second concert following on just over a year from the first.

Earlier in the day he had plucked up the courage to phone his favourite Beatle, Ringo, at his hotel, and was amazed to get through for a brief chat. 'I knew it was Ringo right away. He had a different tone to his voice than the other three, it was a bit deeper. I was dumbstruck to begin with. He was great to talk to, very down to earth and very charming. My pals were astonished when I told them I had got Ringo on the phone. All the girls were going, "What, you did what?" I was already excited about going to see The Beatles that night so this just gave me an extra buzz.'

Tickets for that first Caird Hall concert had been snapped up weeks ago within hours of going on sale. Tayside was gripped by Beatlemania before the term was coined sometime over the next few weeks. This was the last show of a three-date Scottish mini tour promoted by Albert Bonici, the legendary and far-sighted north-east entrepreneur, under the exclusive north-of-the-border agreement he had struck a year earlier with the band's manager Brian Epstein.

'It was a fantastic time to be a teenager and to be a fan of The Beatles,' recalled Brian, now 63. 'You bought all the records, the fan magazines. I grew my hair and I had a Beatles jacket made, brown corduroy. I remember being refused entry to the dance halls in Dundee for having no

Overleaf.
Round Up presenter Paul Young cracks up during the band's second appearance on the popular Scottish Television show alongside fellow Liverpudlian Gerry Marsden.

collar and long hair. Ironically, my hair is longer now than it was then. It was long in the sense that it was creeping over the top of my collar. I got told to get it cut in the salon I worked in. I told my boss that I wouldn't get it cut until I had seen The Beatles but I would get it cut the next day, which I did do or I would have been out on my ear.'

Brian sat transfixed four rows from John Lennon's feet as The Beatles performed a clutch of their own songs including 'Please Please Me' and 'Love Me Do', as well as staple crowd-pleasing covers such as 'Till There Was You' and, of course, the showstopping 'Twist and Shout'. 'The atmosphere was absolutely incredible. Everyone was so happy it was almost a feeling of euphoria. I couldn't hear the first two or three songs and we were four rows from the front. We had a tremendous view. The thing is that you could always hear the songs through the records. The main thing was to see them, to be in the same building. All of a sudden they were right before your eyes. It was like gods coming down from Mount Olympus. I can now easily understand why it was too much for the girls who fainted. The realisation that someone you idolised, you had all the records and read about them in the papers and suddenly there they were right in front of you. Don't get me wrong, I was standing up screaming along with all the girls. It was a fantastic feeling. It was more than I expected it to be. I missed hearing the start of the concert because of the screaming. But you knew what they were singing without hearing them.

'If it hadn't been for the size of the bouncers compared to me then, I would have tried to get up on stage. If I say that to any of my mates nowadays they'll give me a strange look, but that was just the feeling that swept over you at the show. At the time, I tell you, I wouldn't have thought twice about it. The excitement just drew you along. It was all a bit of a blur in some ways. When I heard the next year they were coming back, I was bloody sure I was going to be there.'

In the space of the 12 months that followed, The Beatles blossomed, both as individuals and, equally, as musicians. They were the product of a music industry hothouse that constantly demanded more and more new material. When they hit the stage a second time at the Caird Hall, America had fallen under the spell of the Fab Four. Records tumbled in their wake: 55,000 fans crowded into New York's Shea Stadium for an unprecedented concert at a time when shows on this side of the pond still took place inside turn-of-the-century theatres and dance halls; in March, the top five US singles were all Beatle records; *A Hard Day's Night* – the album and the film – had been released to universal acclaim; and their UK singles including 'All My Loving' continued an unbroken chain of chart-toppers begun by 'Please Please Please Me' some 20 months earlier.

The second Dundee visit was again part of a small UK tour

shoehorned into a schedule already bursting at the seams. And the band were up against a deadline to complete their fourth album, *Beatles for Sale*, in time for Christmas. Against this backdrop, though, Brian Mechan reckons he witnessed a band still on an upward musical curve and not one treading water as the record-tour-record grind began to take an inevitable toll. 'They actually sounded better to me the second time, more confident. They were more professional and, of course, they looked better. They were in silvery grey-blue suits which I suppose made them look a bit more beefed up. They had a lot more of their own songs under their belt. As far as the audience reaction was concerned, I think it was even louder the second time.

'I had been to see concerts before like Tommy Steel and Lonnie Donegan. Paul Anka was the first show I saw. But nothing prepared me for The Beatles. I reckon I paid about eight to ten shillings for a ticket, something about 50p to 60p in today's money. It was a lot of money to me because I was only on about £8 a week. Afterwards, it took me days to come back to earth. It was the only thing people talked about. It was a big thing for Dundee that they came to the city twice.

'The concerts at the Caird Hall are right up there with the best things in my life. I'll never forget them and I'm so glad I went. It would have been rubbish to see them in the likes of Shea Stadium where they would have looked like performing fleas. At least I saw them in an intimate setting where, as I said, you could almost reach out and touch them. It says everything that here we are talking about nearly half a century after the fact. I can always remember saying to my parents that they will always be remembered. I said that the next generation of kids will learn about them in school and I always remember my oldest one coming home and saying they were being taught 'Yesterday' in music. We will never see a band like The Beatles again; nothing will come close.'

And neither, in all probability, will the chance come to speak to Ringo Starr on the phone again.

ABC, EDINBURGH
29 April, 1964

Marilyn Leishman & Stewart Cruickshank

All her loving was poured into The Beatles. At 13, Marilyn Leishman's dedication to the Fab Four was absolute. She had the first two albums, all the singles and was a fully paid-up member of The Beatles fan club. And when she heard the band was set to play their first concert in her home city of Edinburgh, the pieces fell neatly into place. All she needed was a ticket – and to get that all she needed was to persuade her parents to let her queue all night outside the ABC Regal cinema on Lothian Road along with around 1,000 others. It was a hope that, not surprisingly, crashed and burned on the rocks of parental authority.

Crestfallen though she was, however, Marilyn's dream still came true – with a little help from a fellow Beatlemaniac. She said: 'I was in my first year at high school. I was 13. There was only one girl in our year who was allowed to sleep out overnight to queue to get the tickets. Her name was Eleanor Anderson and each person who queued was allowed four tickets. The queue went right round the whole building. I remember people saying they had never seen anything like it. I mean, everyone wanted to go. Eleanor got four tickets and she invited three friends to go with her and I was one of them. There was no way my parents were going to let me queue overnight at that age but they were fine about letting me go to the concert. I was just so excited, I really was. It was such a dream.'

On the day of the concert, Marilyn was a bundle of nervous energy and pent-up excitement. 'Can't Buy Me Love' had just become the band's fifth number one single and filming on their first film, *A Hard Day's Night*, had ended less than a week ago. Beatlemania was rampant and now Scotland's capital city was seeing it up close and personal for the first time. 'You knew it was something special,' said Marilyn. 'The excitement was tangible. You could actually feel it in the air like electricity. On the day of the concert it was just mayhem. I think the police had stopped the traffic in Lothian Road. It was mass hysteria if you think about it now. Everybody was outside milling around, girls and guys. The Beatles always had amazing crossover appeal. We couldn't believe we were actually going to see them, that they would be right in front of us.

'I remember the other acts like Tommy Quickly but we were all there just to see The Beatles. The minute they came on everybody just screamed and tried to run down to the front. The bouncers though were very gentle in those days. I was a screamer. In fact I think everybody was.

'The concert passed in a blur. I remember they had The Beatle suits on, the collarless jackets and at the time we thought their hair was really long but it really wasn't when you look back at the photographs now. I just thought they looked fab. But they could have sung anything because you really couldn't hear it. It was more an experience than a concert. It was very brief compared to concerts nowadays, probably about 30 minutes or so.'

Afterwards, Marilyn and her three friends bounced out of the ABC, walking as if on invisible clouds. 'We were on such a high. I think we were just trying to let it all sink in. I remember we came out and we walked down Lothian Road towards the Caledonian Hotel which at that time was still a station. And I remember we went in there and phoned the ABC to try to talk to The Beatles using the one penny phone box. Of course we had no chance but we were all still so excited by the whole thing.'

This was the first of only two concerts The Beatles played in Edinburgh – they returned in October of that year as part of a UK tour. But Marilyn never again got the chance to see her heroes in the flesh again. She still cherishes the memory. 'Nowadays, when I hear them on the radio or see them in the papers, I tell my kids I saw them and they just say, "Aye right, mum." I don't think they really believe me. I kept my ticket stub for years but I can't find it now so I suppose that would have been proof for them.'

•   •   •

Music was Stewart Cruickshank's first love and The Beatles were the first band to capture his heart and set it racing. He was just 12 years old at the time. Stewart had been given a ticket to see The Beatles through the patronage of a school chum whose parents knew Les Lovell, the dapper manager of the Regal who always wore a white tuxedo and bow tie on the night of concerts. This wasn't Stewart's first time at a gig. He had already seen a number of bands on package tours at the Regal, thanks to parents happy to indulge their son's love of rock 'n' roll music.

Stewart recalled: 'One of my abiding memories is that, on the afternoon of the concert, a helicopter flew over my school, Trinity Academy, and a rumour quickly went round that The Beatles were on board. The whole place came to a standstill and everyone just looked up and started shouting. I don't know if it was them or not – I suspect it wasn't – but they had an extraordinary impact. I remember everyone in the playground just stopping what they were doing and looking up at the sky.

'On the day of the concert, you were just so excited. I was very lucky to get a ticket. In those days, you could really only afford to buy a single or an album once in a blue moon. But it was the era where if you bought a record, you used to wander about quite self-consciously with it under your arm like a badge of honour. School uniform was sacrosanct so the only way you could show your individuality was by carrying the record. The first record that I ever bought was the "Twist and Shout" EP so I used to walk about with that.

'I remember going up Lothian Road towards the Regal and it was just full from one end to the other. If you look at the photographs the kids don't look hip at all. You see the girls wearing Dame Edna Everage-type glasses, these horned-rimmed glasses. The kids weren't hip. They were hip to what was going on but in a fashion sense it was a disaster. It was before the Mod boom.

'There was the odd boutique in Lothian Road but this wasn't Carnaby Street. There wasn't much sign of the swinging sixties in Edinburgh at that time. Edinburgh was quite a snooty city in some ways because of the festival. You grew up with it and you felt as a kid that it was a great and noble city. But when The Beatles came Lothian Road just became a sea of hands. It wasn't like a decade later when the Bay City Roller fans turned up in their tartan regalia. It wasn't the mood of the time. But the atmosphere was just nuts. It was like some kind of social phenomenon had been unleashed.'

'I remember it was a huge event, not least because this was the first time they had been to Edinburgh. The pervading atmosphere was one of bedlam. The kids, and especially the girls, were there to let off steam. And they did. It was viscerally exciting because you knew you were part of a special moment and you felt at the same time you shouldn't be part of it. It was like sneaking in to see an X-rated movie or going to a pub when you're under age.

'When they came on stage, I had never heard so much noise in my life. I don't think I was too bothered though because it was enough just to see them. You had the records if you wanted to listen to The Beatles. In my mind's eye, I can still see them standing up on stage. George Harrison looked impossibly young and he *was* impossibly young. He looked so gawky and the clothes seemed to hang off him because he looked so thin. And McCartney really was a showman even then. I couldn't hear a bloody word Lennon was saying but he was goofing away with the audience. And Ringo was just Ringo, banging away on the drums at the back. But just the fact that those four guys were in front of you was amazing.

'The set included most of the hits up to then and it would have had stuff from *With The Beatles*. People were throwing things on stage. I remember they had to duck to avoid being hit by the likes of jelly babies. When you think back, it was utter madness. It's no wonder that they stopped touring so early in their career. They were unfortunate in the sense that they played live in an era when monitor speakers hadn't really been invented so they couldn't really hear themselves. Their sound just became absorbed in this din, this wall of noise.

'There was a house PA in the Regal but I just remember the Vox amplifiers. There was definite banter between them and the audience but what the hell it was I don't know. It was just this wall of screams. The Beatles show wasn't that long, and there was an air of cabaret about it. They would bow after every song. I think they played the National Anthem at the end, it was all very British. People were expected to stand up but they didn't because they were still going mad. It was bizarre but fantastic at the same time.'

Stewart never again saw The Beatles live in concert. Several months later, though, he saw something that was as near the real thing as dammit. 'I went to see *A Hard Day's Night* on my 13th birthday at a cinema at the back of Edinburgh Castle. For me it was the coolest thing you could do on your birthday and virtually a rite of passage. And once again it was just like being at a live gig. You couldn't hear the dialogue. In fact, I never actually heard the film until seven years later. All the kids were screaming, it was just like being at a concert. My parents were great supporters of me being interested in music so I was allowed to go to all these shows at what some people might consider a young age. But, strangely when you think back, they were very much against The Beatles' long hair, which was considered very effeminate. Yet, if you look back now, their hair isn't long at all. And they look pretty smart in their suits. Compare these pictures of them in Hamburg dressed from head to toe in leather. If they had dressed like that at the height of their fame, parents might have had a point.

Some 44 years after seeing the band in the flesh, Stewart retains an enduring affection for the Fab Four. 'They definitely shaped my musical sensibilities. There may actually have been better bands but they just had their finger on the pulse of change that young people then were going through. The music was exuberant and brilliant. You couldn't get the music out of your head. Looking back on it with the sophistication of modern rock concerts, the show I went to was very primitive. But what it did do was it liberated a generation of people. It was all a long time ago but the music is forever young and so are the memories.'

THE ODEON, GLASGOW
Wednesday, 21 October 1964

Bobby Lennox

When Jimmy Johnstone received the summons to go and see the boss, he didn't need to be told twice, especially when the boss was none other than legendary Celtic manager Jock Stein. When Jock barked jump, wee Jimmy leapt every inch of his 5 foot 6 inch frame.

'You're in the Scotland team to face Finland,' growled Stein.

'Great boss, thanks boss,' replied Jinky, recently voted the greatest player ever to wear the hoops of the famous Glasgow club.

Outside Stein's office, though, Jimmy's face crumpled. Happiness and disappointment merged into a single emotion. He thrust his hand into his jacket pocket to make sure the two tickets were still there. He looked longingly at the two pieces of paper: NEMS presents The Beatles, Glasgow Odeon, Wednesday, 21 October – the same night Scotland's international team faced off against the Finns in a vital World Cup qualifying match at Hampden.

The mercurial little winger with the dazzling feet had won his first international cap that same month. But he hadn't counted on the collision that was looming between his love of football and his passion for rock 'n' roll. Jimmy, a fanatical Beatles fan, knew there was nothing left to do as he thrust his hands deep into his pocket. There was no point in them going to waste. All he had to do was figure out how to break the news to his girlfriend Agnes, who later became his wife.

Out of the corner of his eye, he saw best pal and team-mate Bobby Lennox in the car park outside Celtic's stadium. Some 45 years on, Bobby, like Jimmy a member of Celtic's famous Lisbon Lions, can't recall the exact words as Jinky thrust the two ticket stubs into his hand. 'All I remember is him giving them to me because he couldn't go after being called into the Scotland squad. He was really disappointed. He loved his music and he was really looking forward to taking Agnes to see The Beatles. He was all chuffed because we were all big Beatle fans. So I was the beneficiary of him getting called up by Scotland. I didn't get called up, otherwise I couldn't have gone either. But I was delighted to get the tickets. That was the wee man through and through. If he couldn't go he made sure a pal could.'

And that's how Bobby and his wife Cathy came to be sitting two rows from the front as John, Paul, George and Ringo took to the stage at Glasgow's Odeon Cinema. Before taking their seats, Bobby and Cathy had to wade through the massive crowds wedged into Renfield Street. Traffic was at a virtual standstill as hundreds of teenagers milled around waiting for the cinema doors to open.

'It was absolutely mobbed,' recalled Bobby. 'But it was a happy crowd. When we got in, it was fantastic to get great seats right down the front. We were probably about 20 or 30 feet from the stage. It was nearly on top of us.'

Bobby was used to performing himself in front of noisy crowds that regularly topped 100,000. But nothing prepared him and Cathy for the torrent of screams that exploded all around them as The Beatles tore into their first song. 'It was like nothing I had heard before, just bedlam. When you play football you're so focused on the game you hardly notice the crowd. But I had never heard a noise like this in my life.'

Cathy recalled having to duck under the hail of jelly babies Beatles fans always hurled at their heroes. She said: 'There were Jelly Babies everywhere. It seems so funny now but that's what happened because The Beatles had said in an interview that Jelly Babies were their favourite sweets. We were all big Beatle fans in those days. It was a great time to be young.'

Like Jinky, Bobby had his finger on the musical pulse of the times and was a frequent concert-goer. 'There was a big band on almost every week in Glasgow. I went to see The Everly Brothers and Little Richard but nothing topped The Beatles. They were outstanding.'

Jimmy's reaction to Bobby's concert verdict has been lost in the mists of time. Scotland, incidentally, won 3–1 at Hampden and Jinky lit up a sell-out crowd – just as The Beatles did less than four miles away at the Odeon Cinema.

ODEON, GLASGOW
Friday 3 December, 1965

Josephine Giblin/Frances Clark

Josephine Clark and her pal Margaret emerged blinking from the bright lights of the Glasgow Odeon into the dark night, her ears still ringing from the wall of noise generated by some 2,000 screaming Beatles fans. Barely able to speak, she was walking on air after watching John, Paul, George and Ringo transformed from four figures decorating her bedroom walls to real pop stars she had just seen and heard in the flesh. The fact that she could hardly hear a note at that precise minute didn't matter. What mattered was she had seen them, she had got up close and personal. Well, as personal as you can get amid hundreds of other shrieking youngsters.

But another member of her family had got even closer to the Fab Four, thanks to an ingenious ruse by her mother, who was on duty that night as part of the St Andrews Ambulance Association team, on hand to look after fans overcome by the whole experience. Earlier that night, she 'acquired' a St Andrews uniform for Josephine's elder sister Frances and the get-up became her ticket to the backstage area at the Odeon – and an amazing view of the concert from the side of the stage.

Josephine left the theatre with total recall of the night, but Frances left with Ringo Starr's drumstick. Memories of the sisters' Beatle bonanza came flooding back after she spotted a picture of her mum in the Glasgow *Evening Times* coming to the aid of fans at the concert. Now Josephine Giblin, she said: 'I was amazed to see a picture of my mother in the paper, it brought the whole night back into focus. I went to the concert that night with my friend Margaret. I would only have been 14 at the time. I was a

mad Beatles fan. You couldn't hear any of the music because of the screams. I was definitely a screamer, absolutely. I couldn't speak for about three days afterwards.

'My sister Frances, who is two years older than me and was just as much of a fan, couldn't get a ticket. My recollection is she was very upset so my mother got her a first aid uniform and took her along. She blagged her way in with this uniform and my mother helped her make her way backstage. She stood in the wings and watched the whole show from there. I was very jealous but it didn't cause a major split or anything like that. She had a coffee cup she said Paul McCartney had drunk out of although I don't know if that's true. It's a story that has become part of family folklore but she definitely had the drumstick.'

For her part, Frances has little memory of the night apart from picking up her souvenirs of the show. She said: 'I am amazed at Josie's memory. I laughed when I heard her story because I had forgotten most of it. I remember being disappointed at missing out on a ticket. She said that is why my mother smuggled me in. I do recall my mother was very protective of me on the night and guided me backstage away from the bedlam that was taking place at the front. She knew I would be safer standing in the wings. And that is how I got the drumstick which I hung up on my bedroom wall. I have no idea how I came to have the drumstick but I just imagine Ringo saw me there in the wings with the uniform and gave it to me as he rushed past me to the dressing room.

'I was a big fan, we all were really. It didn't matter how long The Beatles would last, it was all about the moment.'

THE ROOFTOP

Tom Brown

By January 1969, the Sixties had virtually stopped swinging and flower power had withered on the vine. Revolution was in the air as the Soviet Union clenched its iron fist and sent its tanks into Czechoslovakia and students rioted in Paris. In less than two years, the so-called Summer of Love had been replaced by a winter of bloody discontent.

For The Beatles too, the times were indeed a-changing. The Fab Four had long since shed their moptop look. John Lennon and George Harrison had hair that extended beyond their shoulders and it was not unusual for the faces of all four to be framed by large beards. Musically, they seemed as tight as ever, having just released the 'White Album' that November. And, cajoled by Paul McCartney, they were already back in the

Help! I need somebody! Josephine Giblin's mum is on hand to help young fans overcome with hysteria in Glasgow and also manages to sneak her daughter Frances backstage.

Scots journalist Tom Brown got a fan's eye view of the famous 1969 rooftop session – the last time The Beatles played in public.

studio recording a warts-and-all LP that would be backed by a film showing The Beatles at work, rest and play.

But rumours persisted of studio walkouts, business bust-ups and internecine warfare. In the event, the cameras chronicling *Let It Be* captured the dying embers of the world's biggest band. It depicted four musicians pulling in different directions – and tearing each other apart in full view of their horrified fans. As Lennon succinctly put it, the game was up.

So it was against this fractious backdrop that The Beatles decided on one last public hurrah – a live performance that would bring the curtain down on the *Let It Be* film . . . and allow The Beatles to finally exit stage left. Unfortunately no one could agree on the format for the show. McCartney favoured London's Roundhouse Theatre before an intimate audience and there was talk of an amphitheatre in Tunisia. Lennon, who along with Harrison was largely opposed to any live show, drawled: 'I'm warming to the idea of an asylum.'

In the event, The Beatles took the shortest route possible by climbing six flights of stairs and stepping out onto the rooftop of their Apple offices in Savile Row, in the heart of London's austere textile district. They walked into the teeth of a bitter wind, plugged in their guitars and got ready to blow the West End of London away.

Across London, a tip-off reached the newsdesk of the *Daily Express*, then the UK's largest-selling daily newspaper, that something big was going down. Traffic was already backed up all the way along Oxford Street. Tom Brown, a 34-year-old Scots journalist from Kirkcaldy, was summoned by his news editor to hightail it to Savile Row to check out what was bringing central London to a standstill in the mid afternoon. Tom was already a seasoned reporter, having covered a number of major stories, including the death in August 1967 of The Beatles' manager Brian Epstein from a drug overdose.

What happened over the next hour or so left Tom, accompanied by photographer Mike Stroud, with a lasting mental snapshot of the enduring power of The Beatles. And it ended with him being among a handful of people present on the last occasion when all four Beatles would ever play in public – and most definitely the last Scot to watch the Fab Four's swansong performance.

Tom, now one of Scotland's most distinguished journalists and columnists, recalled: 'The thing was we didn't know what we were going to see. All we knew was that something was going down at Savile Row. Now everyone knew that's where Apple was. The Beatles had just spent £3m on buying this property in Savile Row, which was unheard of in those days. It was an outrageous sum. So, although we didn't know what to expect, you could easily put two and two together and figure out The Beatles would be involved.

'We hadn't gone too far in the taxi before the traffic just came to a virtual standstill. It took us halfway along Regent Street and then we had to leg it because the whole place was just nose to tail with cars. Remember, this was just after lunchtime and heading towards the middle of the afternoon. Nothing was moving, it was absolute chaos. As we got closer to Savile Row, we could hear the sound of music but we couldn't make it out because it was just being carried away in the wind. I remember it was bloody cold. All around us, people were looking up at the sky. Everyone was just pouring out of offices and shops and staring up at the top of the Apple building. It was pretty surreal.'

One of the first reporters to arrive on the scene, Tom knocked on the large white door of The Beatles' inner sanctum. He could hear the sounds from the roof echoing down to the street-level foyer. But his request to be allowed in was firmly rejected. 'The logical next step as I saw it was to get onto one of the roofs so we could see what was actually going on. By this time, the streets were lined by hundreds of people just craning their necks to the sky. There was no point in us staying down on the street. So we went across the street to what I think was a textile office and we asked if we could use their lift to get up to the roof so we could see what was happening. I remember it was about five storeys up and then we clambered out.'

Once at the top, Tom and Stroud squinted into the distance at the rooftop opposite. They saw four figures, each of them hunched over their instruments, watched by a motley crew of sound engineers, wives and girlfriends and the customary Beatle hangers-on. About two hundred yards away, The Beatles had turned the tiny rooftop area into a makeshift stage, with wooden planks having been laid out the day before. Cables from the voice and instrument microphones snaked down the stairway of the Apple building to the basement studio.

George Harrison was clad in a black fur jacket and electric green trousers, his black Fender strapped on. John Lennon, carrying his favourite Epiphone guitar, was also wrapped in a fur coat to keep out the bitter chill. Paul McCartney, a broad smile dancing across his face, was dressed in his Tommy Nutter black suit and clutching the famous Hofner bass that still had the set list for Shea Stadium taped to its underside. Ringo Starr's famous hangdog expression was firmly in place, in contrast to the bright red plastic mac he was wearing. And then there was another who slipped in silently to take his place almost anonymously behind the keyboard. American piano virtuoso Billy Preston, a pal of the band since their Hamburg days, had been drafted in at the start of the Apple basement session for *Let It Be* by George Harrison to try to act as an emollient to the internal chafing. And now he would sit in with them for their last public show.

Watching the scene unfold, Tom Brown had no doubt this was an all-star cast. What he couldn't have known was this would the last time all four would be on the same stage together. Tom said: 'We knew right away who it was – it couldn't have been anyone else. The whole place was littered with cables, microphones and amps. There were sound engineers, hangers-on and quite a few girls, including The Beatles' wives and girlfriends.

'There was not much musical appreciation because the sound was just being carried away on the wind. The other thing, of course, is we now know that these were new songs that no one had heard before. So they were in no way recognisable. But you could certainly tell it was The Beatles. I think the surprising thing was seeing all four of them there at all. There had been numerous reports in the papers of bust-ups and suggestions that they had already split up. So it was a big thing to actually see them all together and performing what was in essence an open air recording session. Although I'm not sure how much would have been usable because the sound was so muffled. In terms of the songs, the only one I can remember now that I recognised was "Get Back" and, curiously, the National Anthem.

'My first thought was that, with all that equipment in place, it wasn't a spontaneous thing. You couldn't have all that gear in place just on a whim.

When we got there, it was already underway although I saw about 30 minutes or so. From a distance, they looked to be freezing. Lennon and Harrison had on huge fur coats to keep warm. But they seemed to be enjoying it.'

In fact, The Beatles would perform two versions of 'Get Back' followed by 'Don't Let Me Down', 'I've Got a Feeling' and 'Dig a Pony', before exhuming 'One After 909' almost from their Quarrymen days.

Tom and his photographic cohort may have been mesmerised by the surreal scene playing out before their before their very eyes, but editorial professionalism quickly roused them from their reverie. Sure, it was a happening, of the type which was typical of the late sixties as musicians began to realise the power that celebrity status had conferred on them. Tom's brain went quickly into gear and he took the lift back down to the ground floor. Amazingly, Savile Row police station was located just yards away from Apple's front door. So far, though, there had been no indication from the boys in blue that they were prepared to pull the plug on the free show.

'We went round to the police station and we just asked the obvious question – were they going to stop it? The guy behind the desk said no, they were happy for The Beatles to have their fun. Apart from the fact it had brought that part of London to a standstill, it wasn't doing any harm. At least that's the way he saw it. It was something different in the spirit of the time. So at that point they were happy to let them play. But it was only when a local woollen merchant, I think, complained that they decided to send a couple of the boys round to find out what was going on. One guy told me it wasn't his type of music but they were having fun. When I think about it now, almost 40 years later, it seems amazing that the biggest band of the world could get away with something like that. But these were much different times. It was the last time anyone would see all four of The Beatles playing music in public. I never thought much about it then because no one knew they would split up later that year.'

Tom has gone on to become one of Scotland's best-known and most highly regarded journalists. Of the fact that he was the last Scot to see the Fab Four playing in public he said: 'I have rarely given it a moment's thought. It is the kind of thing that comes up in conversation occasionally, but that's about it. It was widely covered during the time but it would be more widespread today. At that time it was very much a case of here today and gone tomorrow. It may look like a landmark event now, but at the time, the focus very quickly moved on because we didn't have the cult of celebrity that the world has today. Don't get me wrong, The Beatles were huge and this was a big and unusual event, but it didn't dominate world events.'

6. The Scottish Photographers

Harry Benson

The Beatles were the most photographed band in history. Between 1963 and 1970, they lived their lives through a lens, every frame somehow capturing their charisma, every picture framing their personalities. Photographers were given unprecedented access in the days when the word paparazzi sounded like nothing more threatening than a Neapolitan dessert. Flashbulbs popped every few seconds. 'John, could you look here?' 'Just one more, Ringo.' On stage, at press conferences, in the studio, at home, the public's insatiable appetite for all things Fab trapped The Beatles in a Kodachrome-wrapped goldfish bowl. Literally hundreds of thousands of images showed The Beatles' transformation from loveable moptops to psychedelic hippy avatars to rock gods.

Two, in particular, however, have attained iconic status. Taken five years apart, they perfectly book-end a band in glorious ascent – and the same band falling hopelessly apart. The first picture, snapped in 1964, shows four men in their early twenties enjoying a pillow fight at 2 a.m., minutes after hearing they had just notched up their first American number one. Click. The energy pulsating from the picture and the sheer joy on the faces of John, Paul, and Ringo as they leap on George Harrison lying on the hotel bed is a lasting image of a band on the steps of pop music's throne. The second image, hurriedly taken in the summer of 1969, shows the same four men, world-weary, their faces hidden by their long hair, trudging across a zebra crossing. This picture, taken outside the famous Abbey Road studios in London, heralds an abdication. Both pictures are among the most famous of Beatle images – and amazingly both were taken by Scotsmen.

Harry Benson and Iain MacMillan were amongst the top sixties lensmen. But their work with The Beatles elevated them to the major league and changed both their lives forever.

Benson, born in Glasgow, began his photographic career with the *Hamilton Advertiser* before moving on to the *Evening Times* and *Glasgow Herald*. Eventually, ambition took him to Fleet Street and a staff job with the *Daily Express*, then Britain's biggest-selling daily newspaper.

MacMillan was born in the Tayside town of Carnoustie in 1938 and went to school in Dundee. Initially, he was drawn into one strand of the

Opposite top. Three kings and I . . . this picture captures Benson on the other side of the lens for once with Paul, Ringo and George in 1964.

Opposite bottom. Frozen in time . . . Benson rates the famous pillow fight picture as the best he ever took of The Beatles.

city's famous enterprises by becoming a trainee manager for Jute Industries. His real love, though, was photography, an obsession that eventually guaranteed his real life lay through a lens. Like his countryman Benson, MacMillan was soon lured to the Smoke. The city was not yet in full mid-sixties' swinging mode, but its bright lights easily outshone those of Broughty Ferry.

For both men, the decision to take the low road would see them intersect on the celebrity circuit, without ever actually meeting. Their iconic pictures of The Beatles, however, means they share a unique and lasting Scottish connection with The Fab Four.

The story of how Benson was in on the ground floor of Beatlemania in America began when he found himself at a crossroads in his life. Even at 34, he was still a fledgling Fleet Street photographer, but he was up for a *Daily Sketch* assignment to visit Kenya to cover the first anniversary of that country's independence. Instead, though, he was redirected to accompany The Beatles from London for concerts at the Paris Olympia for the *Daily Express* before staying aboard the groovy train for the band's first assault on the United States. He was expected to shadow reporter Derek Taylor who ghosted a column for the paper in George Harrison's name. The arrangement gave Benson unique access to Britain's newest pop phenomenon.

He said: 'I didn't want to go. I was 34 years old and a seasoned photo-journalist. I wanted to cover breaking news stories. But from the minute I heard them at that show, I knew I was on the right story.'

Protest waved aside, Benson and the band decamped to the George V Hotel in Paris. It had already slipped past midnight on 16 January 1964, following a gig at Paris's Olympia Theatre, when The Beatles received a telegram from London. 'Congratulations. "I Want to Hold Your Hand" number one in America.' The band, imbued with the cockiness of youth, had always vowed not to go to America until they had hit the top spot. The beachhead had been secured. Now America, the land of their rock 'n' roll heroes, was braced for an all-out assault of Beatlemania.

Tipped off about the telegram, Benson made his way to The Beatles' hotel suite. He recalled how all four had been hamming it up a couple of nights earlier with a pillow fight. It was a spontaneous, fun-filled moment and, even though Benson was there with another snapper, not one for public consumption. But Benson filed away the incident in his mind. Little did he expect the opportunity to repeat itself so soon. He recalled: 'A couple of nights later, after the show at the Olympia, I'm back with The Beatles. It was very late, they were drinking and in walks their manager Brian Epstein with a cable to say they are number one in America with "I Wanna Hold Your Hand". Moments later they get another cable saying *The*

Ed Sullivan Show wants them. This was big-time news for them, so they were very happy. So I asked them for another pillow fight, and Lennon said this was the most stupid and idiotic thing he'd ever heard. He said it will make us look childish and Paul McCartney agreed with him. So that was the end of that. Anyway, he slips away, Paul's drinking and John goes up behind Paul with his pillow and bangs him right in the back of the head. That's how it started. Then all hell broke loose.'

It was, as Benson later admitted, a moment tailor-made for a photojournalist and a defining moment in his career. These were Britain's new superstars on the top of the hill. Instinctively, he brought his Rolleiflex camera up to his eye and started clicking. The next day, Benson's pillow-fight images were all over the *Express*. And wire services all over the world flooded the paper with requests to reproduce them. Since then, they have been shown at countless exhibitions – and helped pave the way for Benson's entry into American high society.

Looking back, Benson admits he had no idea that the images he took that night would be a lasting testament of a unique juncture in The Beatles' history. He admits, though, that of the thousands of pictures which carry the Benson brand, this remains his favourite. 'I like it because it's a happy picture and I can look at it all the time. I honestly think it is the best picture ever taken of The Beatles. There is an innocence about it, a naivety. It was before drugs, before cynicism. It reflected the times, the optimism of the early sixties. And, you know, it's the greatest group in the history of pop culture. I think they had a tremendous impact and I happened to be rather close to them and I happened to have done it rather well at the time. I still haven't taken my best pictures but for me it doesn't get better than that pillow fight. Looking back, it was the best thing that ever happened to me. The first thing was it meant I was coming to America. The Beatles picture was just so natural. The boys just started jumping up and down on the bed and, before I knew it, they were throwing pillows at each other.'

Benson's bluff Glaswegian manner gave him an in with John Lennon in particular. Lennon was never one to suffer fools gladly and he found in Benson someone who was on the same wavelength. The day after the pillow fight, Benson found himself on the A-list as the band flew to New York for the first of two appearances on America's famous *Ed Sullivan Show*. The avuncular Sullivan was responsible for introducing Elvis to the American masses, his hip-swivelling routine inducing hysteria and outrage in equal measure. Benson was holed up in his hotel when there was a bang on the door. 'John came in and said they were going now and for me to come with them and stay as close as I could or the police would cut me off. Right enough, there was pandemonium trying to get into the car. A

OFF THE BEATLE TRACK 13 –
IN THE FAST LANE WITH GEORGE

Jackie Stewart wasn't the only Scottish Formula One racing driver to be on good terms with George Harrison. Jim Clark, the legendary flying Scot who twice won the coveted drivers' championship, was a hero of George's even before Beatlemania. And their paths crossed at least once as The Beatle's interest in motor-sport started to bloom. Clark, who died in 1968, was, on the surface, less hip than Jackie Stewart, with his close-cropped hair and austere manner. But George had deep respect for anyone who hurtled round the track at speeds of up to 150 miles per hour. More recently, David Coulthard (pictured) found himself in George's company on plenty of occasions as he began his rise to the top of the sport. As he recalled one of the first times he came face to face with one of his musical heroes at a VIP party held for all the drivers following the Australian Grand Prix in Melbourne in 1997, Coulthard revealed: 'George insisted on providing all the champagne. He even played a CD at the party called "Bernie Says" [a reference to Formula One supremo Bernie Ecclestone]. That is what I call throwing a bash, getting one of The Beatles to write a song. He was a big fan of Formula One and also a friend of Bernie which meant he was a regular in the paddock. He could pretty much go where he wanted because of who he was and who he was friends with. I recall he told some great tales that night. It was fascinating listening to him talk.'

policeman tried to stop me getting into their limo and to his credit John said: "If Harry doesn't go, I don't go." Paul, George, Ringo and I got in first and John followed. They were too close for me to take their photo inside the limo (it was not a stretch limo like we have today). They all leaned over and put their heads down so I could get a picture of the fans chasing after us. It all happened in a matter of seconds.

'When we got to the CBS studio, it was the same chaos again. I jumped out first and John kept me next to him because the studio door opened and slammed shut like an elastic band. I sat around with John drinking Coca-Colas, waiting for the show to start. We never went back to the hotel after the rehearsal – it would have been too hectic. And when they went on television, as everyone knows, they were sensational.'

In the States, The Beatles touched every facet of American life. For a country still wreathed in black following Kennedy's assassination, it was an extraordinary and uplifting time. Two days after their first *Sullivan* appearance – a show watched on television by a staggering 73 million people across the US – they were back on Uncle Ed's revolving stage. This time, the segment was filmed in sun-kissed Miami, a millionaire's playground that was as far removed from Penny Lane as you could get. Also in town was Sonny Liston, the brutish heavyweight champion of the world. Liston was in the final days of preparation for his fight with a brash young challenger whose dazzling hand speed was matched only by his verbal sparring. Like The Beatles, Cassius Clay was mouthy, outspoken and an emerging touchstone for a generation.

For Harry Benson, his highly-tuned radar fixed on the moment, it was an opportunity made in photo heaven – two giants of popular culture in the same zone at the same time. So tentative moves were made to soft-shoe The Beatles down to a local gym, not to press the flesh with the man who would later become Muhammad Ali, but with the champ. Liston, though, refused to have anything to do with it. He didn't do photo ops, especially with four scruffy English kids he'd never heard of. Harry quickly turned to plan Benson. He recalled: 'It was my idea to put them together with Clay. While we were cooped up in the hotel, I had plenty of time to watch TV and there was Clay shouting and spouting off poems, preparing for his title fight with Liston. Here was someone The Beatles should meet. When I suggested this to them, John, who must also have been watching the pre-fight coverage, said he didn't want to meet Clay because he was going to lose the fight. The Beatles wanted to meet the champ. I knew I could get them into Clay's gym and I had a journalist's intuition that Clay would make a far better story.'

Benson was forced to change tack, his initial idea still fresh in his mind's eye. His hustle about meeting Liston was still his trump card – he just didn't tell anyone that Liston had counted the idea out. 'The Beatles were expecting to see Liston when I took them to the gym where Clay was working out. The boxer was ready for them. He completely controlled the occasion. He ordered them round the ring shouting, "Who's the most beautiful?" He called Paul the pretty one but said, "You're not as pretty as me."' Clay made the most of it and, for once, The Beatles were reduced to hams. They lined up in a row and pretended to fall in sequence to Clay's punches. But, behind the bonhomie, Lennon only went along with it through gritted teeth. At one point Clay said to Lennon: 'You're not as dumb as you look.' 'No, but you are,' deadpanned a brave Lennon in reply. Later, out of media earshot, he rounded on Benson, saying, 'He made a fool of us.'

Harry, though, didn't care. He had the picture and that was all that counted. Lennon would get over it. Eventually. Benson said: 'They stayed mad at me for a month. It didn't matter, I had lots of assignments coming up.'

When the tour ended, The Beatles made their weary way back over the Atlantic. Benson, though, stayed in the States, his connection to the Fab Four and an unerring talent for being in the right place at the right time earning him a celebrity status of his own. Over the next couple of years, their paths occasionally crossed. But, as is the way of life, Benson and The Beatles ventured down different roads.

When he next hooked up them, for their 1966 American tour, they were mired in controversy. John Lennon's notorious off-the-cuff assertion that they were more popular than Jesus had set off a firestorm in America's Bible Belt. Benson was among a posse of photographers at a press conference in Chicago on 11 August when a confused Lennon, while never apologising, tried to explain his remarks. The chief Beatle, cigarette in hand and what appears to be a saucer of aspirin next to him, cut a forlorn figure as he squinted at the flashbulbs and parried the never-ending questions. Benson's images, seen through the soft focus of events still to happen, neatly capture the slow dissolution of the band.

'They were increasingly fractious. Basically, they were arguing with Paul and a year later Brian Epstein would be dead, leaving the band without a manager. After August 1966, I didn't see any of them again for several years. One day, in the mid 1970s, while trudging along a corridor at LA International Airport, I heard a familiar voice call out a mocking name I never use – Harold. It was Paul, Linda and a clutch of children offering me a ride on one of those electric cars that scoot around airports. This chance meeting rekindled our association and led to several assignments covering Wings and the McCartney family over the years. Through the McCartneys I was also reunited with George. I never did photograph Ringo or John again but in 1985 a *Life* magazine assignment gave me the opportunity to meet John's widow Yoko Ono and her son Sean. She wasn't what I expected and I came to admire her.'

For a time, The Beatles had been wild about Harry, the gruff-spoken Glasgow photographer who was almost one of the boys. Benson, though, was savvy enough to know distance was vital on both sides. And he will always have his memories on film and in his heart. Now 80, he is still working his magic behind the camera on today's generation of pop stars such as Amy Winehouse for publications such as *Vanity Fair* and the *Sunday Times*. Earlier this year, he published a special commemoration of his Beatle portraits, images that, some 45 years on, still bear his unique stamp.

'Imagine me standing onstage next to Paul McCartney at the Paris Olympia, and he says to me, "We want you to cheer for us, Harry." And then I went offstage and watched them play "All My Loving", and it was incredible. It sold me right away. I think I got with them at the right time, right at the beginning, because they didn't really know what was going to happen. Looking back, it's remarkable how well I did. I know that sounds completely self-serving, but the photos just hold up. I got them at the right time. I got them just as they were breaking out and how we always remember them. I look back on it and I know I did well. Other things I would want to do over but The Beatles I wouldn't want to do over.'

Iain MacMillan

While Benson hit pay-dirt in America, Iain MacMillan was making a name for himself on this side of the pond. After grafting for a few years with various publications, he finally clicked with a series of pictures for the 1966 *Book of London*. MacMillan's quirky take on the changing face of the capital, with its bowler-hatted bankers mixed with the mini-skirted debs of Carnaby Street, struck a chord. He approached a London gallery about showing some of his work and met a small Japanese conceptual artist. Her name was Yoko Ono. Yoko had just earned a commission of her own to show her work at the Indica Gallery, a favourite with London's avant-garde and leftfield pop stars. And, at the pre-opening party, she had secured the patronage of one John Winston Lennon.

The tripartite connection between the far-out artist, the millionaire pop star and the Scottish photographer with the hangdog expression seemed, on the surface, unlikely. But somehow, Yoko and John took a shine to MacMillan. And that connection was enough to give his work the kind of exposure it had always merited to a new star-struck public.

MacMillan never craved the public spotlight, happy to let his pictures do the talking. But from the day he got a call from John Lennon in the hazy summer of 1969, his name would be forever linked with The Beatles. By now, the band were in their death throes. Paul McCartney's attempts to keep the dream alive manifested itself in one last group album. Such, though, was the fractious state of affairs that John, Paul, George and Ringo couldn't even agree on a name for what became their final album. One suggestion was to call it 'Everest', after the brand of cigarettes smoked by their engineer Geoff Emerick. But, not surprisingly, the idea of trekking to the foothills of the Himalayas for one picture failed to meet with much enthusiasm. Eventually, it was the deadpan drummer who said: 'Why don't we just go outside, call it *Abbey Road* and be done with it?'

Fair enough. Iain MacMillan's studio was close at hand and he was available. He arrived at 10 a.m. to discover McCartney had sketched out a few rough drawings of what they wanted for a cover. He was given 10 minutes to get the perfect shot of all four Beatles striding across the zebra crossing outside the studios which had been their musical laboratory for eight years.

MacMillan rarely spoke at length about the *Abbey Road* shot,

preferring instead to treat it as just another day at the office rather than let it eclipse his other work. But in an interview to commemorate the twentieth anniversary of that session, he recalled: 'It was a nerve-wracking experience. I had never met all four Beatles together before that day. I remember we had a policeman to hold up traffic while I was up on the stepladder taking the pictures. Surprisingly, there was no great gathering of fans, most people hardly seemed to take any notice.

'I got the job through John, but it was Paul's idea. A few days before the shoot, he drew a sketch of how he imagined the cover, which we executed almost exactly that day. And I was given 10 minutes around lunchtime to do it. They came out of the studio where they had been recording that morning and I managed to take six shots in all. I took a couple of shots of The Beatles crossing Abbey Road one way. We let some of the traffic go by and then they walked across the road the other way, and I took a few more shots. The one eventually chosen for the cover was number five of six. It was the only one that had their legs in a perfect 'V' formation, which is what I wanted stylistically. I have to say even now that the final shot that was chosen still gives me a lot of pleasure.'

Sgt. Pepper's Lonely Hearts Club Band may have broken new ground in terms of cover art, but *Abbey Road* gained a mythology all of its own. The record's release coincided with a grisly rumour that Paul McCartney was dead. Clues about his demise had apparently been liberally scattered on album sleeves since 1966. And, just in case anyone missed them, Iain MacMillan's cover for *Abbey Road* laid an even more bizarre trail. There was Lennon, almost unrecogniseable behind his shoulder-length hair and bushy beard, dressed in the all-white vestments of a clergyman. He was followed in perfect step by the sober-suited Ringo Starr, looking for all the world like an undertaker. George Harrison, dressed in denim shirt and jeans, was the gravedigger. And there was shoeless McCartney playing the part of the corpse with lifelike realism.

The 'Paul-is-dead' rumour caught fire in America and soon swept all over the world. Conspiracy theorists, never slow to jump on The Beatles bandwagon, had a field day. McCartney was barefoot, a sign of death in Greece. And the famously left-handed bass player was holding his cigarette in his right hand. Further evidence could be glimpsed in the number plate of the white Volkswagen Beetle in the background 28IF – 28 if he had lived. Death sells and the furore helped make The Beatles' swansong their best-selling album yet. And it ensured that Iain MacMillan's photograph, one of the last to be taken of all four together, attained iconic status.

Of the mythology that has grown up around the cover, MacMillan was, not surprisingly, scathing. He recalled: 'Paul turned up in his Oxfam suit and sandals and because it was a hot day he decided to do some shots with

Abbey Road. Ian MacMillan's iconic picture of the band striding across the famous Zebra crossing outside EMI's studios in London.

his sandals on and some with his sandals off. Paul checked all the pictures with a magnifying glass – I don't think the other three were particularly bothered. He chose the neatest shot with the legs stretched in almost uniform style and it was pure coincidence that it happened to be the one with his sandals off. From what I remember, he was very much alive.'

Even today, nearly four decades on, fans from all over the world flock to Abbey Road to have their picture taken on the zebra crossing. Not a day goes by without them recreating their own tiny piece of pop inconography. There have been countless imitations, but only one original. Paul McCartney himself called on MacMillan to reproduce the famous shot for his 1994 album *Paul is Live*. Only this time, John, George and Ringo were replaced by Martha, his dear old English sheepdog.

The *Abbey Road* cover made MacMillan a household name in pop art circles and opened other celebrity doors. There was no megabucks spin-off, but the cachet allowed him to continue his association with John and Yoko. In the early seventies, they invited him out to New York to work on album covers and other photographic assignments. Sadly, Iain MacMillan died in May 2006.

Respect from The Beatles was always hard-earned, never easily gained. But Harry Benson and Iain MacMillan gained it in spades. The pictures these two Scots took have become major milestones on the timeline of the Fab Four. Unlike the principals involved, the images never age. Lots of people claimed their five minutes of fame with The Beatles. But Benson and MacMillan can genuinely say: We were there. And their pictures prove it.

Tom Murray

Don McCullin, the *Sunday Times*' celebrated war photographer, made the suggestion sound like an afterthought: 'Bring your camera, you might get some nice snaps.' Tom Murray, a young, ambitious cameraman from Cupar in Angus, didn't need a second invitation and quickly grabbed his favourite Nikon and stuffed two rolls of film into his pocket, unusually picking 35mm colour instead of his preferred black and white. He had no idea what McCullin's assignment was, only that he would be taking pictures of a pop band, possibly for the paper's innovative colour supplement. Murray, not long back from four years working in Africa, was there principally as the driver but was happy to go along for the ride around midday on 28 August 1968. In the back of his mind, he reckoned there might be the chance to shoot a few frames himself. Nothing ventured, nothing gained.

Soon, the two men were bounding up the steps of an old church in

13 13A

London, which was now used as a rehearsal studio. Outside, Murray, who was hip to the latest music, heard what sounded vaguely like the piano chords to The Beatles' latest single 'Lady Madonna' emanating from inside the church. Seconds later, the Scot, no stranger to celebrity, found himself face to face with four men whose features were instantly recognisable.

'As I walked in, I heard someone playing "Lady Madonna" on the piano. I opened the door and went, "Shit!" Paul McCartney was at the piano. I then had a look around and there was George Harrison and Ringo Starr standing over the other side of the room drinking tea. And in the other corner was John Lennon and Yoko. I turned round to Don and said, "Is this the group you're photographing?" He just laughed and said, "Yes, didn't I mention it?"'

For 25-year-old Murray, it was a bizarre introduction to four men who were worshipped as sixties icons. And, although he was there mainly to ride shotgun alongside the more experienced McCullin, the chance to take pictures of all four Beatles in the one place was a heaven-sent opportunity for any self-respecting lensman. Some 40 years later, Murray has good reason to count his lucky stars because the pictures he took that day have been hailed as among the best portraits of The Beatles taken in the fading autumn of the band's career. The shots elevate him to the holy trinity of Scottish photographers alongside Harry Benson and Iain MacMillan whose pictures are today lauded as among the most defining Beatle pictures ever taken.

In a series of extraordinary and intimate images which have gone down in Fab Four folklore as the Mad Day Out, Murray perfectly captured John, Paul, George and Ringo as four guys clinging on to the final fragments of their friendship. Relaxed and acting up for the cameras, The Beatles rekindled the camaraderie that had so endeared them to a global audience five years earlier, as they criss-crossed London to pose at a number of venues including Highgate Cemetery, St Pancras Church and Gardens and Wapping Pier Head, before finishing off at Paul's meditation pod at his home in St John's Wood. There is no evidence of the rancour that within months, indeed weeks, would deflate the Beatle balloon during the tense sessions for the 'White Album'.

Murray today almost has to pinch himself to recall the day he spent photographing The Beatles on the first occasion they had been pictured together for more than a year. His pictures show a band in transition, leaving behind the acid-tinged hippiedom of a year before for an altogether different, rockier image. John had left his wife Cynthia for Yoko Ono. Paul's five-year relationship with actress Jane Asher had crashed and burned, and he was in the middle of a dalliance with American Francie Schwartz. Both women were at the photoshoot, clinging on to their

This eerie picture by Tom Murray was taken at Wapping Pier on the 'mad day out'.

respective menfolk like crabs. George had embraced all things Indian and Ringo had one eye on a burgeoning acting career.

As he let his mind wander back to that summer day, Murray recalled: 'My first reaction when I saw them was I didn't believe it. I just thought, "Oh my God, what do I do now?" I had one camera, two rolls of film, one lens, no flash, no assistant. In those days I would have four or five cameras, flash equipment, a couple of hundred rolls of film before I would consider going out. So I realised I could only shoot outside because the film wasn't fast enough for inside. I thought, I don't have a commission so I'll just shoot what I want.'

Over the course of the day, Murray snapped away, careful to give McCullin his place. But it meant he had the freedom to snap the band at their most relaxed and spontaneous. In one picture, Paul is stripped to the waist and chained to a brick wall at the pier. Another classic shot shows him spouting water in the direction of Murray's Nikon. In another picture, all four are seen side on, their profiles attesting to the changes they had undergone as four individuals. Perhaps, though, the most striking series shows John playing dead on the beach at the pier with Paul, George and Ringo cradling his head in their arms. It was an image that would indeed come back to haunt Murray years later when Lennon's death was real, not imagined.

Without the aid of a crystal ball, Murray could not have known that just two weeks later Ringo would walk out on The Beatles. Tensions in the studio during the 'White Album' sessions had been building for weeks. Cracks were appearing as the record began to look more like a series of solo recordings rather than a group effort. Fed up with the bickering, Ringo, always the emollient that soothed over the cracks, chucked his sticks away. But Tom Murray saw no sign of the band being at odds with each other that sunny August day. 'They were so relaxed with each other. They were such a tight-knit group it was impossible to get in between them. The thing was, it was like four married people. It always split into John and Paul and then George and Ringo. John would say something then Paul would finish it off. They were great fun to be with although it really was a mad day rushing around London. We could only stay, say, 45 minutes in one place before too many people arrived. You couldn't do the same thing now. They would be mobbed in minutes and people would be taking pictures on their mobiles.

'I think they are the best pictures of The Beatles taken that year and it ended up being the last official shoot they ever did. I was in the right place at the right time. It was a golden opportunity and I had a ball. There I was with the four most famous people on the planet. What's not to enjoy? And I'm photographing them.'

7. Fellow Musicians and Friends

Donovan

At the height of their fame, John Lennon, Paul McCartney, George Harrison and Ringo Starr lived like four golden birds cosseted in a gilded cage, prisoners of their own unrelenting fame. They sang together, laughed together, cried together, went on holiday together and made history together. Their personal bond was so strong that very few people were ever allowed to enter their inner sanctum. With the exception of manager Brian Epstein and faithful roadies Mal Evans and Neil Aspinall, no one could get close to The Beatles. The street-savvy Scousers could spot 'fakers' and snake oil salesmen a mile away.

But two men are entitled to claim a special kinship with the band. One was the unimpeachable Bob Dylan whose credentials need no elaboration here. The other was a slightly scrawny kid from the tenements of Glasgow's Anderston district. His special relationship with the biggest pop stars of them all stretched from the smoke-filled recording studios of the swinging sixties to the marijuana-fuelled London clubs of Carnaby Street and from the foothills of the Himalayas to the beautiful Cuillins of Skye.

His name was Donovan Leitch, a child of the fifties who endured the true grit of an impoverished upbringing to become a bohemian icon of the sixties. His self-penned songs, such as 'Catch the Wind' and 'Colours', captured the mood of the times and also chimed perfectly with the Dylan-inspired folk phenomenon sweeping American and British university and college campuses. Indeed, the boy from Glasgow was hailed as 'the British Bobby' – if Dylan was king, Donovan was a prince and pretender to the folk-blues throne, although he would have preferred to be dubbed the Scottish Woody Guthrie.

Donovan was born in April, 1946, in what was then euphemistically called the second city of the British Empire, entering into a world still reeling from the aftermath of the American bombing of Hiroshima and Nagasaki nine months earlier. His father Donny eked out a living as a tool fitter at Rolls-Royce while his beloved 'mammy' Wynn helped supplement the family income by working at a local factory. Money may have been scarce, but his biography recalls a household happy in adversity as a war-ravaged Britain slowly hauled itself off the floor.

At the age of ten, though, the family was forced to move south when

Two of us. John Lennon and Donovan are joint best men at the wedding of 'Magic' Alexis Mardas, Apple's so-called electronic genius.

his dad's job at Rolls-Royce was sacrificed as demand for munitions inevitably dried up, a by-product of the peace dividend. So the family relocated to leafy Hertfordshire, forever leaving behind the grime of Glasgow for the open fields near their new home in the town of Hatfield.

The young Donovan had been influenced by the poetry of Allen Ginsberg and Dylan Thomas, the rock 'n' roll dynamism of Buddy Holly, the hypnotic folk of Ewan McColl and Peggy Seeger and the country blues of Bert Jansch. And then there were The Beatles, whose first album seemed to incorporate strands from all of the above.

In an email interview with me last year, Donovan explained what he believes was the common ground he shared with The Beatles, who he first met in Bob Dylan's suite at the Savoy in London: 'The four guys from Liverpool and I have similar backgrounds. They come from a tough seaport and Glasgow is a river city. We also shared an upbringing with a huge Irish influence. Lennon and McCartney are Irish names and I have an Irish granny. Mix in the literate and musical influences that Scotland and Ireland are famous for and you get a Celtic mix of pals who would get along.

'Of course, we also saw in each other's work a highly skilled level of composition which revelled in experimentation. I absorbed hundreds of popular and eclectic musical styles just as The Beatles did and it showed in our writing. Our working-class beginnings would show in our concern for the world and the millions who suffer under the heel of ignorance and

greed. We had read all the songs in the bohemian library and thought there had to be some way to change the world. Eventually, meditation brought us closer together and we went east to learn how to meditate.

'I was transfixed by the fusion they created on "Love Me Do". This song was a beacon that showed me I was going in the right direction with the Celtic sound I was creating. It was not at all a copy of American folk or pop. The brief we all felt was to discover the root sound from which all music comes.'

Having been initiated into The Beatles magic circle, Donovan occasionally witnessed at first hand the spellbinding creativity the Fab Four brought to their studio work. In the mid sixties, often on a whim, he would pop round to Paul's house in London's St John's Wood to kick back, smoke a couple of joints and talk about their shared craft of songwriting.

Donovan said: 'Paul and I were kindred spirits but we found it hard to write songs together as we both were just too prolific. Any ideas that I had he would immediately riff off into an idea of his own and vice versa. He was so full of songs, I swear that if he fell on the piano, by the time he picked himself up he would have written three new melodies.

'I did not see it at the time but I was becoming a close friend to Paul, a rare confidante to him in his increasingly private world as fame separated him in his reality. One quiet Sunday I was alone, recording new songs on my little Uher tape machine when the doorbell rang. It was Paul on his own. He played a couple of tunes to me on his acoustic Martin six-string.

A young George on holiday in Skye with sister Louise.

The tune was "Eleanor Rigby" but the words had not all come out yet. Then the doorbell rang again. I went to see and found a young bobby. He said a car had been left parked outside illegally, at an odd angle, the doors open and the radio still on. Paul came to the door and the policeman said, "Is it your car, a sports car?" Paul said yes. The Bobby then asked, "Shall I park it for you?" Paul gave him the keys and the car was parked. In those days, The Beatles were treated like royalty. The copper came back with the keys and saluted. Saluted, would you believe!'

Over the years, myths have grown up that Donovan was one of the few outsiders to take part in Beatles studio sessions. Most of them, however, are born of fertile imaginations, particularly those to do with the recording of 'Yellow Submarine' in 1966. Donovan told me: 'I did not play on any Beatle recordings but I wrote a line for "Yellow Submarine". Paul came round one afternoon to swap songs. We were both writing three or four a day. He had a children's ditty and wanted me to add a line where there was a gap. He knew I was adept at children's songs and he was just beginning to write in this genre. I was flattered and wrote, "Sky of blue and sea of green, in our yellow submarine." It is really just phrasing the lines in the song he already had. But it was rare for someone else to add to a song by the four of them.'

Close he may have been to McCartney, but it was to another Beatle that Donovan ultimately gravitated. George Harrison's growing interest in Indian mysticism, Hindu teachings and all things Eastern found a passionate ally in Donovan who also on the cusp of this popular new spiritual awakening. Indeed, his epochal album *Sunshine Superman* – released almost a year ahead of 1967's *Sgt. Pepper's Lonely Hearts Club Band* – heralded the bohemian manifesto before The Beatles told the world that love was all you needed. And when in August of the summer of love, John, Paul, George and Ringo headed to Bangor in Wales to meet the Maharishi Mahesh Yogi to begin studying transcendental meditation Donovan was along for the ride. Seven months later, they all pitched up outside the Maharishi's ashram in Rishikesh, the beauty of the Himalayas spread out behind them and the sacred waters of the Ganges in front of them. It was to be a pivotal moment in all their lives, one that would leave an indelible imprint.

Donovan recalled: 'It was a chance to meet The Beatles far away from pop music and what we were all involved in. It was quite a unique experience to be able to shut ourselves off from everything that was going on. The press was waiting outside but inside the compound it was great. I got a chance to learn and play and hang out with the musicians that I was very impressed by. We were all able to lay back and relax. We played music and George experimented with Indian instruments that were brought in.

George and I were close as we shared the mission to find the reason and cure for the suffering of humanity.

'The Maharishi was quite a relaxed guy, but there was an embarrassing silence in the room. We had all just arrived and nobody was saying anything. We were all wondering what to say. John was so funny and so direct that to break the silence he went up to the Maharishi, who was sitting cross-legged on the floor, patted him on the head and said, "There's a good little guru." We all laughed. It was so funny. John was always very funny. He always said exactly what he felt. John certainly had a wicked tongue but he was honest to a fault. His work proved that. Many people considered him to be very hard and forward. Actually, that's how he protected his sensitivities, by saying exactly what he felt. He was a very sensitive man.

'It was natural that the band and I would be in India. We wanted to discover the inner world of meditation together. For me it was amazing to walk away from fame and be as it were like students again. Imagine just sitting around playing songs for no other reason than making music. Lovely. We dived deep within transcendental meditation. We truly wanted to help ourselves understand and also to help our millions of fans to dive deep down as well. The answer lies within.

'One moment that stands out for me was when George gave me a book called *Autobiography of a Yogi* about Yogananda. I was touched and knew that, of all of the four, George and I were closer as we explored the songwriting that would pass on to the world the lost wisdom of the ages – meditation. He was my spirit brother. We both knew the simple technique was the way to stop the world's suffering if only we would all practise it. He and I had an equal passion for reading, discussing and discovering truths in Vedic science. We were very close in introducing Indian instruments to our music, too.'

Having slipped off the chains of stardom, all five musicians revelled in a new-found freedom. Influences were further shared and absorbed. So prolific were The Beatles that they quickly stockpiled a number of songs that would become the backbone to the 'White Album'. But that record would also owe a significant musical debt to Donovan, whose trademark folk-tinged finger-picking acoustic guitar style can be heard on songs like Lennon's 'Julia' and 'Dear Prudence' and McCartney's 'I Will' and 'Mother Nature's Son'.

'I introduced John to a finger-picking style that I had learned initially with great difficulty. There were only three folk singers in Britain who played this style at the time and any time I tried to learn it from them they refused to play it, which I thought was terrible. But I learned it from this one guy and I taught it to John and he taught it to George. When John

Universal soldier. Donovan, seen here on a visit to Glasgow in 2008, continues to plough his own distinctive musical furrow.

Island retreat. George pictured by first wife Pattie during their trip to the Hebridean isle of Skye to visit Donovan and his family.

learned a new guitar style, he usually wrote a new song. And that encouraged him to write the lovely ballad for his lost mother, "Julia", and "Dear Prudence".'

Arguably, India was the last time all four Beatles would be in perfect harmony away from the studio. Inevitably, the blue skies that had covered much of the sixties gave way to grey clouds towards the end of the decade as the Beatles' dream faded. Friendships were inevitably scattered on the winds of change – but for Donovan the bonds of those far-off days remain intact.

In the summer of 1971 George Harrison and his wife Patti took the train all the way from London to Kyle of Lachalsh with Donovan and his wife Linda to spend a few days on the Isle of Skye where Donovan had a house. Details of the secret pilgrimage to the beautiful Hebridean island only emerged in 2007 when Patti discovered long-lost photographs of her former husband gazing out across the Cuillins and clowning around for the camera on the ferry trip. Wearing a baggy jumper and a woolly, beanie-type hat, and with his hair falling past his shoulders, George is virtually unrecognisable as the innocent young moptop from a decade earlier. Instead, he is very much a mixture of hippy hobo and wandering mystic, happy to indulge in a little bit of fun.

What is equally less well known is that this was not George's first trip to Skye. He once enjoyed a brief family holiday there as a five-year old. And a single picture has survived of George with his sister Louise smiling happily on the famous Scottish island. So the trip to see Donovan could easily have rekindled some happy childhood memories for the former Beatle.

During his few days back on the island, George and Donovan were happy just to wander about. Donovan told me: 'Linda and I were delighted to show our dear friends the beauty of Skye. We had our little one-year-old daughter Astrella with us and George was enraptured by her. As I let my feelings drift back to that long-ago summer, I see four young friends walking the grassy slopes of the island cliffs, gazing out to sea at the shimmering terns and the clear blue sky. All the world was young and the possibility of peace was in every gentle heart.'

Donovan's long-time friend Sam Richards was occasionally part of the company. He said: 'George was a very sweet guy, very humble. We went down to the Stein Inn and had a couple of pints in there. For the most part, Don and him kept themselves to themselves. He signed a couple of autographs but by and large he was left alone. I'm sure the locals were surprised to find a Beatle in their midst but no one bothered him much. I think he was just enjoying some peace and quiet away from all the hassles people like him have to go through. Most of the time they just hung out with each other playing guitars.

George cuts a desolate figure on the ferry that took him and Pattie across from Kyle of Lochalsh to Skye.

'George had travelled up from London and he and Patti got the ferry over from the mainland. I remember it was bitterly cold at that time of year and I gave George a big hug to keep him warm. I don't think he even had a change of clothing. I seem to remember him leaving in the same clothes as he arrived. The weather was so wild I remember him saying you could die out there. So he started fantasising with Donovan about how you could build a tunnel from Don's house down to that boathouse. And they were both talking about how it could be done. They were always joshing with each other, a lot of banter. He was a really lovely fellow.'

Of The Beatles' demise as a working band, Donovan told me: 'What brought us together at first was our work but what tore us apart was super fame. It was the kind of fame that takes your very privacy from you. As it got heavier, the band retreated because of the danger from the madness. "Yellow Submarine" is not a song about a seacraft; it's the protection you build with friends and family when the world turns you into an icon.

'I am always surprised how long a band does stay together. They were together the longest time. We are grateful for the time they were together. It's not easy. I welcomed their solo careers and don't really miss anything. The music of the band is still alive and well. In many ways they were the best friends this planet ever had.'

Lulu

Lulu is as Glasgow as Celtic and Rangers, Tennents Lager and even Irn Bru. Which is just as well. Because to have survived at the top after more than four decades in the cut-throat world of showbusiness requires the grit of someone who is unquestionably made from girders.

Survival has been Lulu's stock in trade ever since as a 14-year-old she was plucked from her home in Glasgow's East End to climb aboard the London-bound showbiz express at the height of the swinging sixties. Within months, her debut single 'Shout' was a monster top ten success and the pint-sized artist from Glasgow formerly known as Marie McDonald McLaughlin Lawrie was the darling of the Smoke. Guest appearances quickly followed on radio and TV shows; magazines formed an orderly queue to listen to the gospel according to the little girl with the big voice; invitations dropped through her door to the top showbiz soirées. 'Shout' was Lulu's ticket to the big time, opening doors into rooms marked 'Star' – and the biggest stars of them all were The Beatles, the band whose pictures had been plastered over every inch of her tenement bedroom in Dennistoun just a few short months earlier.

This was 1964. Lulu was just 15 years of age and no different to millions of other girls whose hormones were in turmoil in the raging maelstrom called Beatlemania. The band had already released three albums – *Please Please Me, With The Beatles* and *A Hard Day's Night* – and a string of number one singles that had raised the bar for British pop in the sixties. Quite simply, Lulu was smitten, cocooned inside her own little Fab Four world. It didn't matter that she had to share her love with millions of other girls all over the world. Unrequited it may have been, but she had an edge that would eventually give her special access to her heroes' world – her own remarkable singing talent and a down-to-earth attitude that would ultimately establish common ground with John, Paul, George and Ringo.

Little Marie had been bitten by the music bug from a young age and regularly sang at Glasgow jive halls such as the Lindella. The attraction lay not in traditional pop music or Elvis's pelvis-pumping rock 'n' roll. No, the young Marie was drawn to American R&B, in particular the gospel-tinged blues preached by Ray Charles and edgier artistes like Sam Cooke, The Drifters, Lee Dorsey and the young Ike and Tina Turner. And she instantly recognised those same Uncle Sam influences between the grooves of her Beatle records.

She declared: 'Like Liverpool, Glasgow was a major port, and this meant it enjoyed a constant influx of foreign ships and sailors. The Americans brought records with them. We were hearing these new songs well before the rest of the country – blues, soul, country and western. We were hungry for it.'

In some ways Lulu has another Glasgow music icon to thank for the moment fate intervened in her life – and he already had his own connection to The Beatles. Alex Harvey had been on the same bill as the Fabs at their first gig in Scotland on 20 May 1960 in Alloa Town Hall and had followed in their footsteps to perform in the clubs dotted on Hamburg's notorious Reeperbahn. So his local hero status was already established the night in 1962 when Lulu waited for him to take the stage in a dark Glasgow city-centre club. When he launched into a larynx-shredding version of 'Shout', already a hit for the Isley Brothers, Lulu was stunned.

'The place went wild. He sang with a female range – high and with so much energy. There was a real anger there, the sound of youth. It was amazing. It was an absolute revelation for me. No other music had ever resonated with me in quite the same way. I knew I had to do that song.'

'Shout', her debut release on 15 April 1964, was a natural fit for her own vocal range, but its climb up the pop charts was given an invaluable nudge by the new princes of pop. Four weeks before the wraps were actually taken off the 45rpm piece of vinyl, 'Shout' was previewed on *Ready Steady Go*, the highly influential pop show hosted by Cathy McGowan and

Girl with kaleidescope eyes. Lulu with Paul and John not long after 'Shout!' hit the top of the pops.

Keith Fordyce that could make or break fledgling careers. On this particular Friday, the guests included John Lennon and Paul McCartney and one of the first songs up for judgement was 'Shout'. Back in Glasgow, Lulu was glued to her parents' black and white TV waiting for her brother Billy to run back from the local chippie with the traditional Friday night fish and chips.

Lulu recalled the moment Lennon and McCartney gave 'Shout' the kind of celebrity endorsement you couldn't buy. As Cathy chatted to them about the week's new releases, Lulu watched transfixed at the grainy black and white images on the screen as John Lennon delivered his verdict. 'Well, my favourite is a song called "Shout",' said John. 'It's by a girl called Lulu.' Six hundred miles north, Lulu's jaw dropped to her ankles. She ran to the window, thrust it open and leaned out. Her brother was hurrying down the street, carrying the fish and chips while stuffing them in his mouth. And her words echoed down the street: 'Billy, they picked me. They picked me.'

Lennon's 14-word approval helped guarantee 'Shout''s rapid ascent to the top of the charts. Nine months later, Lulu's own celebrity cachet assured her a VIP place in the wings at London's Hammersmith Odeon when she saw The Beatles perform in concert for the first time. And the moment they met is still vividly imprinted on her mind. Lulu told me: 'I would do lots of radio shows like *Saturday Club* where you had to pre-record the music. Different bands would come in and do their session so I would come in maybe after them. The Beatles had done theirs so our paths never properly crossed. I was always just missing them. But the official meeting really was at the Hammy Odeon.

'The Odeon could hold about 3,000 but there seemed to be twice as many as that. Most were screaming girls and, of course, they were all about my age. I felt like I was just like them except I had this privileged position at the side of the stage. I was just standing watching them at the encores when Paul came off the stage and just shouted, "Oh look, it's Lulu." I was just amazed that he knew who I was. Then I was invited into their dressing room. I couldn't believe it. I thought Paul McCartney was gorgeous and he had great hair. I have always been hair-obsessed. And I will never forget seeing Paul wet his hair under a tap and then shake it dry. It was fabulous. He had a great haircut. Of course, coming from Glasgow there are two important things that you must know about – the best shoes and the best haircut.

'I was so nervous that I couldn't think of anything to say but I think they knew that. But have you any idea how profound that moment was for me? When I was young, my whole bedroom was covered in pictures of The Beatles. It was wall-to-wall Beatles. Then of course I turned 14, went to

London, made a record and then I was kind of hanging with them and stuff like that. Who did I fancy? Well, I had a big crush on Paul, then John then ultimately the whole band!'

Although London has been her home for more than 40 years, Lulu's accent still echoes with traces of her Glasgow roots and she lets out a high-pitched laugh when I ask her if she was disappointed at meeting her heroes in the flesh. 'Are you kidding? I wasn't disappointed at all. I was a teenager with raging hormones. I wasn't thinking with my intellect, let's put it like that.'

No matter what unspoken thoughts of lust may have been running through her mind, Lulu never had to worry about any of the Fabs crossing the line. In fact, given her tender years, bands like The Beatles, The Animals and The Stones tended to wrap her in a protective blanket. She said: 'Liverpool isn't so unlike Glasgow. Because we were all in the same business and were so young, there was a camaraderie. They were very protective in a way, all the bands were. There was a wee sister kind of thing going on. They treated me like a little girl and sometimes it would irritate me. But I was terrified of the whole thing as well. I was quietly shaking in my boots.'

By this time, the Lennon-McCartney production line was at its peak. They often gave songs away to other artists such as The Stones, Tommy Quickly and Peter and Gordon. The sight of that double-barrelled songwriting credit on the label almost always ensured a hit record, but Lulu says she would never have exploited her growing friendship with The Beatles to ask them for a Lennon-McCartney original. Neither would she ever have asked them for advice about handling the pitfalls of fame.

'No, I would not have done that. I was shy and not presumptuous. I know my place. I was always slightly in awe of them and I don't think I'm like that with a lot of people. It was like your first boyfriend or something or the first time you saw them on the TV. It was just an experience you never forgot. They were incredibly busy but no matter where they were in the world or how hard they were working they always came home and we would meet up in the same kind of clubs. We all gathered in the same kind of places – Eric Clapton, The Who, The Animals, The Kinks, Hendrix. I would be in the group but I wasn't so sure of myself as a young woman. It was a very difficult transition for me to make to leave Glasgow and go into that world where there was a revolution going on. I was coping. But to say I became very close to The Beatles, or part of an inner circle, is not, I don't think, accurate. I knew them, I hung out with them and I loved them, but ask for advice, are you kidding? I'm a Glaswegian. We would not sit down and have a philosophical discussion. The conversation would inevitably be about music.

'Music was the common ground for us. Even though they would think of me as a child, there was a lot of respect. When I did "Shout" not everyone got it right away, but *they* did because that was the kind of music they loved – all that soulful black music, the Stax records – so there was a bond there in the music right from the start.'

That bond endured throughout a tumultuous decade of change and survives today with Paul and Ringo. She was a guest on Jools Holland's New Year *Hootenanny* show in 2007 along with her old pal Paul, both of them looking far younger than they have any right to. And on another programme, they performed a fantastic version of 'Brown Eyed Handsome Man' from Macca's *Run Devil Run* album of old rock 'n' roll favourites from both their childhoods.

By her own admission, though, Lulu forged closer links in the sixties with three Beatle wives – Cynthia Lennon, Pattie Harrison and Maureen Starkey. She says: 'I would hang out a lot with the girls. I'm a bit of a girly girl, a woman's woman.'

It's often said that if you can remember the sixties, you weren't there. Well, Lulu was there and she does remember most of it. She shunned the drugs and the excess-all-areas hedonism which, in part, defined the second half of the decade. Yet, she was an eye-witness to some of the era's most significant occasions, such as the launch party in Brian Epstein's house for *Sgt. Pepper*. She was also present on the night Paul met Linda Eastman in the Bag O' Nails club in Soho and they all decamped later to Lulu's house for an impromptu party.

Lulu has enjoyed a career whose longevity is shared by only a few others from that time. Understandably, she prefers to live in the here and now rather than leaf back through a lifetime of memories, the good, the bad and the ugly. Occasionally, though, her thoughts naturally drift back to more innocent and carefree days when a young girl from Glasgow's East End found herself on first name terms with the biggest band on the planet. Asked why she became such good pals with The Beatles, she takes her time to choose the right words.

'I am more serious than I come across a lot of the time. Let's face it, they were full of fun but they were very serious about the music. And that maybe translates. The serious side of me is the same as theirs. There's a similarity there, we are all northern and keep our feet on the ground. I agree partly that they were a product of the times, in the right place at the right time, but they had a special talent and that helps obviously. To be a huge success you can't just be a singer because there are a lot of great singers out there. It's the package, the whole deal, that's important and they had it in abundance.

'It was a period in my life I will never forget and I will always be grateful for that moment in time.'

Davey Johnstone

MADISON SQUARE GARDEN
Thursday, 28 November 1974

The show began with a quiet buzz of audience expectation, a ripple of excitement and a growing sense of awareness that this would be no ordinary Elton John concert. The fact it was Thanksgiving Day only added to the atmosphere as thousands took their seats in the hallowed New York venue. Rumours had been circulating for days that the flamboyant British singer, fêted as the biggest pop star since The Beatles, planned a special holiday surprise. Elton, though, had managed to keep a tight lid on his plans and not a word had leaked out in advance. So when he strode to the front of the stage midway through the concert and made his show-stopping announcement, it was greeted with jaw-dropping astonishment: 'Ladies and gentlemen, it's my privilege and your privilege . . . John Lennon.'

Out of the darkness, guitar round his neck and dressed all in black with heeled cowboy boots strode the man who epitomised the spirit of The Beatles. The man who, along with Paul McCartney, George Harrison and Ringo Starr, encapsulated the beating heart of the sixties. The noise that came from the seats below sounded like a tremor running through the heart of Manhattan. It was nothing more than an emotional outpouring of love for Lennon, making his first appearance on stage for more than two years. Elton appeared to wipe away a tear as Lennon, chewing gum but looking deathly pale, stared out at the sea of cheering souls in front of him.

Standing just a few feet away was Davey Johnstone, Elton's long-time guitarist and a man whose own dreams had been inspired by the person now sharing the same stage with him. For the Edinburgh-born musician it was a moment of musical nirvana, an occasion that would forever be imprinted in his mind's eye. Not least because merciless fate would decree this was the final time Lennon would ever appear and sing before a concert audience – and Davey would be the last Scot to witness at close hand the charisma and magic of Beatle John singing on stage.

In a rare interview, Davey let his mind flow back downstream to that night in New York. He also talked of his friendship with a man who, beneath all the legend and folklore, was at heart a musician's musician, a man who wanted desperately to ensure his songs still mattered to a new generation of fans.

Davey told me: 'Before the show, John was so nervous. He was green because he hadn't played live for a while. Normally his complexion was

Overleaf. *Imagine that.* Davey Johnstone rehearses with John and Elton for their ground-breaking 1974 show at Madison Square Garden, NYC.

porcelain white anyway but he was green. He was nauseous and a total bag of nerves. He was convinced he was going to throw up. But we had done a rehearsal. A very quiet rehearsal in, I think, the Record Plant or some small studio in New York. It went well and he was fine at the rehearsal. But when it came to the Garden date, he was totally shitting himself. Just before the show I would tune up all the guitars. This was 1974 and we didn't have guitar tuners or roadies who did that. John came in looking like death warmed up and he said would you tune the guitar and I said of course. I said, "Are you okay?" and he said, "No, I'm not okay. I am so nervous. How long till we go on?" I said about 20 minutes and he laughed and said, "Oh in The Beatles we used to get a bit of fanny about now. They used to bring in these chicks and we would have a quick one." I was just cracking up thinking long live rock 'n' roll. God bless The Beatles. They opened so many doors for guys like us.

'The gig when we got on was totally rocking out. It was just a brilliant atmosphere and the crowd reaction was unbelievable. Madison Square Garden is probably *the* place on the planet. There are other venues that have tried to rival it. One of them actually was Greens Playhouse in Glasgow because the audience would always go nuts. The stage is on the second or third floor so when the audience went wild it looked as though it was moving. It felt like there was an earthquake going on when Elton introduced John. There was a rumour going around that someone was going to come on but nobody knew who it was. In a place as high profile as New York, some people may have put two and two together but when Elton introduced John Lennon we were all amazed at the reaction of the audience. I mean, we knew he was coming on but it was just one of those moments where the hairs stand up on your back. When John walked out it was like one of those moments you never forget in your life. It really was a life-changing moment when you saw him appear at the front of the stage. He was all in black and he was great.'

Lennon and Elton sang 'Whatever Gets You through the Night' – John's first American number one single and the reason for his appearance alongside Elton – and 'Lucy in the Sky with Diamonds', the first time he had ever sung the *Sgt. Pepper* album track in a concert environment. And for an encore, they performed 'I Saw Her Standing There', the song which was the first track on The Beatles' first album, *Please Please Me*, released a long decade earlier. John couldn't resist a tongue-in-cheek dig at his former songwriting partner when he name-checked the song as having 'been written by an old estranged fiancée of mine called Paul', adding nervously that he wanted to hurry up so he could get off stage and be sick. Then he was gone, exiting to an even more deafening clamour than the one that 20 minutes earlier had greeted his arrival.

Within minutes the exhilaration of playing on stage had kicked in and John, notoriously impulsive, was already letting his mind wander with all sort of possibilities about the future. That future suddenly materialised in the form of his estranged wife Yoko Ono; that night marked the beginning of their eventual reconciliation and the resurrection of Lennon's public image, which had taken a battering since he embarked on his infamous 18-month long 'lost weekend'.

Davey said: 'When it was over he was thrilled that he had done it and was glad to be back on stage and playing with our band. Because, you know, any artist wants to remain current. Even though he was John Lennon he still wanted to be flavour of the month in the same way that Elton works hard at being today. How does it rate with all the shows I've done? Definitely one of the biggest moments. As much as a show can move you there's a lot you can forget about, a lot of it is like a dream that will just go by you. It was truly a seminal moment for all of us. If all of the people who said they were at that show had been at that show, Madison Square Garden would have held about 150,000 people. As it is it holds about 20,000. Everybody I've met in New York says they were at that gig. It was one of those shows where people stopped you in the street to talk about it.'

Without doubt it was a momentous night in the long history of the Garden, for the fans, for Lennon, for Elton and for lifelong Beatles' fan Davey. Unknown to the Scottish guitarist, however, the night's magic was only just beginning. After the show, Elton's party, high on the success of the evening, decamped to the Copacabana nightclub at the Pierre Hotel for the traditional après-gig party with the celebrities of the day such as Uri Geller and David Cassidy. Naturally, Lennon went with them and schmoozed everyone with his insider tales of Fab Four debauchery and camaraderie, much of the bitterness of the split four years ago having slowly seeped away. It was a fun occasion. Davey stayed a while before eventually slipping away from the crowd and heading back to his hotel room. Around midnight, the phone rang and he heard the familiar voice of his boss on the line.

'Elton called me and he said, "Listen, John wants to come over and hang out with you, is that alright?" And I was like, "Is that alright? Of course, send him over." At half twelve John came over and I proceeded to play him stuff like Ry Cooder and Little Feat, bands he had probably never heard of, stuff I was really into at the time. We talked and I discovered he had spent a lot of time in Edinburgh which I didn't know about. He had an auntie there who lived near Murrayfield Stadium and I said, "Christ, I've just bought my folks a house in Corstorphine." He would talk about places I knew and say he used to go there every year. I was saying come on, get out of here, but it was true.

Overleaf. *New York state of mind.* Davey Johnstone (far right) along with the rest of Elton's band, before John joined them on stage at Madison Square Garden to sing three songs.

'The time we spent after the show in my hotel room is probably my most cherished memory of John. We spent six hours playing music, talking, finding out little things about each other. What was cool about it was I was able to ask him stuff as a friend. I was a fan but I was more on his level because we had done the same kind of things so it wasn't like me acting like a fan or something. I would ask him things like, "You know that harmony on 'Hey Jude', how did you come up with that?" And I would mention other things and he would basically say it was like Motown or Stax records. He was so giving of information. He was totally open. The stuff he came up with was totally from the heart. It was pure John Lennon and to me that was the special thing about him and it always will be.'

The Madison Square Garden gig – the product of an outrageous bet – was the high point of a superstar friendship between Elton and Lennon, the seeds of which had been sown five months earlier. In June, Elton and Davey, along with the rest of the band, were among the passengers enjoying the last voyage of the luxury liner the SS *France* as it headed for its final port of call at New York. The band used the five-day trip from Southampton to write and rehearse songs for the album that became *Captain Fantastic and the Brown Dirt Cowboy*.

Davey recalled the sequence of events that eventually led to John and Elton getting together. 'John had called Elton a few times and they had gotten quite friendly over the phone. John was a big fan of our band. He kept on saying you guys are the best thing I've heard since we've been around. We were amazed. What a compliment! We were all massive Lennon fans. So it was only really a matter of time before we got together in some form or another. So I met him when we got off the boat at New York. It was incredible to meet him but he was very down to earth, couldn't have been nicer. It was a lovely moment.'

John immediately strong-armed Elton to take part a couple of days later in the first of the sessions that would eventually produce the album *Walls and Bridges*. It was an astute move on John's part, knowing the hot young turk could perhaps add a little of his own lustre to the Lennon legend. And so it was that on 17 June 1974, Davey joined Elton at the famous Record Plant Studio to add his distinctive piano chops and backing vocals to three songs, including 'Whatever Gets You Through The Night'.

Davey said: 'John was so grateful he said to Elton, "Well what can I do to repay you for this?" And, of course, Elton said, "Well if it goes to number one will you get up and play with us at Madison Square Garden on Thanksgiving Day?" and John was like, sure, whatever. His career and personal life wasn't perhaps in the best shape at that time. He didn't think in a million years that was going to happen, that he would have a number one record. Plus, he was just not into the idea of performing at that time. But of course, the single did go to number one and Elton called him and said, "It's time to make good on your promise." And that's how John came to perform with us at the Garden. Amazing, really, when you think back on it now.'

So thrilled was Lennon with Elton's virtuoso piano work he had no hesitation in accepting an offer to hang out with his band at Caribou Ranch studio in Colorado where the first tracks to *Captain Fantastic* were due to be laid down in the next couple of days. John ended up playing and singing on a reggae-tinged cover of 'Lucy in the Sky with Diamonds', although he had to call in Davey when, perhaps suffering a sudden attack of nerves, he needed to be reminded about the chords to one of his most famous songs. For Davey, this was a priceless opportunity to get to know his hero on his own turf. And he soon discovered John was more the willing musical collaborator than the stellar Beatle of legend.

He said: 'It always amazed me how humble he was. He would say to me, "You can use my guitars for the session." And he would say, "You're the guitar player, can you tune it for me?" All the time I'm thinking, this is fucking John Lennon, this is absolutely brilliant for me. We had a great time, he was such a sweet guy. He was the best. I think we were all ready for the cynical, funny, slightly cruel John Lennon that you hear about. But, to be honest that side of him rarely surfaced. Any time it did it was always in a humorous context and he would have us all falling about. It was great having him around. He was one of the lads, as simple as that. We were all huge Lennon fans. We just had a great time together.'

Within less than a year, Lennon's life had undergone yet another typical metamorphosis. Reconciled with Yoko, the couple celebrated the birth of their son Sean on 9 October 1975, Lennon's 35th birthday, an event that signalled his retreat from the public spotlight for five years. Elton was named Sean's godfather.

Davey has remained a vital mainstay of Elton's band, his *de facto* on stage musical director, and is surely one of the best musicians Scotland has ever produced. But destiny decided his path would cross with that of John Lennon one more time. He bumped into him at the same record studio where they had once played on 'Whatever Gets You Through The Night' and where they had rehearsed for that magical night at Madison Square Garden. It happened at the back end of 1980. John was working on his comeback album, *Double Fantasy*. Davey said: 'Everything was great and he was just loving life. He was happy. It was quite apparent earlier that there was an unfinished situation in his life with Yoko. Finally, he was enjoying being who he was.'

Hamish Stuart

Hamish Stuart is standing onstage at Brazil's famous Maracana Stadium, gazing out at an ocean of more than 184,000 faces, then a world record for the number of people attending a rock concert. 'Unbelievable' does not begin to describe the experience. His face is a mask of concentration as he cranks out the familiar rhythm guitar chords to The Beatles' classic 'All My Loving'. It's a song that is planted deep in the memory, a flashback to the carefree days when the same Paul McCartney tune echoed happily round a teenager's bedroom on Glasgow's south side. Then a quick glance 10 feet to his right reveals the singer, his Hofner bass guitar raised high at its normal jaunty angle, his face so familiar, his voice belting out the words to the song.

'I just had to pinch myself,' recalled Hamish. 'Here I am playing a Beatles song onstage with Paul. It was a pretty surreal moment but a great one.'

As a teenager, Hamish, like millions of others all over the world, had been hooked on The Beatles. And, like those same millions, he dreamt of playing rock 'n' roll music just like John Lennon, Paul McCartney, George Harrison and Ringo Starr. Except for Hamish Stuart the dream came true and he became one of that rare band of musicians to have shared the stage with not just one Beatle but two. As well as being an intrinsic part of Macca's band for several years, Hamish is also proud to have joined the line-up of Ringo's All-Starr touring band.

But that samba spectacular at the Maracana in Rio on 4 April 1990, was the high point of his time with Paul. Along the way, though, Hamish

Hamish (second from right) with Wix, Blair Cunningham, Paul, Linda and Robbie McIntosh.

Stuart has steadfastly crafted a reputation as one of Scotland's finest musicians and soul singers. After earning his spurs in the melting pot of bands that existed in Glasgow in the late sixties and early seventies – in particular with Dream Police – Hamish got his big break when he joined the ranks of The Average White Band. Their innovative white man's soul sound scored with hits like 'Pick Up the Pieces' and a string of outstanding albums such as *AWB* (also known as *The White Album*), *Cut The Cake* and *Soul Searchin'*. The band's success, like that of so many others, eventually faded under the strain of commercial pressure, but for Hamish Stuart it became a gateway to respect from his musical peers and a ticket to working with some of the biggest stars in the business.

In the past 35 years, he has worked and written music with such luminaries as Chaka Khan, Diana Ross, Quincy Jones, Smokey Robinson and Aretha Franklin. His honey-soft vocal style allied with his abilities on bass and guitar also brought him to the attention of Paul McCartney in 1988. At that time, McCartney was stuck in the kind of creative rut that has peppered his career since The Beatles split in 1970. He had enlisted the help of Elvis Costello to see if he could reignite the creative spark that was again missing following the critical and commercial failure of his 1986 album *Press to Play*.

Pleased with the results of his songwriting collaboration with Costello – regarded by many as having a Lennonesque cutting edge to his lyrics – McCartney began casting his net for a studio band, with one eye on perhaps going back on the road. At that time, McCartney was managed by Richard Ogden, who had in the past done PR for The Average White Band. Hamish said: 'Richard asked if I would be interested in playing with Paul. He said Paul was putting a band together and did I want to go round? He said it's a very informal jam session. So I decided to go over and see what happens. It was an exciting offer to get, especially being such a big Beatles fan as a kid. I had never met Paul before. I had met Ringo a couple of times in LA, but with Paul our paths had never crossed. It was a bit daunting but when I got there Paul was very amiable. It was, "Come in, have a cup of tea." He gave me a tour of the studio where he has all his treasures, the Bill Black bass that was used on "Heartbreak Hotel". It was all very relaxed. He just said, "Let's have a play and see what we come up with." We did that first day and it seemed to go well. Then I got a call saying we were going to start in February with Elvis Costello producing these songs.'

The sessions for *Flowers in the Dirt* marked the start of a musical collaboration with Hamish that lasted for five years. As well as this album – which was hailed as a cracking return to form for McCartney – Hamish played on the follow-up, *Off the Ground* and the *Unplugged* album. He also joined Paul on two mammoth world tours. Accompanying Hamish as a new Macca recruit was former Pretenders guitarist Robbie McIntosh, keyboard wizard Wix, drummer Blair Cunningham, and of course Linda McCartney. Arguably, it became the strongest line-up of any of McCartney's solo career bands.

Music first struck a deep chord within Hamish in his early teens as he discovered the songs of Chuck Berry and other rock 'n' roll heroes. But he remembers one major formative experience: 'The first concert I ever went to was a Beatles show at the Concert Hall in Glasgow in October 1963, a few days before my 14th birthday. I won tickets from a competition in the Glasgow *Evening Citizen* – there were five questions and I knew the answers because I was a fan. I went with my older cousin and she stood on her feet and screamed the whole time but I just kept sat there listening. They opened with 'Roll Over Beethoven' which I could barely make out and then the audience settled down a bit and the songs became clearer.

'"She Loves You" had recently come out and it was the newest thing that they played. I was beginning to think at that time . . . four guys, guitars . . . Maybe this is what I could do. I'd been singing for a while and had just formed a school group and seeing The Beatles spurred me on. I got my very first album, *With The Beatles*, as a present that Christmas of 1963.'

That piece of plastic, played on a portable record player, fired a million musical dreams for the former Queen's Park Secondary youngster. 'The Beatles inspired me to start playing. I started playing guitar by learning Beatles tunes off *With The Beatles*. Obviously on that one there are tunes like 'Money' and 'Roll Over Beethoven' that were kind of straight ahead. Initially, I gravitated towards the ones that had the Chuck Berry vibe. I remember that *A Hard Day's Night* was a really important album as well. It was when that album came out that I really started learning the guitar properly. There were chords I had never heard before. They were exploring at that point and that really opened up new ground for me.'

In his five years, with McCartney, Hamish could watch at close quarters a real music legend at work – from inside the studio to huge arenas to intimate settings such as London's Roundhouse, the venue for the live recording of the band's *Unplugged* album. 'The *Unplugged* thing was a really nice experience. It was lovely to play all these great tunes. Paul is a perfectionist and is meticulous when it comes to detail. He never laid down any conditions, but we all naturally felt they should be done the way they were originally. These are songs that a whole generation know and love so none of us wanted to tamper with them.'

The last time Hamish saw Paul was at the London memorial concert in 1998 for Linda McCartney, an occasion naturally tinged with sadness for both men. 'Linda was very good in the band, very professional. She was a real member of the band in every way. I was devastated when she died,' said Hamish. 'I think he probably needed to change things after he lost Linda. Getting together again with the same group of people would probably have been a bit weird. He had to move on, I'm sure.'

But if Hamish reckoned that was the last chance he would get to hit the stage with any of his boyhood heroes, he was in for a pleasant surprise. Ringo Starr put in a call asking Hamish to join up with his All-Starrs for a number of gigs in America. And in 2008 he signed on again for a whistle-stop American tour, making him one of Ringo's most loyal stage compadres. Looking back on his first tour of duty as an All-Starr, Hamish said: 'Ringo was great, a real sweetheart. He likes to play and he wants the band to have a good time and he likes the music. It is not loose, it's well rehearsed. He and I got on great, he is just so funny. He kept cracking me up. There is a really nice atmosphere in the auditoriums and that is down to the way Ringo is.'

Hamish has continued on a very individual musical path taking in session work, production and mentoring new bands. Would he relish the chance to huddle round a mic with Paul again if the call ever came? 'Absolutely. Anytime, anywhere.'

Jack Bruce

One was the Quiet Beatle and the other was the Quiet Cream. Neither sought out celebrity. But something in the way they played elevated George Harrison and Jack Bruce to the premier league of sixties music icons. Harrison's melodic guitar lines were integral to Lennon and McCartney's songs, while Bruce's jazzy bass lines and powerhouse vocals were the perfect match for Eric Clapton's sinewy lead chords and Ginger Baker's pounding beat in Cream.

Both emerged from tough working-class backgrounds in two of Britain's biggest and toughest inner-cities, each of them being rebuilt from the ravages of Hitler's bombs. Harrison was the product of a loving family unit in the uncompromising Liverpool suburb of Speke. Bruce enjoyed a similarly warm upbringing in Bishopbriggs to the north of Glasgow, in what is now East Dunbartonshire.

Both had to stand their ground in the face of corrosive and combustible inter-band egos. For Harrison, always the junior partner in The Beatles, that meant ushering his songs past the formidable talents of Lennon and McCartney. Equally, Baker and Clapton could be just as abrasive as the no-nonsense Scot who would happily and dogmatically fight his own corner. Different bands...shared values...deep respect... good friends.

OFF THE BEATLE TRACK 14 –
STEADY AS A ROCK

When Paul McCartney hits the road on tour, he literally puts his life in the hands of a Scot who has become his most trusted minder. Mark Hamilton founded Rock Steady security almost 30 years ago after deciding there was more to life than driving lorries to deliver fruit and veg round Edinburgh for a living. Rock Steady was created when Mark was just 19. Soon, he was organising security – the word bouncer is not in the company's lexicon – at pop concerts at the Odeon in Edinburgh and Glasgow's legendary Apollo Theatre. The fact there was rarely any trouble at gigs involving some of the biggest bands on the planet, including Wings, The Rolling Stones and Led Zeppelin in the seventies, was concrete evidence police and city fathers had plenty of faith in Rock Steady.

Mark first encountered Paul McCartney when Wings came to play the Odeon and Rock Steady were responsible for ensuring the former Beatle didn't encounter the full body hysteria of a decade earlier. And that set in motion a friendship and business relationship that is as strong today as it was then and has given Mark a ringside seat at McCartney shows all over the world from Canberra to the Kremlin. So far he has been on three world tours. Highlights include shows in Brazil's Maracana Stadium, Rome's Coliseum, the New Orleans Superbowl and a groundbreaking gig in Moscow's Red Square in front of Russian President Vladimir Putin.

'Red Square especially, was a highlight,' remembered Mark. 'Mr Putin, who's a huge Beatles fan, personally showed us – Paul and myself – round the Kremlin. Gorbachev was there too and Moscow's mayor. To see these guys, world figures, hanging about backstage at a McCartney gig, it fascinated me. Probably Paul too. I suppose I'm still something of a groupie myself, even at my age. Security for the concert in Red Square took on a special significance for many reasons and wherever we went the crowd reacted with an intense fervour.'

Now 51, Mark told the Edinburgh *Evening News* of the first time he came face-to-face with Beatle Paul. He recalled: 'I first met him when he brought Wings to the Odeon. I've never known him anything other than approachable. I got him to sign my business card backstage that night and I was over the moon when he sent me a thank-you note and I got a "thanks to Mark Hamilton" mention on the sleeve of *The Beatles Anthology*. He's a very decent person to work for. He's fair. Make no mistake, though, there's a helluva responsibility in my job. Lennon and what happened to him crosses my mind. There are nutters everywhere and we are confronted by disturbed people.'

In a face-to-face interview at Glasgow's Royal Scottish Academy for Music and Drama, Jack told me: 'As a musician I would rate George the highest of all The Beatles. I think his songs were among the great songs that they did. He was tremendously underrated because it was always Lennon and McCartney.

'I had a lot of time for him. And he went on to do great things after The Beatles as well, like all of them did. I think you can credit George for a lot of people becoming aware of Indian music and Ravi Shankar. I was already into that kind of music anyway but George really made it happen. So that will always be part of his legacy as well as the work he did with The Beatles.'

Jack Bruce's musical journey began at a very young age. Indeed, you could say music is part of his DNA since his parents were both accomplished singers and self-taught instrumentalists. 'My home was very musical. My mother sang Scottish folk songs and my father was a huge traditional jazz fan of people like Fats Waller and Louis Armstrong. But my older brother loved modern jazz. There would be literally physical fights in my house between my father and brother arguing about the role of the saxophone in jazz or something, real punch-ups. Music is a valid part of my background. I didn't adopt music, music adopted me.'

The family moved around a lot; in fact, one online biography suggests he attended 14 different schools before ending up at Bellahouston Academy on Glasgow's south side. Any frustration over this slightly nomadic upbringing, however, was offset by Jack's growing love affair with music. He sang in a local church choir, took up the cello and began pursuing an interest in classical music. His prodigious talents soon earned him a coveted place at Glasgow's celebrated Royal Scottish Academy of Music and Drama. Already, though, his creative talents were running in tandem with a stubborn streak that saw him quit the RSAMD at the age of 17 partly because, it is claimed, he said he knew more than the teachers.

So in 1960, having dropped out, Jack, confident in his own abilities, pointed his musical compass south. London – a melting pot of influences including jazz and blues, as well as moon-and-June style pop – was calling. He first hooked up with the Murray Campbell Big Band, playing double bass on a tour of clubs in Italy. On his return, he drifted towards the capital's blues scene and, like so many others, hooked up with Alexis Korner's celebrated Blues Incorporated. Korner's band would become a launchpad for some of the sixties' best musicians, including Eric Clapton, Jeff Beck and Jimmy Page. This incarnation also included organist Graham Bond and drummer Ginger Baker. And eventually, all three took flight to form their own group. The Graham Bond Organisation granted each of them the freedom to pursue their own blues visions away from the more structured disciplines of Korner's band.

The Graham Bond Organisation was hugely admired but commercial success eluded them, despite the acclaim heaped on the release of two studio albums. And tensions soon surfaced in the studio, notably between Bruce and Baker. GBO often erupted into GBH as the two musicians refused to give way over the inevitable 'musical differences'. There were numerous stories of the pair sabotaging each other's equipment and trading blows on stage.

Something had to give and Baker used his muscular seniority to have Jack fired from the band. Jack then joined John Mayall's Bluesbreakers. The ever-shifting ranks of Mayall's outfit at that time included the 19-year-old Clapton, whose dazzling fretwork was already the talk of clubs all over London and beyond. Bruce and Clapton's musical rapport was instant and with Baker still on the fringes of Jack's circle, the three formed Cream in 1966.

Within 18 months, Cream were celebrated as rock's first supergroup. Their style was a fusion of blues and jazz textures aligned with powerhouse pop that attracted a cult following from fans all over the world and quickly earned the respect of their peers. To his own surprise, Jack emerged as the main vocalist and the main pen behind such classic songs as 'Sunshine of Your Love', 'White Room', 'I'm So Glad', 'Politician' and 'I Feel Free'.

For all the adulation, however, Jack, strongly influenced by The Beatles, longed to write the definitive pop single, forsaking the kind of freeform, extended solos that had become the hallmark of Cream's live shows. As it happened, Clapton had struck up a solid friendship with George Harrison, a bond that eventually saw Eric playing guitar on the Fabs' 'White Album' classic 'While My Guitar Gently Weeps'. Harrison repaid the favour by joining Cream in the studio to co-write and play on 'Badge', arguably the nearest they came to Bruce's idea of powerhouse pop. However, that was not the first time Jack had met any of The Beatles.

He told me: 'I first met The Beatles at a party held by The Moody Blues. They were quite famous for their parties. It happened about the beginning of Cream. It wasn't a proper meeting really because there were lots of other people there. But I think I said hello. The first time I met any member of The Beatles properly was when I was playing with Scaffold on "Lily the Pink". Ringo came in. I remember him saying, "Who's that?" and pointing at me. We have since gone on to become great friends but at the time it was a slightly inauspicious introduction.

'The first time I met Paul McCartney properly was when my first solo album *Songs for a Tailor* came out and he rang to congratulate me, which was very nice of him. He asked me to bring it round to Apple to play it to the guys, which I did and they all gave it a big thumbs up. So to get that kind of validation from The Beatles was great. Then I got to know John

Lennon very well in 1974 during his fallow period. He called it his lost weekend but it was rather longer than a weekend. We got quite friendly and used to hang out a lot with Harry Nilsson who I also worked with later on as well.

'George played on *Songs For a Tailor* but I had already met him when he came in to play on "Badge". We didn't have any outside musicians playing with Cream, he was the only one, along with our producer Felix Pappalardi. Eric had been doing a lot of stuff with George and they were very good friends. But "Badge" was a great song for us. George was brilliant on it. It took a lot of takes. Usually with Cream we did things very quickly – normally three takes, four takes tops. But we spent a whole day on "Badge", about 40 takes. George played rhythm. He played very high chords, very inventive chords, which I suppose gave it a bit of a Beatley sound. But the interesting thing is that everyone thought he played the bridge solo because it sounded so Beatley but it was Eric who did it. George couldn't be credited in those days because of studio contractual obligations so he was credited as L'Angelo Mysterioso.

'"Badge" was on Cream's last album. It gave me the idea of asking him to play on my first solo record. I always thought he was a great player but I didn't know if he would fit in with what I was doing. But it worked out very well and I was very pleased with the results. It was very nice of him to do it since I don't think he was playing sessions for other people at the time. I don't think there was any trepidation on his part about playing with the other musicians I had, but it was more the fact that we were doing it live which could have been a little unnerving. I had a lot of really good jazz musicians working on the album. It was all live with horns. It wasn't maybe a way that he was used to working. So he was quite nervous but he was the first one in for the session and by the time everyone else arrived at Morgan Studios he was very warmed up. And he played great. The song was a rhythm and blues track and he was very comfortable.

'He was a really nice guy, just like everybody says. Very sweet, very spiritual, very generous.'

Nevertheless, Jack never again combined forces in the studio with a man he often called his personality counterpart in The Beatles. When George succumbed to cancer in 2002, Jack delivered a fulsome tribute on his website to the Quiet Fab. He wrote: 'I am really shocked and saddened to hear of the death of George. Along with all of his contemporaries as well as millions throughout the world, I mourn the passing of a musician whose sensitivity and spirituality touched all of us. Apart from his work with The Beatles and his important solo recordings, George was one of the first in the sixties to bring the influence of Indian culture to the attention of the world, thus changing the direction of music for all time . . . I always felt a special empathy with him, the Quiet Beatle as I was the Quiet Cream.'

Long after Cream imploded in 1969, Jack Bruce continued to plough his own musical furrow with a string of projects that reflected his musical diversity and creativity. At one point he even joined one of Ringo Starr's All-Starr band line-ups for a number of highly successful gigs in America.

'I still find it very enjoyable to stand up and scream into a microphone. I would probably get bored not keeping busy. It's very difficult to keep a band together. There's a very sparky energy to the people I play with. I'm after the real thing. I'm not interested in playing it safe. That would bore me. I want to make my own statement, to get my own ideas across. But I do like things like playing with Ringo. Ringo's tours were like a travelling party and we all got the chance to get up on stage and sing our hits.'

In 2007 Jack made a rare visit to his Glasgow roots for a look back at a career that has survived more twists and turns than the Monaco Grand Prix. Forty-seven years after walking out of the Royal Scottish Academy for Music and Drama to pursue his own musical dream, he was back at his alma mater for a ceremony in which part of the school was named the Jack Bruce Zone, a signpost which the school hopes will encourage more budding musicians to follow the path of one of its best-known sons.

Nowadays Jack is happier talking of his pride in his family, especially daughter Natascha, who is already pursuing her own musical journey. 'I wouldn't discourage her. There's a big world out there,' he said. For Jack, though, music is still his thing, a hobby that became a passion that elevated him to the ranks of the very best and gained him the recognition of a grateful world . . . including John, Paul, George and Ringo.

Andy White

The early evening chill was beginning to nip at his cheeks when Andy White walked briskly through the front entrance of Abbey Road studios. The date was 11 September 1962. So far, the sixties were far from swinging, but gradually the times really were a-changing. There was an air of social upheaval, a mood captured by a younger generation hell bent on sweeping aside the old order and stamping their own imprint on the world.

For Andy White, a 32-year-old session drummer from Glasgow, nothing marked this day as being anything out of the ordinary. By the end of it, however, he would have earned himself a secret footnote in the story of the biggest band the world has ever known. He was early, punctuality being a prerequisite for freelance musicians clamouring for work in London's burgeoning rock 'n' roll scene. Andy's services were much sought-after, his reputation having been honed while playing with such

And the beat goes on. Session drummer Andy White looks very dapper in bow-tie. He had no reason to believe The Beatles would be so big.

varied stars as Billy Fury and Marlene Dietrich. He was a safe pair of hands, a stark contrast to those younger drummers who struggled to hold down a solid backbeat, thereby destroying hours of precious recording time.

Andy took up drumming in a bagpipe band when he was 12 years old, and by 17 was ready to turn professional. He spent most of the fifties playing swing and trad jazz. Among his more notable rock 'n' roll gigs were the 1960 sessions where Billy Fury recorded *Sound of Fury*, which is usually thought of as the first great British rock 'n' roll album. Sandwiched in between his various concert engagements were recording sessions for the likes of Anthony Newley, Frankie Laine and German film legend Dietrich.

Today's gig amounted to little more than another day at the office. He had received the call a couple of days earlier from EMI. A young group from Liverpool called The Beatles were due down for their second session. The name meant nothing to Andy. EMI Producer George Martin had already detected a spark of potential in the mouthy Scousers. At their first session a week earlier, the band had barnstormed through a string of rock 'n' roll covers plus, unusually, a song they had written themselves called 'Love Me Do'. Martin liked the song with its bluesy harmonica riff and unusual chord changes. But he had already pinpointed drummer Ringo as the weakest link at that first session. Time was money and Martin was not prepared to write off expensive recordings because of poor musicianship. So Andy was on standby to lend his technical expertise and drive The Beatles' rhythm section into a higher gear.

By the time the band trooped into Studio Two, Andy was already behind the drums. Not surprisingly, colour drained from Ringo's face. He had only just been recruited to the band a couple of months earlier after fans' favourite Pete Best had been shown the door by John, Paul and George in cahoots with new manager Brian Epstein. So his confidence as the new boy was already waning – and now another drummer was sitting behind the kit.

Indeed, Martin was unaware Best had been fired and had been surprised by Ringo's appearance at the 4 September session. He hadn't been impressed by Best either and, at that point, had booked Andy White for the 11 September session rather than record with what he felt was a sub-standard drummer. George Martin quickly explained to Epstein his reasons for hiring Andy. Ringo, he said, could still play on the session, perhaps with a tambourine or some other percussion instrument. Gutted, the newest Beatle had no option but to go along. In the studio, George Martin's word was law. At least for the time being.

All this, of course, didn't register on Andy's radar. His job, simply, was to play the drums. Band politics were someone else's problem. After polite introductions, Andy went to work, his ear for what was required quickly feeding into the recording. Over the course of the next two hours, Andy played on three songs, each of them penned by Lennon and McCartney: 'Love Me Do', 'Please Please Me' and 'PS I Love You', with Ringo on maracas.

By about 6.45 p.m., George Martin had arrived back, having earlier left an assistant to oversee most of the session. The songs were in the can and Andy's cheque was in his pocket. He walked out of Studio Two and never saw The Beatles again.

Weeks later, 'Love Me Do' was released as The Beatles' first single with 'PS I Love You'. 'Please Please Me' became their second single, released on 3 January 1963. Their debut album, also called *Please Please Me* was released on 22 March 1963, and contained all three songs. Naturally, Andy's work was recorded in the EMI studio log. But, when The Beatles rode the elevator to fame and glory, his contribution was glossed over in the glut of history books that followed. As far as history was concerned, Ringo Starr had played on all The Beatles' records. Andy saw no reason to say anything different. He had been paid for his work and slipped unobtrusively back onto the carousel of session work for other artistes.

Two decades passed before the public discovered how an unknown Scottish drummer had helped take the Fab Four on another small step to Beatlemania. It was only with the release of a commemorative twentieth-anniversary 12-inch vinyl version of 'Love Me Do' and 'PS I Love You' that details began to emerge of his contribution. Then, of course, there was confusion over which tracks Andy had played on and which ones featured Ringo. The truth is the band's debut single features Andy drumming on 'Love Me Do' and its B-side 'PS I Love You'. The band's first attempt at 'Please Please Me' was a slow soft-shoe shuffler with Andy on drums but was scrapped in favour of the reworked, uptempo version released on 11 January 1963, as The Beatles' second single.

Andy's small contribution may have for years been airbrushed from history, but he has never forgotten the day he played with The Beatles. Now living in New York, he has rarely spoken of the session. But I tracked him down and found a man happy to talk about his work and keen to dispel a couple of Beatle myths along the way. He recalled: 'It happened that Ron Richards was the producer at that session, not George Martin. George couldn't make it and asked Ron if he would stand in. George arrived towards the end but Ron Richards was the sole producer. I had probably been a full-time session drummer for two or three years by then. Ron used me a lot at that time and decided to book me for this date.

'I remember meeting The Beatles for the first time. They were nice guys and their music impressed me. Ringo was very pleasant, a good guy. George was pretty quiet and retiring. And, of course, John and Paul were

OFF THE BEATLE TRACK 15 –
KEEN MR MUSTARD

Outside of his music, Paul McCartney's other huge passion is food, not so much eating it as insisting it is always meat-free. And one man who got on the inside track of Macca's crusade to turn the world veggie was Scottish celebrity chef John Quigley. John, who now owns Glasgow eaterie Red Onion, teamed up with his Beatle hero when Paul hit the road in 1990 to promote *Flowers in the Dirt*. John explained: 'I was working for a company called Eat Your Hearts Out. When I first got the job I was just amazed. I was a massive Beatles fan and still am. It was phenomenal job for me. It was also a really high-pressured situation. Eat Your Hearts Out were on eggshells. They are now the biggest rock 'n' roll catering company in the world because of that tour. It was nine months solid, 160 people a day. Everything had to be right.'

Top of the food chain agenda, obviously, was a zero-tolerance approach to all meat products. It was a culinary code of conduct rigorously enforced and one that everyone was expected to live by. But John said: 'The driving force behind this at the time was Linda. She wanted a vegetarian tour, everything had to be vegetarian. To my knowledge I don't think it had been done before. I mean, you're asking these big hairy-arsed American boys who live on three cheese-burgers a day to tuck into a bowl of vegetarian lasagne. It was a massive challenge to keep everyone happy. At lunch and dinner times there would be six different options. You would do pastas and things that were obvious. Linda introduced a thing called TVP, textured vegetable protein. They were very strict about food. Anyone selling from a hot dog stand or Kentucky Fried Chicken – and these are big hockey arenas – they bought the concessions out so no one would be selling meat.

'On a personal level, they were brand new, two human beings who were so down to earth. It was a huge operation but as soon as you got to the heart of everything, by that I mean Paul and Linda, it was "this is easy, stop fussing." Linda did like her guacamole really lemony, so if that was in her dressing room she was really happy. Paul's a happy guy with his quiche, potato salad, coleslaw, he likes his carbs.'

John's gig with the McCartneys took him on a UK tour and a string of European dates and guaranteed him a front-row seat at what was billed as Paul's great return to live performances. And for such a huge Fab Four fan, he admits it was a thrill of a lifetime to see one of his heroes play the songs that were the soundtrack to his own youth.

the leading lights. Each one had his own ideas as to what would make the music work best, and they'd play off each other, throwing jokes back and forth. I spoke to John and Paul mostly, they were the composers and knew the routines of the songs. There was no written music involved, we had to discuss the arrangement of each song then try them through till Ron was satisfied enough to start recording. I thought the music was very good because it was original. Most groups were recording covers of American hits at that time.

'I never spoke to Ringo or George that day other than to say hello when we were first introduced. All my time was taken up working with John and Paul. I've no idea how the band felt about Ringo's omission or how the rest of the lads reacted. I was too busy. I did enjoy the session. The music was original and interesting, not another day at the office. The session could be considered a milestone in Beatles history, but it didn't do my musical career a great deal of good. Although it was known in the business about my playing on those tracks, publicly no one was supposed to know it wasn't Ringo.'

In 1995, The Beatles released their six-CD *Anthology*, a collection of rare tracks, studio oddities and outtakes. Among them were songs played on by Pete Best and Andy, notably the discarded slow version of 'Please Please Me'. But while Best collected a deserved windfall in royalties – a rumoured six-figure sum – Andy's remuneration was zero. This is entirely proper because he was a simply the hired hand – and he got paid for an honest (quarter) day's work.

Andy recalled: '*The Beatles Anthology* meant nothing financially to me, because I didn't have a royalty contract with EMI. So I didn't and never have received residuals for playing on those songs. That's just the way it was. You were paid for a job and you did it to the best of your ability.'

Ringo Starr, of course, remained an integral part of The Beatles until the band split in 1970, his place as one of rock's most revered drummers assured. Not surprisingly, though, the sight of Andy White sitting behind his drum kit that September morning remained a bone of contention between him and George Martin for years. In the *Anthology* book, Ringo recalled: 'Oh George wanted me out. He told me to sit in a corner and play the tambourine. On my first visit to EMI in September, we just ran through some tracks for George. I remember we did "Please Me" because while we were recording it I was playing the bass drum with a maraca in one hand and a tambourine in the other. I think it was because of that that George used Andy as "the professional" when we went down a week later to record "Love Me Do". Andy was previously booked anyway because of Pete Best. George didn't want to take any more chances and I was caught in the middle. I was devastated that he had his doubts about me. I came down ready to roll and was told, "We've got a professional drummer." He has apologised several times since, has old George, but it was devastating. So Andy plays on the "Love Me Do" single but I play on the album version. Andy wasn't doing anything so great that I couldn't copy it when we did the album. And I played virtually everything after that.'

George Martin has subsequently agreed he was too quick to judge Ringo. He said: 'I didn't give him a chance to begin with. He suddenly turned up at a session – I didn't know he was coming and I booked Andy White, and I said, "Well Andy's here and he's paid for, so he's going to play. You can join in on tambourine if you like. When I heard him [Ringo] he was much better than Pete Best, he gave it more solidity, and, in fact, he was more raucous than Andy White, and it fitted the group anyway. He was pretty rough in those days, but pretty good.'

For his part, Andy was able to monitor Ringo from afar as The Beatles' career went into orbit. And, like any of his profession, he has stoutly defended the drumming of Richard Starkey MBE. 'On "Love Me Do" and "Please Please Me", for example, it wasn't a matter of Ringo copying my playing. The band had been playing those songs for some time and I did what was asked of me, so, what was to copy? Ringo did well on subsequent recordings because he supplied what was required, a good solid back beat. End of story.'

Across the pond, Andy has carved out an outstanding reputation among the country's piping and drumming community. He served for many years as a popular drummer for the Eastern United States Pipe Band Association. But a reminder of his link to the Fabs hits him every day when he gets into his car, for his New Jersey licence plate number reads 5THBEATLE. Other traces of his wry Scottish humour also remain intact. He acknowledges that he has now become the answer to a Beatles trivia question.

If he met a perfect stranger and sensed he might make a good friend, how long would he wait before revealing that he once played with The Beatles? A month? An hour? Five minutes? He thinks about it for a moment. Then he laughs. 'I think it depends on how much I wanted to impress you.'

Wallace Booth

Wallace Booth sank back in the chair and let the words wash over him. 'Would you be interested in becoming The Beatles' road manager? I'll pay you a handsome salary.'

The question came from Brian Epstein, a blossoming player on the

Liverpool music scene whose family owned NEMS (an acronym for North End Music Stores), one of the city's largest record shops. As always, Epstein was immaculately groomed and dressed, wearing a two-piece suit and silk tie. He was debonair and his clipped tones betrayed an upbringing of wealth and privilege.

Wallace, in contrast, was a no-nonsense Aberdonian, a 22-year-old who had grown up on the tough side of the tracks in the Granite City. For more than a year, he had worked part-time as a bouncer in Liverpool's Cavern club, alternating his shifts with his dream of winning an Olympic gold in wrestling.

The Cavern, owned by Ray McFall, was then a magnet to kids who were drawn to a new craze sweeping the capital of England's north – beat music. Its exponents were four young Scousers whose live shows and songs inspired a cult-like devotion in their young followers. Most people believed The Beatles were on the cusp of something special. Epstein especially was prepared to gamble his reputation on their musical talents, having decided to act as the manager who would lead them to the promised land of pop stardom.

But Wallace Booth was not ready to take that risk. And it took him seconds to tell Epstein: 'Thanks, but no thanks.' Instead, he recommended his fellow bouncer at the Cavern, six foot six Malcolm Evans, a post office worker who was ready to throw it all in and accept whatever new challenges life had to offer. And in that instant lives were changed and destinies altered.

Wallace, who now lives in the Perthshire village of Comrie, said: 'Epstein summoned me to his office in Whitechapel in Liverpool. It was very swanky, very posh. And he said to me the boys, meaning The Beatles, want you to be their road manager. Would you pack your job up? He was prepared to pay good money, much more than I was used to. But I said no, I'm an athlete and I'm training for the Olympic Games. Honest to God, I wasn't interested. So he said to me, "Is there anyone else you can recommend?" And I said, "Well there's big Malcolm Evans." He was begging for the job. He worked with me as a part-time bouncer at the door at the Cavern but he wasn't a hard sort. He was a big amiable lad. So I went back to the Cavern and said to Malcolm, "Brian Epstein wants to see you about a job." All I know is that after that he got the job as The Beatles' road manager. And he travelled all over the world with them. He had only been working at the Cavern for a few months when this happened.

'I have never regretted my decision for a second. No one knew how big The Beatles would become so I could have ended up with egg on my face and back to square one. The other thing was that my whole life revolved round my training as a wrestler. I was already the British champion but I really wanted to lift the gold medal at the Tokyo Olympics in 1964 so all my ambition was targeted on that. If I had gone with The Beatles I would have had to sacrifice my own dreams and I wasn't prepared to do that. The funny thing is that big Mal turned up at the Cavern one December with a Mk 10 Jaguar, a beautiful car. The Beatles had bought it for him for his Christmas. He said to me, "Aren't you jealous?" but I wouldn't have changed a thing. I've had a very full life and not had any reason to look back once and wonder at what might have been. I wasn't envious in the least.'

Growing up in Aberdeen, Wallace was the youngest of a family of six. His father died when he was two, leaving his mum to eke out a living to raise the family on her own. In 1959, while still in his late teens, he answered an advert in a local paper for 'journeymen or apprentice joiners'. He was stunned to discover the job trail led him out of the North-east to Liverpool, a city that was still recovering from the effects of the Luftwaffe's bombing raids. 'My family all said I shouldn't go because Liverpool was rough and tough but I just thought that'll do for me,' he recalled.

The Scottish youngster had already shown he could take care of himself through his interest in sport and, specifically, wrestling. He was lean and muscular and dedicated to his training. But he was also a normal kid who liked nights out. 'After I went to work in Liverpool I would ask the people I worked with where the young ones went at the weekend. The most popular place at that time was the Locarno in Derby Street. I went there for nights out at weekends. One night I was just standing around minding my own business where a fight broke out. I saw this guy with a bow tie and four punters were kicking hell out of him so I ran up to help him. And it so happened he was the manager and he was from Glasgow. He was so pleased at what I had done he offered me a job. I was working part-time earning 15 shillings a night [75p] from 7 to 11 p.m.

'I was only there a couple of months when Paddy Delaney, who was head bouncer at the Cavern club, came up and said the Cavern was getting so busy with new groups that he needed some more bouncers. Up to this point, the Cavern had been mainly a jazz club but McFall was changing all that. I wasn't so sure about the offer, then he said it's £1 a night and I jumped at it. Five bob at that time was a gallon of petrol and a pound of steak. There was no choice, and that's how I came to work at the Cavern.

'But you never saw such a dive in all your life. There were no fire exits, nothing. It was a health inspector's nightmare. You would not dare stand against the walls because they were running with sweat. The entrance was only three foot wide. I would say it was little more than a death trap at the time because you used to get hundreds of kids in there.'

OFF THE BEATLE TRACK 16 –
TAKE A SHAND SONG

George Martin was the studio mastermind at Abbey Road whose careful hand on the tiller steered The Beatles into the calm waters of pop perfection. But before the Fab Four changed his life, George was fine-tuning the recording process for the doyen of Scottish country dance music. Jimmy Shand may sonically be as far removed from The Beatles as you can get, but in the mid to late fifties he was a major recording star who was signed to EMI label Parlophone, the same label that later became home to the Fabs. In 1955 George was appointed head of Parlophone, which was on the outer rim of the EMI radar, known more for comic recordings that mainstream pop. Slowly, though, George began to transform the label's fortunes, first by recording The Goons and then tapping into the popular artistes of the day outside the pop/rock 'n' roll mainstream. Among them was Jimmy Shand, Scotland's accordion king, whose toe-tapping ceilidh waltzes were huge favourites on BBC radio shows such as *Housewives' Choice* and *Two-Way Family Favourites*. He teamed up with George on a number of recordings, the best known of which was 'Bluebell Polka'. Jimmy, who came from Fife, wasn't the only traditional Scottish artist to work with George Martin. The legendary producer also oversaw sessions by Kenneth McKellar and Moira Anderson as well as a little-known Glaswegian crooner called Bob Inglis who went by the slightly more exotic stage name of Roberto Inglez, in keeping with his Latin-American balladeer image.

Wallace quickly became a familiar face at the Cavern on Friday nights. Eventually, though, he took on Saturday and Sunday stints as well as the jazz lovers surrendered their haunt to the new groups emerging from the ashes of skiffle music. In the vanguard of this new musical wave were Gerry and The Pacemakers, The Searchers, The Remo Four and, of course, The Beatles. Pete Best was still the band's drummer when they made their Cavern debut on 9 February 1961. Wallace was not on door duty since it was a lunchtime gig but that one-hour set marked the start of an amazing relationship between The Beatles and The Cavern that lasted until their final appearance there on 3 August 1963.

Wallace quickly built up a solid friendship with the band who, not surprisingly, called him Jock. And he saw at first hand the chain reaction The Beatles unleashed as news of the highly-charged shows in their grimy underground lair quickly spread. Queues of kids snaked all the way from the club's entrance down to Whitechapel, creating a conga line of feverish expectation. And then they would be crammed down the 18 stone steps into this claustrophobic hothouse.

'I had never seen anything like it,' recalled Wallace. 'There were a lot of other good bands, but no one generated the excitement that The Beatles did. It was manic. They had an incredible effect on the audience. The girls would go mad to get near them. They used to have me on the dressing room door and you used to have to go through the crowd and everything. The girls used to go crazy to try to get in their dressing room. They would offer you anything. I could have been in my element but I wasn't interested. I just wanted to do my job. I never really paid that much attention to the music. My job was to keep them out of trouble. But I was still on very friendly terms with them. It was so hot inside the Cavern that they used to come to the front door just to cool off and get some air. And that's when you would talk to them most.'

Ultimately, the band's destiny did not include Pete Best, the moody-looking drummer with the swept back hair who, ironically, was the favourite among the band's female followers. He had already taken part in The Beatles' first recording session for EMI in June, 1962, but had failed to impress producer George Martin. In truth, Pete had long been on the outside of the band looking in. His personality was an awkward fit compared with the more zany natures of Lennon, McCartney and Harrison. And that trio all had their doubts about him musically. In the end, though, it was Epstein who was called on to do the dirty work and Pete was sacked on Thursday, 16 August, hours before the band were due to take the stage at their favourite venue. Three nights later at the Cavern, Ringo Starr was behind the drums and the Fab Four were finally in place. Permanently.

Wallace Booth was an innocent bystander when it came to internal band politics. He was just the guy at the door. But he couldn't helping feeling sorry for Pete, a boy with whom he had struck up a good rapport. 'He was an easy-going fella and he had been with them a long time. I had a lot of sympathy for him. I just thought, "What price loyalty?" He used to come up to the door to find me just to have someone to talk to. I'm not saying they didn't like him but he just seemed to be on the outside, not quite on the same wavelength as the others. It was as if he wasn't a fully-fledged member of the group. The story I heard was that he refused to cut his hair in the same style as the others. He looked more like a rock 'n' roller. He was a big favourite with the fans, especially the girls because he was a good looking fella.

'But they were all quite different. Paul was great, George was quiet, I got on well with Ringo but John Lennon was one troublemaker. The amount of times I had to go down to sort fellas out that he had been cheeky to or arrogant with. He was a smart mouth and I don't mean that as a compliment. He knew all the bouncers would be on his side and he could afford to shoot his mouth off. He always stayed friendly with me but I never liked him. It was no wonder so many guys wanted to whack him. I knew him for three years, three nights a week. We had to stop people trying to fight him.'

Some four decades after these tumultuous days, Wallace has long since come to terms with the fact that he passed up a lift on the Beatle bandwagon just as it was about to head for the stars. Instead, he remained dedicated to his wrestling training, devotion that paid off with a silver medal at the 1966 Commonwealth Games. Later, after giving up the grip and grapple game, he went into the nightclub business in Liverpool and became a personal trainer and friends with Scottish sporting stars like footballers Graeme Souness and Asa Hartford.

Of those heady days manning the door at the Cavern, he is philosophical. 'They were great times because we were all young. We all lived for the moment but I never had any reason to think I made the wrong decision in turning down The Beatles. I was an athlete and all my focus was on training. I was proud to represent my country. That's something you can't take away from me. Who knows? The Beatles could just as easily have been an overnight sensation and never heard of again.'

The Marmalade

John Lennon sarcastically called it the toppermost of the poppermost, a rallying call to The Beatles when spirits reached rock bottom and the endless struggle to 'make it' was the musical equivalent of running up a hill backwards. For any band, success in the sixties was measured in a single digit that sat at the top of the pop charts, the weekly barometer of public taste. If you hit the top spot in the hit parade you became part of an exclusive club in which fame and fortune was there for the taking.

In November, 1968, membership of that club was handed to five guys from Scotland. They were The Marmalade, the song was The Beatles' reggae-tinged ditty 'Ob-La-Di, Ob-La-Da' and it bestowed on them the accolade of being the first Scottish group to make it to number one.

Long before they were retooled as The Marmalade, Dean Ford, William 'Junior' Campbell, Pat Fairlie, Graham Knight and Alan Whitehead had toiled away on the Scottish club circuit under the somewhat dubious soubriquet of Dean Ford and the Gaylords. Their hard graft and top-notch musicianship quickly brought them to the attention of London talent spotters desperate to latch on to the Next Big Thing. No

one seriously put Dean Ford and the Gaylords in that bracket, but potential to crack the charts was evident. All they needed was the right song.

Eventually, The Marmalade's act, a blend of R&B and Motown tunes, was seen by London booking agent Peter Walsh, who brought the band into his roster of groups such as The Tremeloes. Next stop was Swinging London. Said bass player Graham, 'We had to go and live in London because they didn't have such a thing in Scotland as recording studios. The band was like Scotland's Cliff and The Shadows, that's the way the whole thing was modelled. By the time we got down to London, other bands had funny names and our manager decided that we should change the name. He was just sitting having his breakfast one day and staring at a pot of marmalade and from then on we were The Marmalade. Simple as that.'

The Marmalade appeared at such hip London joints as the Scotch of St James, the Cromwellian and the Revolution. These were the favourite haunts of sixties rock royalty after a hard day's night in the studio. The band were delighted to get a regular gig at the Speakeasy and it was there that they first touched the hem of a Beatle's garment. Even 40 years down the line, Junior Campbell remembers the moment clearly: 'We had just become Marmalade and we used to play in there about three times a week. It was a real jumping gig, where all the trendy people went. We got there

early one day. We used to do a lot of Motown stuff and we were rehearsing one of the numbers we were going to do. It was early, about six o' clock. There was no one there, the club wasn't even open and we heard this clapping. And then suddenly out of the darkness appeared Paul McCartney with a cine camera. And he went round us all shooting this film.

'It frightened the life out of us. It was like God coming down the stairs. That was the first contact we ever had with The Beatles. In the clubs you used to see them all the time, hanging out with the Monkees or The Stones or The Who. We never spoke to them on those occasions because they were the higher echelons and we were just a wee band. I can't remember exactly what he said but it was along the lines of, "Great stuff, oh you're left-handed as well." It was like the first time you meet a hero footballer, you don't know what to say. It was *Sgt. Pepper* time and they looked fantastic.'

It quickly became the norm for The Marmalade to find themselves in the same social orbit as The Beatles, The Stones, The Who and Jimi Hendrix without actually mixing with them. 'There was a little corner at the Scotch of St James that was The Beatles' corner. No one else could sit there but it was all very friendly,' said Graham. 'Thing was when you got into these place there wasn't any star-gazing. It was just blokes doing a job. We were all musicians and you could speak to anybody. If you saw Paul

McCartney at the bar you would just say "hi" and get on with it. No one mobbed them or anything like that. There was hero worship, but they were just normal people. At the Speakeasy you'd have The Who, the Hollies, Jimi Hendrix . . . everyone just having a chat.'

In the studio, meanwhile, The Marmalade continued to pray for some chart success. They hit paydirt with 'Lovin' Things' which was a top five UK hit. However, like all things, a breakthrough was tough but following it was even tougher. As songwriters, Campbell and Ford's talents were never in doubt. Record company demands, however, piled on the pressure and heightened expectations, leaving the band at the mercy of shark-finned music publishers and silver-tongued song pluggers desperate to offload their substandard tunes. Occasionally, though, a nugget emerged. The Marmalade recorded 'Loving Things' which was a minor UK hit and 'I See The Rain' which charted in Holland. And they also cut a version of 'Everlasting Love', but the song was released by The Lovin' Spoonful and went to number one, leaving The Marmalade to rue the fact they had been the victim of record company politics.

'The fact was we needed more songs,' recalled Graham. The band approached various song publishers, including Dick James, who worked with The Beatles. 'He promised us he would give us "Ob-La-Di, Ob-La-Da" which was on The Beatles' "White Album" which had just come out and no one else would get it. We had actually heard the song before it was released and it was just a funny song. Dick James was trying to plug a song by another in-house writer but it wasn't what we were looking for. He played "Ob-La-Di, Ob-La-Da" and I just laughed and said I like that one. He gave me an acetate and I took it back to the guys. We all came back with different songs. We played all the songs from the various music publishers and that one stuck out like a sore thumb. After all, it was a Paul McCartney song so it had one of those melodies that just sticks in your heard. It's infuriatingly catchy.'

Junior Campbell recalled the chain of events slightly differently from his old bandmate, and doubts that, on first hearing it, anyone knew it was a Beatles song. 'I think it was Pat and Graham who went round the publishers. They went to Dick James and he said, "I'm going to play a song to you that'll be a hit." I don't think they knew it was The Beatles, I don't think anyone did. Pat phoned me and played it over the phone and I thought that's a really good song. You knew right away it had potential to be a big hit.

'As a band we were working up north, Stockton-on-Tees I think it was. I remember we flew back to London and we recorded the song that night. We did the whole thing in a night. A horn arrangement was put on in the morning and then it went to press.'

Graham said: 'It came out the week after the "White Album" was released. Then, of course, Dick James in his wisdom gave it to about 16 other acts. It was all money, money.'

Nevertheless, 'Ob-La-Di, Ob-La-Da' began its steady ascent up the charts, boosted undoubtedly by a touch of Beatles magic and a typically annoying-but-catchy McCartney melody. And when it finally reached the pop peak, all those hours spent grafting in seedy dives, the endless drives up and down motorways and the interminable studio time slipped away.

The Marmalade spent five weeks at number one with 'Ob-La-Di, Ob-La-Da', a song The Beatles never released as a 45. But, applying 20-20 hindsight vision, the band today are unanimous that 'dooblo-doobli' as Junior calls it, proved to be more a curse than a blessing. 'It was the least favourite of all the band's records. Apart from anything else, it was a cover, and it was a Beatles cover. We were friendly with The Tremeloes who were in the same management stable as ourselves. And they sent us a telegram saying under no circumstances should you release this. It will be a very bad move for the band. And of course we said fuck off. In retrospect, although it was hugely successful, it didn't do us a lot of favours. It is easy to be wise after the event, all those kilts on Top of the Pops. It was embarrassing.

'We never saw The Beatles until about three weeks after the song came out. Alan Whitehead met McCartney in one of the clubs and said thanks very much for the song and McCartney said it's a pleasure. And Lennon made some comment that he thought ours was the best version.'

In truth, though, The Marmalade's chart success was short-lived. They never again found themselves at the pinnacle of the pop chart. The band continued for a few more years before key members such as Dean and Junior decided, in time-honoured fashion, to explore other musical interests. Graham, however, has kept The Marmalade flag flying high and on the night I spoke to him was in fact on his way to a gig at Pontin's holiday camp in Minehead. And once again, as he has done thousands of times before, he would sing the little song about Desmond and Molly Jones that has helped to pay the mortgage down through the decades. He still plays several hundred gigs a year under the Marmalade banner, maintaining a toe-hold in showbusiness thanks largely to the magic of that Beatles song. But he jokingly admits its familiar melody can still cause him to sit bolt upright in the middle of the night, wrenching him from a soothing sleep.

He said: 'I'll be playing it tonight so it's helped to keep me in the business all those years. But, I'll be honest, I have nightmares about it. I wake up in the night screaming about "Ob-La-Di, Ob-La-Da", but I have a lot to be grateful to the song for. It has become The Marmalade anthem. And there are a hell of a lot worse songs to be remembered for.'

Mean and moody. White Trash were inadvertently at the centre of a storm in their home city of Glasgow.

White Trash

White Trash were a gritty five-piece Glasgow rock band . . . and by 1969 they'd broken their balls to break into the big time. Relentless gigging in their Scottish heartland had cemented a reputation founded on the twin pillars of musical craftsmanship and a rock-solid fan base. When they came to the attention of The Beatles' fledgling Apple record label, they were hopeful that some Fab Four fairy dust would fall in their direction and give them their moment of glory. Unfortunately, White Trash's moment coincided with *Abbey Road*, The Beatles' swansong album and the last time all four collaborated on a record. Instead of riding the rocket to fame, White Trash were given a ringside seat as The Beatles crashed and burned amid bitter recriminations.

In 1968, Ian Clews, Fraser Watson, Timi Donald, Ronnie Leahy and Colin Hunter-Morrison had taken the low road south from Glasgow with stars in their eyes and hope in their hearts, dreaming of that lucky break that would propel them into music's big league. At that time, they were called The Pathfinders, and they were eking out an existence playing gigs at hip joints like the Scotch of St James, the Cromwellian and the Marquee. The band had recorded a demo of a barnstorming version of Carole King's 'The Road to Nowhere', which had long been a mainstay of their live set. Tony Meehan, the former Shadows drummer, now an A&R man with Decca, was plugging the track at several record companies in the hope of winning The Pathfinders the break they so badly wanted. But all of them turned it down – except one.

Fraser Watson recalled: 'We were playing the Cromwellian one night. We were pretty pissed off playing in what was virtually an alcove. We just felt a bit down because we didn't think we were moving at all. We were sitting in what was virtually a wee broom cupboard when Tony came in and said, "Guess where I've just been. I've just met George Harrison and let him hear your single. McCartney also heard it and The Beatles are going to release it on Apple." We were just stunned. Apple had only just been started and The Beatles were being swamped with tapes and demos from anyone who had ever picked up a guitar. It was the biggest thing on the planet at that time. We just went, "Fuckin' hell!" It was like a dream.'

The Pathfinders now found themselves under the Apple umbrella in London's Savile Row. They had allies in Derek Taylor, The Beatles' legendary press officer, and Richard Di Lello, an afro-permed Californian who was Apple's resident house hippy and who became a real champion of the band. The first priority was to drum up press interest in the band, and that meant a change of name and a shift of focus. Di Lello suggested calling the band White Trash, a name that guaranteed controversy and coverage.

'Road to Nowhere' was rush-released in the spring of 1969 after the band got wind that up and coming session singer Lesley Duncan had recorded it as a single. But it died a death after radio stations and the BBC refused to have anything to do with a band called White Trash. Looking back through Apple-tinted specs, Fraser said he had no problem with the change of name. 'By that time The Pathfinders was sounding a bit passé. We needed something a bit grittier, something that would get us noticed a bit. We didn't think there would have been a problem over the name but in hindsight it meant we couldn't get played on the radio. The BBC wouldn't touch the song with the proverbial barge pole and we couldn't get on *Top of the Pops*. That's a real drawback when you're trying to sell records. I think Apple even paid for a video to be shot but it was never aired. The BBC said the name was offensive. We couldn't understand it. But things were very different back then and we just felt that the establishment was against us because of the band's name. To this day I don't think it was offensive.

'Some copies had already gone out and they had to be recalled and the name altered so they just scored out the White and we became Trash. It was a bit of a sell-out but that's just the way it was to get the single played. The fact is a lot of people did like the record. We met George Harrison, he just walked into the press office with the denims on, long hair, and he shook our hands, said he loved the single, it was going to be great. He was very friendly. But there was a lot of pressure within The Beatles during this period and George actually walked out for seven days while we were there.

But it was all hushed up. The Beatles were recording what eventually became *Let It Be* in the studio in the Apple basement. He was very friendly, very laid back. It was just like talking to a pal. We were maybe a bit starstruck but, of course, we were all trying to be cool in the company of a Beatle. It is amazing when you look back. But George was great.'

Disenchanted, White Trash continued on the gigging grind as the rot slowly began to set in at Apple. But they were about to become innocent accomplices in the great *Abbey Road* album heist.

The album had been mixed but not mastered and five acetates – one for each Beatle and Apple chief Neil Aspinall – were in Aspinall's office. Fortified by encouragement from Derek Taylor, Di Lello mustered all his courage to confront McCartney personally about the future of White Trash. And surprisingly, his rap that this bunch of Scottish roughnecks could become an Apple money-spinner if given the right material got the nod. 'All right,' said Paul. 'Tell them to go ahead and make some demos and then we'll listen to them and see if there's enough material for an album.'

Unknown to McCartney, however, Taylor, a true member of The Beatles' inner sanctum, stole into his boss's office and liberated an acetate of the unreleased *Abbey Road* and handed it over to White Trash. 'I can't really remember what our exact reaction was,' recalled Fraser. 'Derek just told us to give it a listen and pick the most commercial song. It was a finished demo. Derek put his neck on the line for us.'

The song they chose was 'Golden Slumbers' merged with 'Carry That Weight', both tracks mainly Paul McCartney compositions. And when McCartney heard White Trash's version, he went tonto. 'He was livid. He thought we might just have done a wee demo. Instead, we gave it the full works. We recorded the basic tracks with Tony Meehan in Trident studios and then we finished it up with a 10-piece orchestra. And, of course, it was due to come out before *Abbey Road* was released. I can understand why he was so angry. After all, they were his songs and we'd stolen a bit of a march on him. But anyway there was this huge row and he said it wasn't to go out. Derek Taylor then decided to go and see Lennon. He knew if he could get a majority of Beatles on his side it didn't matter what McCartney thought. Lennon said it sounded great and he even let us use a reception he planned for a press launch. George Harrison gave it the thumbs up and Ringo just went along with John and George. So that was that. And it was actually released the day before *Abbey Road* came out. It might have been that the other three were getting back at Paul over all the business problems at Apple but we didn't care. We just wanted our record out.'

In his book, *The Longest Cocktail Party*, Di Lello revealed how he drew up a press release to accompany Golden Slumbers and unwittingly

provoked a storm of protest in the band's home town of Glasgow. The press release contained the following passage: 'White Trash come from Glasgow, the most violent and tempestuous city in the British Isles. A city in God's own country, inhabited by the devil's own people. A city that reeks of desperation under the cold, gray wash of the Scottish skies. They played their way through every club in the Gorbals, the Glasgow slum infamous for its rampaging gangs and razor kings, slashings, pummelings, stompings and copious pints of red blood in the gutter's sunset.'

Reaction in Glasgow was, predictably, off the scale. Banner headlines in the *Sunday Express* screamed: 'Trash Pop Group Disowned by Lord Provost' and brought condemnation from the high and mighty, in this case the city's chief constable and Lord Provost Donald Liddle: 'The members of this group may come from Glasgow but to my mind they are not Glasgow boys any more – they are orphans. In my opinion, this kind of publicity for publicity's sake is despicable. If this is the way you sell a record, I can only hope it's a flop.'

Today, Fraser can still laugh at the controversy the band generated. 'It was just written as a joke but it caused complete outrage back home. The Lord Provost was saying we had brought shame to Glasgow. It was a load of nonsense. But we just took the view that any kind of publicity was good publicity. The reaction was mad, totally over the top.'

White Trash, though, were perhaps on the right label at the wrong time. The Beatles idealistic dream for a company that would embody, in McCartney's words, a kind of Western communism, was fading along with the end of the sixties. Before the final embers were extinguished, however, White Trash hitched a ride on the Magical Mystery express, that included a drug-fuelled stop in Amsterdam when they ran out of money and had to rely on John Lennon to bail them out so they could get back to Blighty.

The band was due to sing 'Road to Nowhere' on the Dutch equivalent of *Top of the Pops*. Fraser takes up the story. 'We recorded the piece for the programme then they asked us if we fancied playing the Paradiso Club in Amsterdam, which was one of the big underground ballrooms. We had been due to go back to London that same day but we said we would do the show. I think we were paid 40 quid and an ounce of hash. In the end, I think we stayed for about five days and it was always a hassle getting paid. At the end up, when we totalled all our bills, we were £150 short. And the hotel wouldn't give us our passports back. So we phoned up Dutch EMI who promptly said it was nothing to do with them. They said we would need to speak to one of the Beatles to get an advance. We were really worried that we wouldn't get back home. We didn't have a penny between us. Luckily, John Lennon was staying at the Amsterdam Hilton. He had just got married and this was the first of the famous bed-ins.

'Richard Di Lello, myself and Ronnie Leahy and Clewsy trooped along to the Amsterdam Hilton. The place was full of journalists. We had to wait two hours before we could go up. We went up to see John and Yoko and brought them a couple of joints in an envelope and gave them to him with some brown rice. There was a guitar in the room and he occasionally mucked about a bit on it. But it was all very friendly. John was in great form and put everyone at their ease. But here we were in John Lennon's bedroom.

'It was on all the news bulletins and newspapers and we were for a short while right in the middle of it. You could hear the kids in the street shouting up to John. He was quite shy, he wasn't on an ego trip or anything. It was all very calm and mellow. We talked about music and what was happening in the world. He was just great. We were there for about an hour. They were there doing their thing for peace and had just got married so we talked a bit about the wedding and that. Anyway, we explained the situation and John said he would see what he could do. It was all sorted out in the end and Apple paid our bill. And we got paid enough cash to get back to Britain.

'It was a crazy time but it was also a magical time. We didn't make any money from it and there were times when we were literally starving. But I didn't have any regrets then and I don't now. The thing was we were a right good band.'

Fionna Duncan

Fionna Duncan watched in bemusement as the gaggle of teenage kids snaked round the outside of Liverpool's Cavern Club. As one of Scotland's foremost jazz singers, Fionna had become a regular at the venue as she and her band The Clyde Valley Footstompers criss-crossed the country night after night.

Despite the advent of skiffle and rock 'n' roll, jazz had kept its place in popular entertainment. Songs by Acker Bilk and Kenny Ball still sold in their thousands, the smooth tones of 'Stranger on the Shore' crackling out from radios and record players all over the country.

But right now, as she watched those kids queuing outside the Cavern, Fionna knew she was witnessing the turn of the tide, the moment when jazz finally handed the conductor's baton over to the new kids in the orchestra pit. In this case, the new kids were four local youngsters who called themselves The Beatles. And the hysteria they were creating was a shock to the former Rutherglen Academy pupil who went on to become one of Scotland's most stylish jazz singers. Looking back some 45 years,

Fionna readily admits she's forgotten more than she can remember about the times she shared a stage with what could be termed a pre-pubescent Fab Four.

'What I remember most is these funny looking wee boys all dressed in black. I thought it was a laugh. Imagine calling yourselves The Beatles. Did you not know that's not really a cool thing to call your band? And then the next thing they're all over the place so what did I know? I got it all wrong.'

Fionna and The Footstompers were more likely to be found at Liverpool's Mardi Gras, an upmarket club run by local entrepreneur Jim Ireland. Occasionally, though, the band fulfilled engagements at the Cavern. Fionna said: 'The Cavern was not a patch on the Mardi Gras. It was smelly and dank and you wouldn't take your mother there, let's put it like that. One night we noticed all these girls queuing up to get in. That in itself was unusual. You would queue to get into ballrooms but not jazz clubs or a club like The Cavern. These kids were just so young, right out of junior high. But they were lovely. I mean, I was 19 or 20 at the time and felt ancient compared to them. But this queue told us right away there was something different happening. I took one look at them and right away didn't think they were jazz fans. But they were great and very receptive to what we were doing.'

Fionna's instincts were right on the money. In between her own gigs, The Beatles had virtually set up camp at the Cavern, alternating between lunchtime and evening sessions. And the storm they whipped up was only a precursor of the mania that would grip the whole world within a few

OFF THE BEATLE TRACK 17 –
RANGERS BEFORE BEATLES? NOT ON YOUR TELLY

Glasgow schoolgirl Marian Orr once took on the mighty BBC after it scrapped plans to broadcast a Beatles TV special in favour of showing Rangers getting thumped 6-0 by Real Madrid in a European clash in October 1963. Marian, a pupil at Hillhead High School and daughter of the Reverend David Orr, minister of Govan Old Parish Church, was incensed at the decision to put football before the Fabs. She collected more than 3,000 signatures from disappointed Scottish Beatles fans and also enlisted support from politicians. She fired off her petition and was amazed when the Beeb backed down and promised to screen the show in Scotland. Marian told the *Daily Record*: 'The Beatles are more important than any old football match.'

short years. Fionna said: 'These four wee boys came on and I just stood at the side laughing. They were good fun but I didn't see them as the next big thing. They were just a band. But the place erupted into one outburst of screams. No one clapped. They screamed even then. And I just thought, oh no, I can't take this. I moved out because of the screams, not because of the band. It wasn't really my audience. The only other person anyone had screamed for like that was Frank Sinatra when you had the bobby-soxers.

'What I do remember is they were all smartly dressed. This was not long after Brian Epstein took over the management of The Beatles and smartened them up. And the other thing was that Ringo Starr was not in the band, it was Pete Best on drums. But you could just tell that something was in the wind, there was a change in the air. Looking back, The Beatles did change everything, especially for jazz groups. None of the bands went back to the Cavern once The Beatles got a foothold.'

Lonnie Donegan

Nineteen fifty-six was the year when two messiahs emerged from a barren musical landscape and converted teenagers John Lennon, Paul McCartney, George Harrison and Ringo Starr to a new religion – rock 'n' roll. One was a 21-year-old truck driver from Tupelo, Mississippi, whose sexual swagger and raucous singing style generated enough raw heat to power up a small town. The other was a wiry 25-year-old former squaddie from Mill Street in Bridgeton in Glasgow's East End, whose nondescript appearance and country-tinged vocals belied a gritty talent that would define British rock 'n' roll for the next five years.

Elvis Presley may have been God in the eyes of The Beatles but Lonnie Donegan was the man who spread the new gospel, a sort of John the Baptist figure paving the way for the emerging deity that would change music forever. History tells us that the opening seconds of 'Heartbreak Hotel' sent a shockwave through the first generation of post-war teenagers. Five months later, however, Lonnie's 'Rock Island Line' lifted the curtain on a new form of music; skiffle was DIY rock 'n' roll and it provided the trigger for the 'Savage Young Beatles' – and countless others – to pick up a guitar. The beauty of being in a skiffle band was that almost anyone could play the instruments – all you needed was a washboard, tea-chest bass and a guitar and you were away. For the 15-year-old Lennon, this was the sign he had waited for all his life. When he formed the Quarrymen it was from Lonnie Donegan that the band took their cue – not Elvis Presley.

'We all loved Elvis,' said Lennon. 'But songs like "Rock Island Line" were very influential. It made us realise that anyone could play in a band. Lonnie Donegan made a big contribution to my musical education. And when I got together with Paul and George, we discovered we were all big Lonnie fans so there was common ground to start with.' Indeed, Lennon, frustrated at not being able to pluck out chords on his first guitar, was on the verge of binning the instrument until he heard Lonnie plonking away on "Rock Island Line". And suddenly, realisation dawned that perseverance might eventually pay off with this type of music.

Lonnie was born Tony Donegan in 1931 into a musical family – his father was a classical violinist. Within two years, though, the family had decamped to London's East End as job opportunities in Glasgow dried up. He explained: 'It wasn't a good time for employment anywhere in Glasgow particularly and among musicians especially. No one's going to pay a classical violinist to give them a bit of Tchaikovsky when they don't have enough bread to eat. So he packed up his red-spotted handkerchief and hiked down to London. I was about two and a half at the time. I didn't return to Glasgow until I was eight. When the Blitz started in London, I was shipped back north. We lived in Duke Street in Dennistoun and I went to Whitehill School round the corner. When things calmed down I went back down to London where I remained.' Throughout his life, Lonnie spoke, not unnaturally, with a pronounced cockney lilt but he always regarded himself as a Scot. 'You can leave Glasgow but it never leaves you.'

Eventually the family relocated to Manchester, and Lonnie quit school at 14 to work as a clerk in a stockbroker's office before joining the army at 18, carrying out his National Service in Vienna. He had already shown an interest in music – against his father's wishes – and taken up the guitar. He became a huge fan of American folk and blues. When the young Donegan saw his hero American singer Josh White in concert his mind was made up. In 1950, he formed his own jazz combo, the Tony Donegan Jazz Band. At one of their earliest gigs, a tongue-tied MC confused him with the great American blues guitarist Lonnie Johnson and introduced him as Lonnie Donegan. The name stuck. Tony was dead . . . long live Lonnie.

Word quickly spread of his stage performance and his banjo-playing dexterity. Fellow jazzman Chris Barber suggested a partnership and a friendship was born that was to last the lifetimes of both men. Barber's band specialised in New Orleans 'trad' classics, but also included a splinter group that bashed away at 'skiffle' versions of American folk songs and blues during the intervals.

Lonnie's version of Leadbelly's 'Rock Island Line', a song about slavery in the Deep South, was so popular it soon found its way into the band's main set. In January, 1956, the song was released as a novelty single under Lonnie's own name and bucked record company expectations by becoming a huge hit on both sides of the Atlantic – the first time a UK musician had crashed the top ten at home and in America. 'Rock Island Line', with its pulsing rhythmic intensity and earthy simplicity, caused a sensation and sold more than a million copies. Lonnie was instantly crowned Britain's king of skiffle and millions of kids picked up a guitar in homage. The song earned him the equivalent of £3.30 but set him on his way.

Within weeks, he was guesting on *The Perry Como Show* in America – appearing in comedy sketches alongside Ronald Reagan – and earning $800 dollars a shot. All this happened almost at the same time as Elvis started preaching his own gospel.

Now ploughing his own musical furrow having split from Barber, Lonnie was free to make more of the music he loved. For the next five years, chart-topping songs like 'Cumberland Gap', 'Puttin' on the Style', 'Nobody's Child' and 'Love Is Strange' guaranteed him a permanent place in the pop firmament. He also set off on a gruelling 52-weeks-a-year touring schedule. Lonnie loved the stage and was a natural performer, a trait that endeared him even more to a rapidly-growing fan base.

When he played five nights at Liverpool Empire in 1956, among those clutching tickets were a 15-year-old Paul McCartney and an even younger George Harrison. Both boys lived near each other and found they spoke the same musical language – and Lonnie's records often provided the kind of common reference points that overcame the 17-month age gap. Paul and George were the only Beatles to have ever seen Lonnie live, but it seems reasonable to conclude that seeing their idol in concert helped point the way towards a musical future.

Lennon rarely went to live shows, preferring instead to concentrate on honing his own style, having now ditched his mother's banjo for a proper guitar as he attempted to whip The Quarrymen into a proper band. On 6 July 1957, The Quarrymen were booked to play two short sets at the summer fête of St Peter's Parish Church in Woolton. Among the songs Lennon reckoned were good enough for public consumption were Lonnie's 'Cumberland Gap' and 'Puttin' on the Style', proof of the reverence he had for the Scots singer. And so it was that John, then just 16 and having consumed a few illegal beers for Dutch courage, took to the makeshift stage on the back of a lorry and sang his heart out. Watching from the front was a chubby-faced, doe-eyed schoolboy from the Liverpool Institute on a day when all the stars seemed to line up in a magical constellation – the day that Paul met John.

Fellow Quarryman Colin Hanton believes Lennon's life may have veered in an entirely different direction had it not been for Lonnie. He said: 'John had tried taking lessons for the guitar but had packed it in because he decided it was going to take forever to play music properly. But then Lonnie Donegan came on the scene and said all you need is three chords and something you can bang – a rhythm section or whatever. So overnight everybody joined a skiffle group. They realised that you didn't have to be particularly musical or talented as long as you could keep a tune.'

Between 1955 and 1962, Lonnie racked up 30 songs in the top 30. But the ever-changing landscape of showbusiness is rarely kind to those who helped draw it in the first place. By 1963, The Beatles sat atop pop's throne and Lonnie had long become a victim of music's inevitable *coup d'état*. Skiffle was skewered by the rise of guitar-based bands like the Fab Four so, in a bitter irony, the king was killed by his courtiers. His last big hit was the whimsical 'Does Your Chewing Gum Lose Its Flavour (On the Bedpost Overnight)?', a comic song that pointed Lonnie in the direction of the cabaret circuit.

But Lonnie's career refused to die. He continued recording throughout the next four decades and toured constantly. And such is the cyclical nature of the music industry, his star rose again towards the end of his life when a new generation of pop stars, including Brian May and Mark Knopfler, realised the debt they all owed the wee man from Glasgow. In the early nineties, George Harrison acknowledged his IOU to Lonnie when he formed The Travelling Wilburys with Bob Dylan, Tom Petty, Roy Orbison and Jeff Lynne. The band only made two albums but running between the grooves of the mainly acoustic-based songs was the sound of skiffle, the simple music that had so fired each of the musicians when they started out on the long road to rock 'n' roll stardom.

'Lonnie was a much bigger influence on rock than he was ever given credit for. He was a big hero of mine,' said George. 'Lonnie and skiffle seemed made for me. It was easy to play if you knew two or three chords and you'd have a tea-chest and a washboard and you were away . . . "Oh the Rock Island Line is a mighty good road . . . "'

In 1997 Lonnie received an Ivor Novello lifetime award which was followed by an MBE in 2000. His devotion to life on the road affected his health, however, as a series of heart attacks took their toll and curtailed his tours. But, with a spirit that could easily have been forged in the furnaces of Beardmore's steel foundry just a mile from where he was born in Glasgow, Lonnie refused to hang up his guitar.

Eventually, though, that heart that had caused so much concern stopped pumping. Lonnie died on Sunday, 3 November 2002, halfway through a UK tour. It may sound clichéd but isn't that the way he would have wanted to go? He was 71 and his passing came just less than a year

ELEANOR RIGBY . . . IN BEARSDEN

Life for Eleanor Trickett was ticking along nicely when she wed her teenage sweetheart Alex in 1964 at the height of Beatlemania. The fact that her married name was now Rigby stirred not a ripple of interest – until two years later when The Beatles released their seventh album *Revolver*. And there, leaping out from between the grooves was Paul McCartney's masterful slice of social comment about a sad and lonely old spinster called, as the world now knows, Eleanor Rigby. Overnight, Eleanor went from anonymous new bride to a girl with one of the most famous names in the world.

However, unlike the Eleanor in Paul's song, Eleanor was never lonely and went on to raise a family of four in Bearsden near Glasgow while managing an estate agent's in the city's Byres Road. 'I always thought Eleanor Trickett was a terrible mouthful and I spent my entire youth wishing I could get rid of it,' she told Glasgow's *Evening Times*. 'I met my husband when we were both 14 and when we married I was glad to have his name.' Then her whole world was turned upside down when The Beatles released 'Eleanor Rigby' in August 1966 as a double-A-side single with 'Yellow Submarine' . . . and the search was on to find the real-life Eleanor.

When journalists turned up at her door, Eleanor was mortified. 'The papers hunted me non-stop. I was embarrassed.' Over time, though, Eleanor credits the song for helping her land good jobs and gaining new friends. Never a day goes by without a comment. It brings a smile to everyone's face. The usual question is, "Were your parents Beatles fans?" But it's a super name and in my line of business, it's terribly important. It's definitely helped my career. I've even had clients follow me when I've changed jobs simply because they remember the name.' Although she's a Beatles fan, she resisted the temptation to buy the song when it came out. Likewise, she never saddled any of her children – Karen, Carl, Sven and Alexis – with any Beatle-connected name. But that didn't stop them from being the butt of jokes. 'As soon as the girls said their name was Rigby, back would come the question, "And what's your first name, Eleanor?" They would say, "No, that's my mum." '

For the record, the origins of McCartney's 'Eleanor Rigby' contain a surreal twist. The author himself claims the name was not based on any real person, although the actress Eleanor Bron, who starred with The Beatles in their second film *Help!*, may have subconsciously been on his mind. But, amazingly, a headstone bearing the name Eleanor Rigby was later discovered in a Liverpool cemetery near where Paul played as a child. Incidentally, the song's central character was initially called Daisy Hawkins before it was changed.

after George Harrison had joined Elvis and John in rock's Valhalla.

Paul McCartney paid him this tribute: 'When we were kids in Liverpool in the late fifties, we loved rock 'n' roll and we loved American artists, but the man who really started the craze for guitars as far as I'm concerned was Lonnie Donegan. Lonnie was the first person we heard of from England to get the coveted number one on the charts with Rock Island Line and we studied his records avidly and even did a few of his numbers. We all bought guitars to be in a skiffle group and it was this craze that swept the country. Lonnie's great vocal style was, and still is, highly original, and his love of the blues and early folk music is something we all could relate to very easily. So for those of us there, in those early days, he was the man. In later years, I grew to know him as a friend and was not in any way let down. He was a great guy with a true love of good music and many of us owe him a huge debt of gratitude.'

Ivor Cutler

The story of The Beatles includes a multi-layered supporting cast of childhood friends, family, musicians, actors, businessmen and a whole host of other acquaintances who left their mark on the band. Undoubtedly, though, Scottish humorist Ivor Cutler was the most unlikely addition to The Beatles' entourage. From the outside looking in, they were at opposite ends of the showbusiness spectrum. The world according to Cutler was a surreal playground of absurd misadventure. One critic dubbed the Glasgow-born comedian, poet, actor, painter and songwriter as grit in the oyster of respectability, a stupid genius who revelled in his eccentric image.

The Beatles seemed light years away from Planet Cutler, a place inhabited mainly by weedy undergraduates and fully paid-up members of the sixties underground movement. Closer inspection, however, reveals the Fab Four and Ivor Cutler had more in common than one might expect. John Lennon, Paul McCartney and George Harrison especially shared Cutler's love of all things silly. Lennon's two books *A Spaniard in the Works* and *In His Own Write* were both heavily influenced by the nonsense prose of the Goons, Lewis Carroll . . . and Ivor Cutler.

In 1967, the worlds of Ivor Cutler and The Beatles collided in a supernova of psychedelic silliness and hippy self-indulgence. Wrapped up in the free-spirited hedonism of the summer of love, McCartney's head was bursting with ideas. *Sgt. Pepper's Lonely Hearts Club Band* was already in the can and now Paul was hatching plans for The Beatles' third film. The idea behind *Magical Mystery Tour* was not exactly set in concrete: hire a

Paul McCartney and Scots humorist Ivor Cutler take a break from filming the band's third screen outing, *The Magical Mystery Tour*.

bus, spray it in Day-Glo colours, get a load of C-list actors, and a make-it-up-as-you-go script, hit the road – and film the whole damn thing.

As loose as the idea seemed, McCartney, in his own mind at least, was metaphorically driving the bus. One night as he watched TV at his home in St John's Wood in London, he saw Ivor Cutler performing a sketch on a late-night BBC show. His appearance triggered a lost memory of Cutler's more eccentric musical recordings, and gave birth to an idea for the Scottish comic to hop aboard the *Magical Mystery Tour*. Not one to waste time when the lightning bolt of inspiration strikes, McCartney got hold of Cutler's number from the actors' directory *Spotlight* and instantly called him up.

Later Paul recalled the circumstances surrounding his first face-to-face encounter with comedy's most bizarre figure. 'I saw him on the telly and was amused and impressed by his laconic sense of humour and by his Scottish wit . . . So I called him up and went, "Hello Mr Cutler, this is Paul McCartney." And he said, "Oh yes," in that gentle Scottish accent. "I'd like to invite you out to dinner." So he accepted the invitation, we went out to dinner and we had a lovely evening. He's a very precise spoken Scottish fella, very quiet but real entertaining, real nice bloke. Very sensitive. I'd seen him on the telly with his very dour Scottish accent that I liked very much. And he used to play this little Indian hand harmonium. He had a song I liked called "I'm Going in a Field", just a lovely little song. I used to want to record that with him.'

So it was that Ivor Cutler was cast as the tour bus guide Buster Bloodvessel. The wee man in his NHS specs and ill-fitting conductor's tunic arguably stole the show from the four pop stars. Suddenly, playing against type, he was a leading man. Up to then, Cutler had been a regular blot on the fledgling British TV landscape. Mainly, he popped up on shows like *The Acker Bilk Show* and *Late Night Line-Up*. But his appearance in a Beatles film shoved him a good few rungs up the ladder of fame, a celebrity he neither wanted nor felt comfortable with.

It was all a long way from Cutler's roots in Glasgow's Gorbals and Ibrox. His Jewish parents and grandparents came to the UK at the end of the 19th century in the wake of pogroms in Eastern Europe. They thought their ship was bound for America only for them to go up deck to disembark and gaze out on . . . Govan. However, the family stayed and Ivor was born a yardarm's distance away and only 100 yards from Ibrox Park, leading to the myth that his first scream coincided with the roar from the crowd as a goal was scored.

An occasionally troubled childhood followed, and he may have suffered at the hands of anti-Semitic teachers. His deeply-held socialist views were formed at an early age after seeing kids hobble into school wearing little more than ragged socks as shoes. Leaving school at 15, he took a job as an apprentice fitter at Rolls Royce before entering the RAF where he trained as a navigator. But he was not cut out for a career with the flying squad, his dreamy take on the absurdity of life and death incompatible with the seriousness of the job in hand. Ivor enrolled at Glasgow School of Art and also studied to become a schoolteacher, a job that seemed in sympathy with his growing love of prose, poetry and music. And it was teaching, he claimed, that unlocked his creativity and convinced him to hawk his nonsense songs round Tin Pan Alley.

Eventually, a promoter liked what he heard and introduced Cutler to the comedy producer Ned Sherrin. Sherrin was amused by Cutler's surreal folk music and booked him to appear on BBC television. Later in life, Cutler almost always veered away from the path of commercial respectability. He was happiest treading the boards with his one-man show at the likes of the Edinburgh Festival, the ideal platform for his zany take on life. But when Paul McCartney called that summer night in 1967, he risked his hard-earned reputation as the darling of the campuses. Typically blunt, he was unfazed by McCartney's fame and The Beatles' stardom. Nevertheless, at the age of 43, Ivor Cutler signed up for the *Magical Mystery Tour*.

During their conversation over dinner, as McCartney sketched out the idea swirling inside his head, Cutler even had the audacity to come up with the name for his own character. McCartney said: 'So in the film he became Buster Bloodvessel and he was very good and very helpful. His romantic interest was Ringo's Aunt Jessie, the fat woman played by Jessie Robbins and we got him on the sand where he drew a big heart round her. We'd say that's nice and it would be part of the sequence.'

Curiously, Cutler's big romantic scene was at the heart of a heated dispute between The Beatles and the BBC who had bought the rights to show *Magical Mystery Tour* on Christmas Day, 1967. Paul Fox, the head of the BBC department with whom McCartney was negotiating, took offence at the sight of Cutler and Jessie having a seaside smooch. Indeed, it would be another 22 years before Britain's TV audiences were apparently able to handle the sight of two middle-aged people kissing when the scene was reinstated for a 1979 TV screening.

Cutler never cashed in on his brush with Beatles fame. He hated the notion that people only wanted to talk to him because he had been in a Fab Four film. Any mention of *Magical Mystery Tour* in interviews normally received a scant or scabrid response, although Cutler could, from time to time, be mischievous in his recollections. He once said: 'Between scenes, I was surreptitiously filmed as I sat in Raymond's Revue Bar watching a stripper, wiping my spectacles on the dirty raincoat they had given me. My hand was moving at abdominal level. It looked . . . questionable.'

His long-time agent and friend Martin Pople said: 'He obviously really enjoyed it at the time . . . Lennon and he were kindred spirits, McCartney not so much. Yet Ivor did say that of the songs he was performing at the time he could detect his influence on Paul McCartney. And I think if you wanted to you could delve deep into Lennon's stuff and see Ivor's influence there.'

Indeed you could. Listen to 'Strawberry Fields' and 'I Am the Walrus' and it's impossible not to detect a surreal vein running through it, the likes of which bore some of the hallmarks of Ivor Cutler.

Ivor Cutler died in London on 3 March 2006, at the age of 83. Even in the twilight of his days, he continued to see the world through a fish-eye lens and never embraced convention. As is the cyclical way of things, he was enjoying a new level of appreciation from the uber-generation of bands such as Franz Ferdinand and Orbital when he finally shuffled off the stage. Cutler also allied himself with that quirky bastion of eccentricity, the Noise Abatement Society and, in a typical absurdity, always spoke loudly on its behalf. On being told, following major heart surgery in the late 1990s that he did not have long to live, he said: 'When I do die I shall be glad to get away from loud pop music and motor cars, but I shall miss, insofar as when one is dead one can miss anything, the beautiful kindnesses of those people to whom courtesy comes naturally.'

Gordon Smith

The words were out before Gordon Smith had a chance to stuff them back in his mouth. 'I play one of your songs on guitar.' The claim, stated quite matter-of-factly, was either an act of astonishing bravado or sheer brass neck. For the song in question was 'Blackbird', Paul McCartney's hauntingly beautiful acoustic ballad from The Beatles' 'White Album'. And the man sitting directly across from the former Rangers footballer was the same Paul McCartney whose famous Bambi eyes were suddenly wide with interest.

'You can play "Blackbird"? McCartney's tone betrayed more than a little surprise. Acting on instinct, the former Beatle stood up and left the room only to return seconds later with an acoustic guitar. And then, right in front of Gordon's eyes, he ran through the whole finger-picking song, chord perfect and in perfect tune. Then, as the last chord died away, he looked at Gordon and said: 'Is that how you play it?'

McCartney was having a laugh but it was a moment that will live with Gordon Smith until his dying breath. 'It was one of the most fantastic moments of my life, very special,' said Gordon, who, in 2007, was appointed chief executive of the Scottish Football Association. 'The truth is that when he stood up and went out of the room and came back with the guitar I nearly died because I knew he would ask me to play it. Luckily for me, though, Paul plays left-handed and I play right-handed so that was my great escape, really. I can actually play it, but it's one thing strumming away at home to sitting across the room from Paul McCartney. It was just so surreal to be sitting there with one of The Beatles, my favourite band of all time, and he's singing one of his most famous songs. Not bad for a boy from a council house in Stevenston.'

It was the culmination of an unlikely friendship that had begun two years earlier when Gordon was still part of a highly successful Rangers side. In December, 1979, Gordon, his wife Marlene, sister Elaine and younger brother Billy were among a sell-out crowd who packed the Glasgow Apollo to see Wings, the band that had helped McCartney rise Phoenix-like from the ashes of the Beatles split. In Glasgow, even rock legends can often take second place to footballers and Gordon, as a high-profile Old Firm player, could not escape recognition. When someone asked him for an autograph, he was happy to oblige. As he handed back the piece of paper, Gordon's admirer asked him how big a fan he was of McCartney and then added: 'Would you like to meet him after the show?'

It was the kind of showy remark top footballers are used to. But, as Gordon recalled: 'It turned out he was the Apollo's head of security so he was actually for real. He told us to come round to the side door after the concert and he would get us in. To be honest, I still thought he was at it but we decided to go to the side door anyway. There were quite a few people milling around hoping to get a glimpse of Paul. We hung around for 20 minutes or so in the freezing cold. We were just about to call it quits when then door burst open and this guy said: "Who's Gordon Smith? You've to come in and meet Paul McCartney."' All around Gordon was the sight of necks turning in unison to see who had gained this special patronage. As he and Marlene stepped forward, though, a hand stretched out to underline this was an invitation for one person only. But Gordon's wife, heavily pregnant, was having none of that and said: 'If he goes, I go.' That left just Gordon's brother Billy, as big a McCartney fan as Gordon, to stamp his feet in frustration at being left on the outside looking in as his football star sibling schmoozed with a Beatle.

The couple climbed the stairs aware of the chatter coming from the top of the steps. Naturally nervous, they had no idea what to expect. But there was little time for anxiety to take a firm grip – waiting for them at the top were Paul and Linda McCartney, their hands already stretched out in welcome. Conversation quickly turned to that night's show and the Smiths

AND YOUR BIRD *CAN'T* SING

Glasgow band The Beatcombers found themselves on the receiving end of an amazing legal threat from their heroes after a joke about an unreleased Beatles song backfired. The Beatcombers had built up an outstanding reputation as Scotland's premier beat band. They were all huge fans of the Fabs but stopped short of being seen as a tribute band. In the early nineties, it emerged that The Beatles were planning an *Anthology* that would see McCartney, Harrison and Starr adding their chops to two – perhaps three – John Lennon demo recordings to produce the first 'new' Beatle songs for 35 years. The songs were 'Free as a Bird' and 'Real Love', two Lennon tracks that had only been available on bootlegs.

Like millions of excited fans, George Burton, guitarist with The Beatcombers, was gripped by the news: 'I wasn't so interested in "Real Love" because it had already appeared on the soundtrack to the *Imagine* film. But I hadn't heard "Free as a Bird" so my nose was bothering me. I came across the song on a bootleg and one afternoon I was in the studio and sitting at a piano trying to find the chords to "Free as a Bird". Eventually I got it and I thought, you know, that's not actually half bad. The only problem was there were certain parts of the song missing. So we just made them up. We played around with it in the studio and I was surprised at how well it started to work.' In an interview with Fraser Middleton in the Glasgow *Evening Times* to promote their new album, *Eight Arms to Hold You*, George laughingly tossed in a line about 'Free as a Bird'. George recalled: 'I jokingly said we're thinking of putting out The Beatles' *next* single, "Free As A Bird". I didn't think he would put it in anywhere, it just appeared at the foot of his column. But the way it was written it looked like we were trying to pull a fast one on The Beatles.'

But the ripples from George's cheeky comment soon spread right to the heart of The Beatles' inner circle. One morning two weeks later he was still teasing the sleep from his eyes as he opened an official-looking letter at the breakfast table. 'The letter was from a high-powered law firm representing The Beatles and Yoko Ono seeking the destruction of master tapes of The Beatcombers' version of "Free as A Bird", tapes which simply didn't exist. My first reaction was: eh? I couldn't believe it. Anyway I phoned them and said, "Look I think you've got the wrong end of the stick here." We said we've got no intention of releasing 'Free as a Bird', we're very sorry for the misunderstanding" blah blah blah. And that seemed to do the job and they backed right off. But it was a scary moment.'

were not slow in voicing their admiration for the band's efforts. Gordon said: 'We just said how much we'd loved the concert, it was really fantastic. I had seen Wings before, in 1974, but this show was tremendous. They had the pipers there for "Mull of Kintyre" and it was fantastic. He was great to talk to, very down to earth. I kept looking round and seeing all these famous people like Billy Connolly. We had been talking for a few minutes and then I thought he's probably got lots of people to see. So I just said, "Well, it's been great to talk to you, we'll leave you to talk to others." But he sort of said, "What's the rush? Why do you need to go? I know what you mean but I'm enjoying the chat." Then he started talking about football and playing for Rangers. He's actually a big football fan, especially coming from a city like Liverpool but he had never been to a game in Scotland.'

Gordon had good reason to think all his Christmases had come at once. Then he suddenly remembered Billy would be freezing his socks off outside. 'I just mentioned to Paul that my brother would be really disappointed at missing out on the chance to see him. Paul then asked where he was and I said he's standing outside. He then shouted to the same security guy who brought me up to go and get Billy and bring him in. When Billy came up, he was pretty speechless when he saw Marlene and I talking to Paul and Linda. The first thing Paul did was say to him, "So you didn't want to meet me?" The look on Billy's face was priceless.'

Minutes later, the McCartneys did have to break away to circulate round the other guests. Goodbyes were exchanged with a vague promise from Paul saying he's love to check out a game Gordon was playing in. Realistically, though, both men probably reckoned the chances of their paths crossing again were unlikely. Fate, however, had other ideas.

The following summer, Gordon swapped Ibrox for Brighton and found himself playing for a team only a long goal kick away from the McCartney's sprawling farmhouse home in the East Sussex village of Peasmarsh. Hoping to return the hospitality he had received several months earlier, Gordon invited Paul and Linda to be his guest when Liverpool would provide the opposition for his new club. He received a letter back from Paul saying he would love to come, commitments allowing. But as the weeks and months passed, Gordon heard nothing more. He was just beginning to regard his time with Paul as one of those fleeting celebrity moments when, out of the blue, an invitation arrived for him and Marlene to attend a VIP opening night in London for an exhibition of Linda's pictures.

'The two of us rolled up not quite sure what to expect really,' recalled Gordon. 'I didn't think he would remember me. There were quite a few celebrities there such as Billy Connolly – he seemed to be everywhere – and the pop group Bananarama. We bought a copy of Linda's book and we could see her and Paul doing the rounds of everyone in the room. We kind of held back for a long while and then I went up and asked her if she would sign the book for us. She looked at me and said, "Hi there, how are you getting on?" I thought she was just being polite and wouldn't remember us. Then she tapped Paul on the shoulder and said, "Look who's here." She was a very warm person, no airs and graces. Paul asked me all about playing for Brighton and apologised for not being able to see a game.'

Gordon was desperate to get a picture of all four together, but the event's official photographer kept drifting out of sight when the right moment arrived. Eventually, the night drew to a close with Gordon resigned to missing out on a celluloid keepsake of his Beatle buddy. As they said their farewells at the door, Linda remarked: 'You didn't get a picture. Why don't you come and visit us instead?' The jaw-dropping invite could easily have come from a neighbour or long-term friend and not from a member of rock's ruling aristocracy. Nothing definite was arranged but Gordon was convinced in himself that the offer was genuine.

So, several weeks later, he decided to give spontaneity a chance. He and Marlene – as well as three-year-old son Grant and baby daughter Leigh-Anne – set off on a Sunday afternoon in the direction of Peasmarsh to take up Paul and Linda's invitation. After several wrong-turns, they found themselves driving down a narrow country lane. Ahead of them walked a woman with three children and her dogs. 'I recognised Linda right away and that's when I really started to get nervous. I mean we were really just turning up unannounced to see Paul McCartney. I wound down the window and said hi and she just laughed and said, "How are you getting on?" I said we were just out for a drive and we were passing by. She said, "No problem, come on in. We invited you."'

Gordon recalled being stunned by the McCartneys' living arrangements. He may have been one of the richest men in the world but his home and lifestyle were far removed from what you might call typical rock star ostentation. Marlene helped Linda prepare a light lunch while Gordon and Paul picked up where they had left off several months earlier. In the corner, a TV flickered and the highlights of Saturday's game came on, a cue for the conversation to turn to football.

Gordon said: 'The funny thing about Paul was that he was thrilled I knew Kenny Dalglish, obviously because of the Liverpool connection. And I said I know him well and Paul said what's he like, as if he could be just as star-struck as anyone else. It was amazing to think that here was one of the Beatles asking me about someone else. And believe it or not Linda came through at that point with my wife and she said, "Do you know who I really like . . . Gordon McQueen." Linda was a big fan of Gordon, who at that point was playing for Manchester United and I said, "I know Gordon as well." So that was a funny moment.'

This visit, of course, eventually provided the backdrop for Paul's spellbinding rendition of 'Blackbird', a lasting memory of a special few hours. Such, of course, is the nature of lifestyles like McCartney's that it was the last time the two men met.

'The thing that impressed me most was how open he was. We called in on pure chance, it was a bit of bravado on my part to do that, I must be honest. But he and Linda were so down to earth. I was really pleased about that. If you're lucky enough to meet one of your heroes, there's always the chance you might be disappointed, but not on this occasion. To meet someone who is that well known who turned out to be that nice is rare. It was a fantastic thing.

'He was chatting about John Lennon being killed and his own security. He said to me, "I don't have any security but I let people think I do." At the time he was going on the train to places from Hastings to London, with people looking at him and saying, no, it can't be. His kids went to a normal school. But here's something that says it all really. On the night we went to Linda's picture exhibition, one of the last things he said to me was, "How's your brother, Billy isn't it?" My brother couldn't believe that. That's a special quality but then he's a special man. I can't think of anyone who would be able to do that. I haven't seen him since we visited him that day but I know if I did we would just pick up where we left off.'

Jackie Stewart

Sir Jackie Stewart sat by the edge of the open-air swimming pool with his 12-year-old son Paul at their home on the banks of Lake Geneva in Switzerland, their legs dangling in the water. His wife Helen had prepared some lunch for the Scottish Formula One legend's family and their guest, a serene and sinewy figure whose dark hair tumbled over his shoulders, to eat al fresco. All around them, the sounds of their favourite music wafted gently into the warm night sky, floating away on the breeze towards the Swiss Alps. The tunes were all Beatle songs, tunes that in the sixties had formed the soundtrack to so many people's lives, including Jackie's: 'Here Comes The Sun', 'Something', 'While My Guitar Gently Weeps', 'Hey Jude', 'In My Life'.

The only difference this time was that the songs weren't coming from a stereo or radio. Instead they were being strummed on an acoustic guitar by the long-haired man sitting opposite, a man who knew these songs intimately, especially since, for the most part, they bore his signature. And

George Harrison and
Sir Jackie Stewart at
Silverstone race track
during the mid 1970s.

at this point Jackie Stewart felt like all his birthdays had arrived at once as he watched his close friend George Harrison let his fingers find old familiar chords and sing those famous songs.

For Jackie and Helen it was a genuinely magical moment. Here was a real Beatle singing Fab Four songs for them in the most intimate and relaxed of circumstances, unplugged and unadorned by studio production. In fact, most of them had never been heard sung by any of The Beatles outside the confines of Abbey Road. It remains Sir Jackie's most cherished memory of a friendship which began in the gravel pits of the 1969 Monaco Grand Prix and ended tragically too soon.

Sir Jackie recalled: 'We shared many wonderful times. On this occasion, when he was staying with us in Switzerland, we decided to go and watch the French Grand Prix in Dijon. It was not far so we drove there and back on the same day and it was a fantastically clear and warm evening when we arrived home. Helen had prepared a barbecue and Paul, who was 12 at the time, brought out his guitar. George seemed so completely at ease and he just started to play, running through all the great Beatles hits, singing parts of the songs and explaining what the lyrics meant to various members of the band. I remember sitting there thinking this had to be one of the greatest privileges anybody could have, to enjoy such a perfect evening at home with such a remarkable man.'

At first glance, George and Jackie would appear polar opposites. George, having forever purged Beatlemania from his nervous system, was easy-going and spiritually aware. He had a dry Liverpool humour and was at one with his place in the universe. Sir Jackie was a ball of nervous energy, always on the go, defiantly Scottish and driven by a burning ambition to succeed at anything he touched. Both men came from similar working-class backgrounds. Sir Jackie, three years George's senior, was brought up among the heavy industry and distilleries that peppered Dumbarton on the banks of the Clyde. George was raised in Speke, a tough Liverpool suburb best known as the location of the Bryant and May match factory and the Triumph motor hub, both of which provided the area with much-needed employment.

Neither was academic. Sir Jackie's dyslexia stymied any hopes of advancement at Dumbarton Academy, while life at Liverpool Institute held little interest for the young George. Between them, they left school with barely any qualifications to their names. In time, though, both men would go on to graduate with flying colours from the school of life. Sir Jackie would, of course, become a three-time winner of the Formula One world championship between 1969 and 1973 and carve out a lucrative post-racing career as one of Scotland's greatest business and cultural ambassadors. And George's exploits in the world of music, not to mention

his stewardship of Handmade Films and advocacy of Eastern philosophy, guarantee him a permanent place in the pantheon of the world's most influential individuals.

When he spoke to me, Sir Jackie acknowledged the amazing journey both men had been on: 'George was one of the most influential people in my life. We went racing together and I listened to his music endlessly. I don't know if George always was but he definitely developed into a real thinking man. We were very much opposites. He discovered some of that in India. Some of that through religion, some of that through his life. He was a great friend to have, a very loyal friend. He was just a good man, a real gentle man.

'He was a fantastic thinker. He had one of the best minds of anybody I have ever met. He had his own beliefs but as he got older he wasn't someone who couldn't get on with anyone who didn't share that opinion. That was one of the nice things about George. Here was I living a whole different lifestyle than George, a different pace. As time passed we became close, which seemed to confirm the old saying that opposites attract. While I liked to organise my life with military precision, George took a more laid-back approach.

'We never saw each other as often as we should have done. But it never made any difference because our friendship was deep enough that you didn't need that constant communication. We would always just pick up where we left off.

'The thing that most impressed me about him was he was very sincere. He wasn't a bullshitter. George told it like it was. He was very straight. He didn't like people who were fakes. If he said he was going to do something he would do it.'

Jackie and George first met in the playboy principality of Monaco during the Grand Prix in the spring of 1969. Unhappily for Harrison, it was not long after the acrimonious *Let It Be* sessions. Just a week earlier, George, John Lennon and Ringo Starr had signed a management deal with New York accountant/hustler Allan Klein. Paul McCartney remained bitterly opposed to the deal – and was left on the outside looking in. With the band in limbo, George would understandably have been happy to leave behind The Beatles' winter of discontent.

He had always been a keen racing fan. As a youngster, he used to enjoy going to Aintree bike meetings. And when The Beatles hit paydirt, George splashed his cash on the fastest cars the law would allow, the familiar trappings of the hip sixties pop star. So when he wandered the pit lanes of Monaco, he felt right at home among the car technicians, the growling carburettors and, most of all, the drivers. Over the next 20 years, the motor-mad Beatle became a familiar face on the Grand Prix circuit, often flying out to places like Brazil, Australia and Canada to watch the likes of Sir Jackie, Jody Scheckter, Niki Lauda, Emerson Fittipaldi, Ronnie Peterson, Ayrton Senna and Damon Hill burn up the track and mingle in the VIP enclosures.

Over time, his friendship with Sir Jackie grew into a two-way street of enduring affection. So much so that when his career slipped into a creative funk in the mid seventies, George credited Sir Jackie with renewing his confidence and inspiring him to return to the studio. The result was 1979's eponymously-titled *George Harrison* album which contained a song called 'Faster', written as a heartfelt tribute to the Grand Prix specialists he admired so much. The inside sleeve showed the two men strolling in the paddock at the British Grand Prix. When he came to film a video for the song, Sir Jackie pulled off a masterstroke by suggesting he act as George's chauffeur as they hurtled round Silverstone in a Daimler.

'He was never a great driver, although he loved fast cars,' said Sir Jackie. 'He adored the sport. If I went to concerts with him, he could come to races with me. I used to take great joy to begin with in getting him the right credentials. I could take him to places that other people couldn't take him. I knew which corners were best to watch the race from. When he told me he was doing a video it was my idea to be the chauffeur, wearing a white helmet with a tartan band in the same style as my old racing helmet. George loved it and saw the humour in it right away. He had a fantastic sense of humour. I drove the Daimler while, on the other side of a glass partition, George sat in the back, strumming on his guitar and singing the song.'

Sir Jackie and his family were often invited to stay at the Harrison's sprawling Gothic pile, Friar Park, at Henley-on-Thames. There they saw at first hand how he worked on his songs in his custom-built studio. 'It was unbelievable to see him at work running through numbers. He would work and work on a song until it was totally as he wanted it to be – so precisely right that it would almost sound as if it had evolved effortlessly.'

Cruel fate, though, was to intervene and bring their friendship to a premature and tragic end. The cancer first diagnosed in George's throat in 1998 quickly spread to other parts of his body. It's an illness that had already cast its shadow over Sir Jackie's own family so he was only too well aware of its destructive properties. When his son Paul was struck down by cancer, Sir Jackie entrusted his health to the world-famous Mayo Clinic in the United States and he told me how he tried to encourage George to go down the same path earlier than he eventually did.

Sir Jackie was in Scotland when he learned that George had finally passed away. 'I last saw him about a month before he died. He wasn't well

but in the end he certainly died at peace. I was in Gleneagles when I heard the news. Helen and I were getting ready for the day when there was a newsflash on the television. Paul came into the room a few minutes later. We had known he was seriously ill and feared the worst, but the news was still a shock. We stood arm in arm in tears. It was such a sad loss. I had taken him to the Mayo Clinic to try to get him the latest treatment but it was too late. Had we got him there earlier, I believe he would have lasted longer.'

Six months after George's death, Sir Jackie, his wife Helen and sons Paul and Mark were among a very select group of friends who attended a private memorial service in a sunken part of Friar Park, surrounded by the plants and flowers tended so lovingly by the Beatle, who was a dedicated gardener. 'It was a beautiful day,' recalled Sir Jackie. 'Very spiritual, just the way he would have wanted.'

It's impossible to sum up in a few words the bond that clearly existed between the Scotsman and the Scouser who, between them, remain giants in their own worlds. But for Jackie Stewart, Harrison's humility was an insight into how to handle celebrity. 'For me George was a true friend who opened my eyes to so much that I would otherwise not have seen and who in his calm, gentle way, gave me a new perspective on living and dying.'

Gordon Waller

In the sixties, to be a part of the pop scene was to belong to a musical chain gang; everyone famous had a link to someone just as famous. It was like being part of an exclusive club where one introduction opened the door to another level on a staircase that ultimately led to the penthouse suite. But you needed special patronage to get through that last, privileged door.

Gordon Waller was luckier than most. His 'access all areas' came through the musical partnership and personal relationship he had forged with Peter Asher, whose actress sister Jane was the darling of London's society hotspots. She was also the beautiful girlfriend of Beatle Paul McCartney, a couple whose youthful celebrity symbolised the swinging sixties.

When Paul and Jane first hooked up, Peter and Gordon, who was born in Braemar, were happy playing their folk-tinged soft-harmony songs in London coffee bars and pubs. But the onset of Beatlemania in late 1963 tore down all the old conventions and nudged open the door of opportunity – especially for anyone who could boast of being in the Beatle orbit. The two boys had met at Westminster School after discovering a shared love of music. Peter, shy and bespectacled, was a big jazz and folk fan, his

Gordon Waller and pal Peter Asher reaped the benefits of being part of Paul McCartney's social orbit.

interests ranging from Charlie Parker to Woody Guthrie; Gordon, more extrovert than his school pal, championed rock 'n' roll. So they met in the middle, finding common ground in the soft harmony vocals of the Everly Brothers and the songs of Buddy Holly.

At the first wave of Beatlemania, record companies scoured the country for young talent. It was during their regular gig at the Pickwick Club that an A&R man for EMI Records approached them about making a demo.

By now, McCartney had moved into the top room at the Ashers' luxury house in London's fashionable Wimpole Street, which acted as a sanctuary from the incessant pursuit of Beatle fans. Unlikely as it seems, the working-class youngster from Liverpool and the public schoolboy from London quickly found they actually liked each other. Music was the common language between Paul and Peter so it was natural for Gordon Waller to be drawn into the rarefied atmosphere and be on friendly terms with a Beatle. The circles the affable big Scot was now mixing in could not have been more removed from his childhood growing up on Royal Deeside.

One night, McCartney casually mentioned he had a song they might like to have a shot at. Gordon said: 'We'd known them for a while and we were playing in this club in London and they used to come in quite a bit. And we used to talk to them a lot. We had got this recording contract with EMI which was the same record company they were with and we were talking to them about songs to record and also about the fact that our recording manager didn't think any of the songs we did were very good, or not good enough for an A-side single. And Paul just mentioned that he had a song he thought would work well for us.'

'A World Without Love' had been written by Paul at the age of 16 in his home at Forthlin Road, Liverpool, not long, in fact, after he had first met John Lennon. It was far from a classic but, by then, all a record needed was a sprinkling of Fab Four fairy dust to give it a hefty shunt up the charts. It suited Peter and Gordon perfectly. First, though, McCartney felt he had to tweak the words – but he still couldn't work on the opening line without causing Lennon to crack up with laughter. 'Please lock me away . . .' was the cue for the caustic Beatle to dissolve into mirth.

'A World Without Love' was released in August, 1964, as a Lennon-McCartney original and Peter and Gordon's debut single. It reached the top of the charts on both sides of the Atlantic, a feat that made Gordon Waller a key part of the British pop armada that, led by The Beatles, invaded America. In Britain, the song knocked 'Can't Buy Me Love' off the number one spot and became known as one of the best songs The Beatles gave away. In America, Peter and Gordon found themselves mobbed by screaming teenagers when they performed in concert or in TV studios, a fortuitous by-product of British Beatlemania.

Neither Peter nor Gordon fitted the image of would-be pop stars but the six-foot Scottish youngster, with his brown hair combed forward in a Fab fringe, looked the part more than his studious-looking sidekick. Over the next three to four years, the pair enjoyed fair to moderate success, piggybacking on their Beatle sponsor. McCartney would write two more songs for Peter and Gordon. One of them – 'Woman' – was written under the cloak of anonymity, being credited to Harry Webb rather than Lennon-McCartney. It still crept into the lower reaches of the charts.

When Beatlemania gave way to psychedelic rock, Peter and Gordon's homespun image faded and eventually unravelled, and they went their separate ways in 1968. Their music, though, has guaranteed them a place in the pantheon of sixties pop stars. Gordon eventually moved to America where he maintained a career that alternated between music and occasional bouts of acting. Peter Asher went to work for The Beatles' newly-formed Apple record company and also went on to build a highly successful career as a producer for top stars like James Taylor and Linda Ronstadt.

For Gordon the halcyon days of Beatledom seem like a lifetime ago. Still, however, there are moments that stand out. Gordon was present when Lennon and McCartney were piecing together the chord arrangements for the song that eventually became 'I Want to Hold Your Hand'. He said: 'As far as I can remember, John was on a pedal organ and Paul was on piano. The basement in Peter's house was the place where we all went to make our "noise" and they called us down to let us hear this song they'd just written. It wasn't totally complete but the structure and the chorus were there. It sounded great even in that early form.'

The Peter and Gordon story didn't actually end when the pair split. A wave of nostalgia for sixties groups gathered momentum at the turn of the century and Peter and Gordon received several offers to reunite, mainly for Beatle conventions. And in 2005, they covered a distance of several thousand miles and some 38 years by playing in, of all places, the Philippines. Among those delighted at Peter and Gordon's reunion was none other than the man whose song had sent their career skyward all those years ago. Paul McCartney considered himself enough of a fan to wish them both well, perhaps remembering those carefree days in the Asher household when making music seemed the most innocent and productive of pastimes.

Macca's whimsical tribute read: 'What the world needs is Peter and Gordon to sing their songs and remind us all of the fab years they are from. I'm very glad to hear they have got together after these many moons and we are going to help to make a world without love into a love-filled planet.'

Hippy-dippy, maybe, but heartfelt all the same for the boy from Braemar who for a while was part of the big Beatle bubble.

Gallagher and Lyle

Benny Gallagher can still clearly remember the day he reckoned he and pal Graham Lyle finally joined the elite songwriting fraternity. Realisation dawned not in the shape of a big fat royalty cheque but in the shape of a big fat chocolate cake. The clue, though, lay not in the unexpected confectionery but in the fact that the sender was Paul McCartney. The gift was a token of appreciation to the two Scottish musicians on having written a song that was admired by a man who knew a good tune when he heard one.

The song was called 'Sparrow', not perhaps an effort that Scotland's best songwriting team will be mainly remembered for, but still one that signalled their arrival into a bigger league. 'Sparrow' was on the flip side of Welsh songstress Mary Hopkin's 1968 hit 'Postcard', itself penned by McCartney and a follow-up to the huge hit 'Those Were The Days'. All three songs came under the auspices of Apple, The Beatles' multi-faceted new business empire which incorporated music publishing and a record label with a Utopian artistic vision based on the flower power philosophy that there was nothing you can do that can't be done.

Neither Gallagher nor Lyle were hippy kids – their west of Scotland sensibilities were too entrenched for that – although they were nevertheless hip to the winds of change blowing through the music industry. Some three years earlier, both had taken the low road south from their home in Largs. While not exactly aiming to be the next Lennon and McCartney, they were fortified with enough self-belief to have a crack at cracking the Smoke. Both had been writing songs and playing in local band The Tulsans, whose performances brought them to the attention of Decca records chief Dick Rowe – the man who famously, or infamously, turned down The Beatles in 1961. After seeing the band, Rowe was impressed enough to dangle an audition in London in front of the band, a platform they also shared with fellow Scot Lulu and her band The Luvvers.

A couple of records followed for Decca before Gallagher and Lyle decided on a policy of unilateral independence, quit the band and pitched their tent permanently in the capital. Graham recalled: 'Benny was married by that time and I got married soon after moving to London, in 1966. We both had to have jobs . . . We were working all day and the only

Those were the days. Benny Gallagher and Graham Lyle have fond memories of being part of the Apple songwriting club.

time we could write was when the kids had gone to bed.' Benny also recalled the uncertainty that surrounded those far-off days, but admits both possessed an inner drive to chase their musical dreams rather than settle for the nine to five grind. He told me: 'The thing was we arrived down in London on a really iffy publishing deal that wasn't worth the paper it was written on. We were struggling songwriters and we had to have day jobs to pay the bills. One day we were in Caroline House, which was the pirate radio station. Then this guy with a huge Afro hairstyle turned up with a two-track tape recorder. He told us he was looking for songwriters for something that was going to be really big, but he couldn't tell us what it was. We did a couple of songs for him, but thought nothing would come of it so we didn't follow it up.'

The man was Terry Doran, one of The Beatles' fixers-in-chief who was charged with scouting a roster of new songwriting talent to become part of Apple publishing, a venture still so hush-hush only those in The Beatles' inner sanctum knew what was afoot. 'Of course, not long after Terry came to see us Apple was all over the papers and we realised who he was and what he was looking for,' recalled Benny. 'We thought we had shot ourselves in the foot. But God bless Terry, he heard some more of the stuff we did after that and signed us and we got into Apple as writers, for the princely sum of £25 a week, I seem to remember.

'So that was a big step forward for us. We were part of the in-house Apple publishing team, but so were dozens of other songwriters, people like James Taylor, for example, all of us desperately trying to write a hit record.'

Graham said: 'Terry Doran was a mate of The Beatles who had been a car salesman and a road manager. He was an old rocker, really, and the hippy thing was a bit confusing for him, but he was a lovely guy and in charge of Apple publishing. He said, "We're not open yet but we will be in the next two months and I want to sign you." We thought, we've heard that before, but right enough, two months later we got our first paid songwriting job.'

They were based in the Apple studios in Savile Row and given free rein to avail themselves of all the instruments. Benny said: 'Paul sent a letter to all of the Apple writers just after he had produced "Those Were The Days" for Mary Hopkin, basically saying he wanted Apple writers to write the next hit. All the writers wrote something and we wrote our song "Sparrow", which was chosen for the B-side of "Goodbye". That was great. Paul invited us to the studio. And he was great. After we got the message that they had picked our song, the next day a chocolate cake arrived saying, thanks guys.

'Apple was fantastically open in wanting something to work. Without doubt Paul was the driving force then. George was more involved with the Hare Krishna movement, John with the Plastic Ono Band and Ringo just floated in and out. We also did some session work with Mary but it was especially Paul who was driving Apple to be a success. It wasn't that the other Beatles were not friendly or nice, it was just that Paul was the driving force. He is a natural at that. It was a privilege for us to watch him in the studio working with other musicians and then he would turn and say, "Have you guys any suggestions?" And you think, wait, he's with the biggest band in the world and he's asking us.'

Being part of Apple ensured Gallagher and Lyle were put on a £25-a-week retainer, a move that eased the financial pressure they were under and helped free up their musical creativity. 'That was more than we were getting in our jobs and it was terrific. We had to deliver product, though. I know everybody says Apple was total chaos, but at the end of the week we had to come and show them songs. It was great for us,' said Graham. 'Paul was genuinely concerned that the publishing side of Apple would develop. We got two or three B-sides so it was good for us.'

As their talents developed Gallagher and Lyle eventually quit Apple in the meltdown that accompanied the break-up of The Beatles. They went on to play with McGuinness Flint and wrote such memorable hits as 'When I'm Dead and Gone' and 'Malt and Barley Blues' in the early seventies.

Although they gradually went along separate paths, their success has continued as solo songwriters. Both have underlined their credentials as being among Scotland's finest musical exports by scoring chart success with a coterie of A-list stars. Graham co-wrote Tina Turner's multi-million selling comeback single 'What's Love Got To Do With It' as well as Art Garfunkel's huge smash 'Breakaway'. Yet, some 40 years on, both reckon they owe a debt of gratitude to the Beatle who became a mentor and, certainly in Benny Gallagher's case, the relationship continues today through McCartney's ongoing patronage of the Liverpool School of Performing Arts (LIPA).

'It opened so many doors for us,' said Benny. 'We would not have been as good writers had we not gone through Apple. People like James Taylor were there and, although we didn't get to know him, we heard all the stuff so everything kind of rubbed off and influenced you in some way. How much interest did Paul take in Apple? Total. How many publishing companies have a resident mentor? One of the loveliest things that happened was after Graham and I had left McGuinness Flint and were breaking in the US. We were playing a tour with Supertramp and Chris De Burgh. We got to Milwaukee and there was this telegram waiting for us. At the time "I Wanna Stay With You" was riding high in the charts in Britain while we were in America. And all the telegram said was, "Always knew you were great writers, love Paul."

'I have fond memories of Apple. They were fantastic times for us. It got a bit iffy at the end when it was falling apart. But we were treated amazingly well at Apple. There will never be a publishing company like it again. I think had it been allowed to continue, it would have changed the world of music publishing forever. It was sad at the end when the band were breaking up and it got very messy. But all of these things have their time.'

Gallagher and Lyle's place in pop history is assured after more than four decades of writing hit songs and their own personal wounds – inevitable in such a claustrophobic industry – have long since healed. Benny has retained a connection with McCartney after being appointed to the board of LIPA. He said: 'I was delighted to be asked. Paul takes a hugely close interest in what we do here and what we do is try to nurture young talent into reaching its full potential. Paul always comes to the graduations and you can see all these kids light up when they go up to collect their diplomas from him. He is the ultimate survivor and it's always a pleasure to see him.'

Al Stewart

Al Stewart's lungs were still getting used to the good Glasgow air when he suffered what can only be described as a premature evacuation. The baby who grew up to be one of Scotland's most enduring singer-songwriters was whisked down south by his parents within weeks of his noisy arrival into the world. Presumably, though, some of the city's gallus DNA seeped into his bones before his cross-border transfer. Because 17 years later Al showed typical Glaswegian brass neck to get through a mob of screaming fans and a police cordon and worm his way into John Lennon's backstage dressing room.

The venue was Bournemouth's Gaumont Theatre and the date was likely 19 August 1963, four days before the release of 'She Loves You', The Beatles' tremulous fourth single. Stewart was raised in the south coast town but is forever tied to Scotland by birthright, a fact he is always happy to acknowledge. And it is that distinction that allows me to include his Beatles story in this book, a tale Al was delighted to relate in a telephone interview from Los Angeles. Stewart is a brilliant storyteller, so I'm going to let him tell you in his own words just how he came to hoodwink Lennon.

'I was 17. It was summer of 1963. and The Beatles were doing a week at the Gaumont cinema in Bournemouth. It was a package tour in those days. I think it was the week that "She Loves You" came out. Curiously, it was at that time in Bournemouth that they shot that very atmospheric cover for their second album *With The Beatles*. I think it was shot at the Gaumont cinema.

'I was living in Bournemouth. Billy J. Kramer and Tommy Quickly were on the bill, they were all part of Brian Epstein's roster. My friend and I decided we had to go and see them. They were playing two shows a night. I can't remember which day we went but it would have been early on in the week. It was pandemonium. I think that was the week that Beatlemania hit England. They were staying three doors away from the cinema at the Palace Court Hotel. It was only 50 yards away, but they were forever having to deal with getting from the hotel to the cinema and from the cinema back to the hotel. There must have been 2,000 kids there. When I say kids I mean youngsters my age at the time. The screaming went on all day. Whenever one of them appeared at a window it sounded like an aircraft taking off.

'We went to the first show and it was incredible. The Beatles were great. I mean, there was a lot of screaming going on, but at that point you could still hear the songs. I was a huge fan so this was fantastic for me to actually watch them play those songs that I already knew off by heart.

'I don't remember whose idea it was, but we decided we had to meet them. If you've seen *A Hard Day's Night*, you'll know the scene where the police are outside the stage door with their arms locked together trying to keep the fans at bay. Well that was exactly what was happening at the cinema. It was like a scene from *A Hard Day's Night* which at that point was still a year or so away. I turned to my friend and said, "You're mad. Even if you could fight your way through these screaming fans, there is a police cordon." Then he said he had an idea. I think we knew the manager of the cinema, a Mr Watt, I think. So he called up this 50-year-old guy who was already dealing with what seemed like the outbreak of world war three on his doorstep. He was used to more demure shows, not this kind of thing. So my friend got him on the telephone and he says, "Myself and Mr Stewart have come down from London and we represent Rickenbacker guitars and our client Mr Lennon needs our advice on one of his guitars and we need to talk to him. But we can't get to him because of all these screaming kids outside your cinema."

'I'm listening to this thinking he's going to get us killed. I can't believe what I'm hearing. The next minute, Mr Watt goes away then comes back and tells us he's sent down a message to the security detail: "Just give them your names and they'll let you through." We, as bold as brass, then went up to the chief policeman and said, "We're Mr Stewart and Mr Kramer from Rickenbacker guitars and there should be a message for us from the manager." Sure enough, there was. The next thing I know I'm actually walking through the police cordon. And we're doing this in front of thousands of people, many of whom we know.

'Suddenly, we get in through the stage door and we're walking in the backstage tunnels of the Gaumont Theatre. They pointed us down this long corridor and, lo and behold, we're standing outside The Beatles' dressing room. This seemed astounding to me. So we knocked on the door and out comes Neil Aspinall, The Beatles roadie at the time. Now he was not born yesterday and he recognises two idiots when he sees them. He just looked at us and pointed back down the corridor, gently pushed us, not in a nasty way, propelling us back the way we had come away from The Beatles' dressing room.

'As he's doing this – and he's a big guy – I'm trying to look over his shoulder because I was aware of someone standing in the doorway of The Beatles' dressing room and it was John Lennon. He was 10 feet away but it was becoming an ever-increasing distance because we're being pushed in the opposite direction. So I had to say something fast that would distinguish us from the unwashed hordes. I was beginning to play electric guitar so it had to be a techie thing. As I'm being pushed away, I called over Neil Aspinall's shoulder to John Lennon and said, "Why are you not using your Fender amplifier any more?" Which was the single best thing I could possibly have said to him, of course.

'Lennon is bored. He's got nothing to do between the two shows. And he's just sitting around. As it was, he was very upset that he couldn't use his Fender amplifier. Suddenly Lennon goes into this diatribe about Fender amplifiers. He just kept saying, "Fookin' Brian, it's all his fookin' fault. Here we are with fookin' Voxes. If I had my way I'd throw them off the fookin' pier." He goes into this spiel about Vox amplifiers and how he doesn't like them and Epstein had signed the deal with them. We got him off that and he was a bit more cheerful.

'We then asked him about his Rickenbacker which was the fictitious reason we had managed to get this far. So he goes into his dressing room and comes out holding it and playing it. My hands are already sweating because I'm in such close proximity to a Beatle when he hands me the guitar. The only thing that was going through my mind at this point was I'm going to drop it. I put it round my neck and started playing, probably a Chuck Berry riff or something. Then we started talking about things that basically rock groups talk about, like what's the best place to play, what's the best place to hang out in Bournemouth.

'After about five minutes, he's bored and takes his guitar back. He said, we'll get a party together and invite you out and we were delirious. It never crossed our minds that he didn't mean it. It was time for us to go but as we turned to leave he suddenly said, "What did you think of the show?" If you remember, in those days, amplifiers were kind of one-directional. Where we were sitting was right in front of George Harrison's amplifier. The show was great and I heard a hell of a lot, especially the sound of the lead guitar. And I proceeded to tell Lennon this, saying, "I couldn't hear you very well because of George." So he starts to mutter, "Bloody George" under his breath but I didn't think any more about it. Until the next day. And this is the point of the story. This is my claim to fame. I woke up the next day and got the *Bournemouth Echo* and it had a review of The Beatles show. It said the first show was fantastic and The Beatles were great and everything was wonderful. But the review of the second show was very short. It said unfortunately in the second show John Lennon played so loud we couldn't hear anything else – and I realised I had been the cause of this. No matter what I did during the next 45 or so years, the one thing I can always say is I ruined a Beatles show by getting John to play his guitar too loud. Even after all these years, I can still hear myself saying to him I couldn't hear you because of George's amp.

'Flushed with this success, we then decided we would spend the upcoming weekend hanging out with The Beatles. We knew we couldn't use the same ruse again so we got into their hotel by pretending to be reporters from the *Bournemouth Echo* and that's when we met the others. Ringo was coming down the stairs and he quickly sussed we weren't who we claimed to be and he just said, "Yer mates went that way," and pointed to the door. And then we went over to talk to George Harrison and that worked very well because he thought we were reporters and was just chatting away.' In a career spanning four decades, Al has established a reputation for songwriting excellence, signalled by his seminal album *The Year of the Cat*. This is how he summed up his youthful encounter with The Beatles: 'It was fantastic to get that close to them, especially for someone like me who was trying to get into the music industry. Looking back, I'm amazed we got that far. But when you're young, you don't think of the consequences. You just go for the moment . . . and in this case it worked.'

Jimmy McCulloch

Jimmy McCulloch was the top guitar for hire who could have been Scotland's Jimmy Page. Instead, the virtuoso musician whose dazzling fretboard skills so impressed a Beatle ended up like Jimi Hendrix, another tragic victim of life in rock's fast lane.

When Paul McCartney founded Wings in the aftermath of The Beatles' break-up, it was Jimmy's gritty lead guitar work that helped the band really take flight. There had already been a number of personnel changes before Jimmy stepped aboard in 1974. At that point, Wings were a three-piece band consisting of McCartney, Denny Laine and, of course, Linda McCartney, and they were riding high on the success of *Band on the*

Run, the album that marked the former Beatle's welcome return to form.

Two years earlier, Jimmy had been one of a number of session musicians to play on a Scaffold album that was being masterminded by Paul's brother Mike McGear. From that came an invite for the young Scot to lend his precocious talent to a tentative Linda McCartney album called *Seaside Woman,* recorded in secret under the banner of Suzy and the Red Stripes. Unknown to him, though, this time Jimmy had actually been auditioning for a permanent role in Wings. And when McCartney got set to hit the road in 1974 he called up the young Glasgow guitarist whose musicianship had left such a big impression.

For Jimmy, aged just 20, it seemed like a dream gig. Five years earlier, he had left his parents' home in Cumbernauld near Glasgow carrying little more than a case of clothes and a guitar and headed for London. With him was his brother Jack, an excellent drummer. The year was 1969. Music was undergoing something of a metamorphosis in the late sixties and early seventies. As The Beatles – and The Rolling Stones – exited stage left, a new breed of musicians stepped forward to claim their place in the spotlight. And the new currency was guitar-based heavy rock, typified by the likes of Cream's Eric Clapton and Jack Bruce, Led Zeppelin's Page, Deep Purple's Richie Blackmore and the extraordinary American Hendrix. Sonically, they ushered in a wave of musical innovation whose impact was felt by a new generation.

Jimmy McCulloch was no different from millions of other teenagers who idolised these new guitar-playing gods. He first picked up a guitar at the age of 10 and, with his brother Jack on drums, formed his first band,

One of the earliest pictures of Glasgow guitarist Jimmy McCulloch (back right), after he had joined Wings.

The Jaygars. Mum Lilian provided ardent backing for both her sons but Jimmy had already shown signs of a special gift for the guitar. Mrs McCulloch told me of Jimmy's passion to learn the songs he heard on the radio and TV, especially those of The Beatles.

'He practised from the moment he got up in the morning until it was time for school. And then he would come in at lunchtime and start again. The Beatles were his heroes. He was too young to have seen them live, but he had the records and he listened to them all the time. He had a terrific ear, everything was by ear. He would hear a song on radio or television then pick up a guitar and get it very quickly. He was an average pupil at school but he found something in music that he could do very well.'

Music quickly became the focal point of Jimmy's life and, with Jack, he managed to persuade local promoters to get them gigs on the lower rung of bills at the likes of the Greenock Palladium and, eventually, Glasgow's Barrowlands. That gave them a shot of watching up close bands like The Hollies, Manfred Mann and even The Who.

Soon, whispers of Jimmy's prodigious talent spread and reached the ears of The Who's Pete Townshend. At just 15, Jimmy was lured down to London to play with Townshend's protégé group Thunderclap Newman. And within weeks he could add a number one single to his fast-growing CV as the band's 'Something in the Air' soared to the top of the charts.

Thunderclap Newman quickly imploded but Jimmy was never short of work. The precocious young Scot was the talk of studios all over the

Soaraway star . . .
Jimmy, far right, gets
up close and personal
with Wings fans.

capital. He toured with John Mayall and formed his own band called Bent
Frame for a while before hooking up with legendary Scots band Stone The
Crows. In June 1973, he joined Glasgow band Blue with former
Marmalade guitarist Hugh Nicholson but quit after a few months. Next up
was a brief spell with a band called Tundra.

Jimmy, though, was beginning to lose his musical direction and badly
needed some ballast to anchor his ambitions. So when Paul McCartney's
offer came, Jimmy eagerly took it up. McCartney's star was once again on
the rise following the release of *Band on the Run* the previous year. Re-
energised, McCartney was back in the studio within months to record the
follow-up, *Venus and Mars* – and Jimmy was right by his side. Jimmy soon
got a glimpse into life with a superstar. McCartney whisked the entire
Wings entourage off to Nashville for a bonding session.

Work, rest and play was the theme of the month-long stay. As usual,
McCartney had a pot pourri of songs already stirring in his mind. The first
song they recorded was 'Junior's Farm', a hoedown rocker inspired by the
McCartneys' rustic lifestyle on the Mull of Kintyre in Argyll and their main
home in Sussex. Initially, the song was played at a bluesy mid-tempo canter.
But when Jimmy worked out a lead guitar part, the song took off like a
NASA rocket. The time-change infused the song with a charge of energy
and jolted it into an entirely new direction. McCartney was delighted and
suddenly 'Junior's Farm' was promoted from album filler to hit single.

It was a good start for Jimmy. Next up, the band headed for New

Orleans to record tracks for the *Venus and Mars* album. Jimmy was relishing his time in pop's premier league. His confidence was so high he even had the Glasgow gall to persuade McCartney to run through some songs he'd written himself. McCartney, perhaps chastened after his experience of freezing out George Harrison's songs in The Beatles, agreed to give them a go. And one of them, a high-tempo rocker called 'Medicine Jar', made the final cut for *Venus and Mars*, one of the rare times McCartney gave democracy its head and let other band members' songs on an album.

Venus and Mars was a huge success, containing such McCartney gems as 'Listen to What the Man Said' and 'Letting Go'. The former Beatle's career was on a roll and the obvious next stop was to tour on the back of two highly successful albums. By the time the UK tour kicked off in Southampton, Wings were as tight musically as they were ever going to be. Venues had been sold out months in advance and McCartney even unlocked his vault of Beatle songs to perform the likes of 'Yesterday', 'I've Just Seen a Face', 'Blackbird', 'Lady Madonna' and 'The Long and Winding Road', the last three being sung live for the first time. Jimmy's mum remembered: 'One of the shows was at the Glasgow Apollo and it was marvellous. You just felt there was so much following for Jimmy because the fans knew he was the lad from just down the road. It was probably my proudest moment.'

The UK and Australian tours were a resounding critical and commercial success and infused the band with another charge of confidence ahead of the European and American legs. However, off stage, cracks were already beginning to appear. Jimmy was like a kid who had been given the combination to the biggest sweetie jar on earth. And naturally enough, he helped himself to as much candy as he wanted. Groupies, booze and drugs were a rock star's backstage tick list and Jimmy was soon in a freefall of hopeless hedonism. Alcohol, especially, became a problem, not to mention the ever-present spliffs and the lure of harder drugs. Midway through the US tour, McCartney spotted the obvious dangers and tried to warn Jimmy to temper his lifestyle. But stubbornness ran through Jimmy McCulloch like a vein. Headstrong and full of the impetuosity of youth, Jimmy spurned his employer's words of wisdom.

Bad feeling slowly crept into his relationship with McCartney and matters came to a head during a show at Boston. As the band waited backstage to go on for their encore, Jimmy was nowhere to be seen. McCartney chased back to the band's dressing room only to find his lead guitarist swigging from a bottle and refusing point blank to go back on stage. McCartney, as professional a performer as music has ever known, snapped. In a blind rage, he grabbed Jimmy by the scruff of the neck and frogmarched him back to the stage as the rest of the band watched in

open-mouthed astonishment. McCartney later dismissed the incident as concert cabin fever, but the damage had been done. In her memoirs, Denny Laine's wife Jo Jo revealed the faultlines in the relationship between the two Macs. And she even went so far as to allege that one night, McCulloch, high on drink and drugs, crept into McCartney's room armed with a loaded pistol. According to her account, he pointed the gun at the sleeping superstar – but bottled out of pulling the trigger. Instead, he slunk back to his own room, muttering under his breath how much he hated Paul McCartney.

McCartney acknowledged the bad feeling that simmered between the two musicians several years later in the 2004 Wings DVD retrospective *Wingspan.* He said: 'Jimmy was a great player but he had an attitude. This is rock 'n' roll – people do have attitudes; you can't expect everyone to be choirboys.'

When the tour ended, Jimmy was retained to play on the next Wings album, *Wings at the Speed of Sound.* Again, he squeezed one of his own songs, the self-explanatory 'Wino Junko', into the grooves between hits like 'Silly Love Songs' and 'Let 'Em In'. Relations were approaching breaking point, however, and reached a nadir when the band retreated to a boat in the Virgin Islands to record the mediocre *London Town* album. Jimmy knew it was time to move on.

The split came when Steve Marriott called Jimmy to invite him to join the relaunched Small Faces. By then, Jimmy's Wings had been well and truly clipped, stifled by being a bit player in a band fronted by an ex-Beatle and his own ambitions to eventually front his own group. His CV was undeniably impressive and his standing musically had never been higher. Away from the studio, however, Jimmy was losing himself in a trough of excess. His drug intake, which had graduated to speedballs, cocaine and heroin, was gargantuan. And booze was never far from his side. To many, it seemed like Jimmy was pressing the self-destruct button.

On 27 September, he was found dead in his Maida Vale flat. He was just 26. Cause of death was given as a suspected drugs overdose. Traces of morphine, marijuana and alcohol were found in his body. His ashes were scattered alongside his grandparents at Dunottar Cemetery near Clydebank.

In the years since, McCartney has rarely spoken about Jimmy. In *Wingspan*, he said: 'He was always a little dangerous. As an older guy I did try and warn him a couple of times, like what's going to happen when you're 30. You've got your whole life ahead of you. But he liked partying too much and was getting into too many things. In the end he was just too dangerous for his own good.'

Jimmy McCulloch was the best guitarist Wings ever had. In the end, he penned his own epitaph in the words of 'Medicine Jar', a tragic premonition of self-inflicted, drug-addled burn-out if ever there was one.

Campbeltown Pipe Band

It was the most unlikely pairing in pop – the Beatle and the bagpipes, the pied piper and the pipes. Somehow, it should never have worked. Especially as it was recorded in the teeth of the punk rock maelstrom that was tearing down the walls of Britain's musical old guard. But the extraordinary 1977 alliance between Wings and the Campbeltown Pipe Band produced the unthinkable – a song that toppled The Beatles' 'She Loves You' as the biggest-selling non-charity single in UK chart history.

Even today, more than 30 years after it was released, 'Mull of Kintyre' still retains its historic status and unique Caledonian charm. And it immortalised in song a little corner of Scotland, as well as giving a bunch of ordinary Joes – among them farmers, electricians, joiners, shipyard apprentices and schoolkids – a glimpse of the celebrity that constantly enveloped a Beatle.

Campbeltown Pipe Band will forever be associated with the song that stayed at the top of the British pop charts for nine weeks in 1977. Although recorded in the summer of that year of the Queen's Silver Jubilee, the song had actually been echoing inside McCartney's head for a couple of years. Bootleg versions dating from 1975 show the melody was already forming, although the words, eventually co-written with Wings co-founder Denny Laine, were still unfinished. Something was missing, that vital ingredient that can lift a song from the mundane to the magnificent. And for several months, Macca's mind meandered over how he might try to breathe new life into the tune.

Since buying High Park farm a decade before, McCartney had blended easily into the fabric of Campbeltown. Almost everybody in the town had brushed shoulders with their famous occasional resident at some time, notably at the annual local agricultural show, where the sight of a welly-booted Beatle, Linda and the kids was not uncommon.

The real local music legend, though, was not Paul McCartney – it was Tony Wilson, the ebullient and popular pipe major of the town's pipe band. Tony's standing was untouchable in an area where the pipes are a potent symbol of Scottish identity. The two men knew each other from a distance and eventually Tony received an invitation to head up to the farm to hear McCartney map out a musical idea. Over a dram, McCartney hauled out his guitar and played Tony a bare bones version of 'Mull of Kintyre' and then invited him to let rip with the pipes to see if they could find some common ground.

Paul said: 'Tony decided it would be a bit too loud indoors so we went out into the garden and he starts tuning up. I took my guitar out and found out what key he was in because I don't know anything about bagpipes. So we worked it out.'

An accomplished musician, Tony could not have been prepared for what came next. McCartney, who can't read music, simply asked if he would be able to score the song for the bagpipes . . . and would his band play on the record? And he sold it with the argument that Scotland didn't have a modern song that properly reflected the country's heritage.

At the band's next meeting in a local church hall, Tony nonchalantly put Macca's idea before the body of the kirk where it received a tentative thumbs up. Leading drummer Campbell Maloney said: 'Not everyone was in favour. Some people didn't think it was the right place for a pipe band. But the overall feeling was we should give it a go.' Teenage schoolboys Ian McKellar and Jimmy McGeachy, the youngest member of the band, went with the flow, too young perhaps to appreciate the significance of the pact the band had entered into. Ian told me: 'Tony came to the band one night and told us he had been approached by Paul McCartney. He said he had a song that he thought would benefit from having the pipes played on it. We thought he was winding us up, but it turned out to be absolutely true. It was a fairly simple tune and simple melody so we spent about seven

Paul and Linda with Jimmy McGeachy, the youngest person to play on the song that was an homage to their Argyll hideaway.

weeks learning it. And then we went up to his farm to record it in the studio he had there. Paul did mean something to me. I was never a massive fan of The Beatles at that age but now I can look back and see exactly what they did. Some of the boys were a bit overawed by the whole thing, but I think I took it in my stride. I wouldn't say I was star-struck, really.'

Equally unfazed by Macca's legendary status was Jimmy who, like millions of teenage kids at that time, rocked to The Clash and The Pistols. Paul had always been in the town since I'd been growing up. There was a wee bit of a buzz at the time because he was Paul McCartney, this huge icon. You would occasionally see him going for his groceries in the town, walking about. And no one bothered him. And his daughters Mary and Stella would hang around the town as well with the young farmer fraternity. It wasn't that big a deal with me, to be honest. I didn't have a great reaction to the actual song at the time because I was right into punk. I was more interested in the musical angle rather than being star-struck about him.'

It was a Tuesday night when about 12 members of the band crammed into the back of a minibus with their pipes and drums. They headed up to McCartney's studio, a split-level facility that was a derelict barn when the farm was first bought. Wings had just returned from the Virgin Islands where they had been recording the album *London Town* on a boat. So the

RAK mobile equipment had been shipped to Argyll to allow the band to continue recording when the mood took them.

Jimmy recalled being mesmerised more by the instruments on display on the mezzanine than playing on a record with a former Beatle. 'He had had all these amazing guitars including the Hofner violin bass and the Rickenbacker that he used in the *Wings Over America* tour. There was a whole rack of them and a fantastic drum kit. His whole team was there to record us including Geoff Emerick, who had been The Beatles' engineer. So he was taking it very seriously.'

Led by Tony Wilson, the band recorded the pipes first to a backing track of the song and, after listening to a playback, McCartney was thrilled. Ian said: 'I remember we did it in just one take and Paul was blown away by it. He just said, that's it, and we were finished. We knew what we were doing because we had done plenty of rehearsals. The band was all prepared. Tony had hand-picked the pipers and drummers, the ones he thought were best.'

An hour later, about 11 p.m., it was the turn of the drummers to add their parts, which were then double-tracked to beef up the sound. Drummer Campbell Maloney said: 'Paul told me he wanted a simple beat, I played it and he said fine, and then he recorded the whole thing. At the end of the recording he played it back and I'm not kidding, it was brilliant. It made the hairs on our back stand up.'

Song in the can, Paul was delighted with the result but sceptical about how this world-weary, tartan-tinged waltz about a remote part of Scotland would go down. You could almost hear the sound of knives being sharpened. According to McCartney, though, it was the lads in the band and Geoff Emerick who convinced him to hurl caution into the heather and go for it. He said: 'When we finished it, the pipers all said, "Aye, it's got to be a single, that." . . . I thought it was a little too specialised to bring out as a single, you would have to bring out something with more mass appeal. But they kept saying, "Oh, the exiled Scots all over the world. It'll be a big single for them."'

Thoughts then turned to shooting a video for the song that Paul and EMI had slated for a possible Christmas/New Year hit. The song resonated with kitsch Scottish sentiment, ideal for Hogmanay and the festive period and could become a new 'Auld Lang Syne'. The video began with McCartney strumming his guitar outside his farm before being joined by Denny and Linda. And then it cut to the band, this time padded out to its full complement, marching in the distance across the white sands of Saddell beach. In keeping with his man-of-the-people image, Paul had invited dozens of locals to take part in the video and they can be seen joining in the happy singalong round a giant log fire on the beach, the 'flickering embers going higher and higher'.

When it was released on 19 November as a double-A side with 'Girls School', critics reckoned McCartney had scribbled his musical obituary. This, after all, was the year of hissing Sid Vicious. 'No More Heroes', snarled The Stranglers. Some radio stations stuck to the B-side 'Girls School', a jagged-edge rocker that was the very antithesis of 'Mull of Kintyre'. Not for the first time, though, McCartney's songwriting touched a chord with the public who bought the record in their thousands. It finally burst through the punk barrier to crash land on the top of the charts and it stayed there for seven weeks.

Even in today's age of digital downloads, the stats behind 'Mull of Kintyre' are staggering. It spent 17 weeks in the British charts and had sold more than half a million copies 21 days after it was first shipped to record stores. And by 14 January, the first song credited to McCartney-Laine edged past 'She Loves You' by Lennon-McCartney to become the biggest-selling UK single of them all. Eventually retail figures showed a total sales tally of 2.5 million, which meant it was bought by one in 30 of the population. Punks and all.

All of a sudden, Campbeltown was the music world's capital of cool and a tourism mecca. Lachie Mackinnon, of the local tourist board, was quoted as saying: 'Normally we get about 500,000 to a million visitors a year in Kintyre. But from the letters we have had already, that total will be up by about 20 per cent and the letters are still flooding in. It's even sold the pipes to the Arabs, Libya, Saudi Arabia and Dubai. They are offering the Scots £30,000 a year to go out and teach their military bands the bagpipes.'

For the boys in the band, it was their ticket to undreamt-of celebrity. There were numerous photocalls, and newspaper and TV interview requests poured in from all over the country. Media attention went into overdrive. The pinnacle of all this fame was an appearance on Saturday, 10 December, on *The Mike Yarwood Show*, then the most watched TV gig in Britain. It was Paul's first television performance in three years and he would be backed by the country's unlikeliest pop stars – the Campbeltown Pipe Band. The trip to London to film a new video for the Yarwood show as well as a blitz of London radio stations was the moment the success of the song finally dawned on those band members chosen to go. Ian McKellar reflected: 'That is when it really hit me. We were treated like superstars. We were staying in top hotels. I wish I had been five years older because I would have taken it in a lot better. Some of the older guys were out all the time but I couldn't get into pubs and the like. But I still had a great time.'

Of course, this type of fame is fleeting. When 'Mull of Kintyre' began its inevitable slide down the charts, so the spotlight on the Campbeltown Pipe Band slowly faded. Everyone gradually went back to their day jobs. But McCartney had one last trick up his sleeve before the band slipped permanently off the stage. Buoyed by the success of the single, a rejuvenated Macca drew up plans for a British tour to promote Wings' latest album *Back to the Egg*. It couldn't take place until the end of 1979 – two years after the release of 'Mull of Kintyre' – because the family took time out after Linda had given birth to baby James. Three Scottish dates were pencilled in as the wrap-up dates when Wings took flight in November for their 19-date jaunt round the UK. On 15 December, the band would play Edinburgh's Odeon, the scene of Beatles concerts some 15 years earlier, before finishing up with a double-header at the Glasgow Apollo.

The legendary Glasgow venue was packed out for both shows, but the second one has gone down in folklore for an encore that no one before or since has matched. As the sounds of 'Yesterday' faded away, Macca eventually led the band back on for a final bow. And, as he plucked at the opening chords of 'Mull of Kintyre', the Apollo erupted in a cauldron of patriotic fervour. Then halfway through the song, the stage parted and emerging from the dry ice in full Highland dress was the Campbeltown Pipe Band, the pipes and drums blasting into the famous auditorium.

It was a seminal moment for McCartney and the band, the high water mark of a partnership that had created a special piece of pop history. Weeks of secret planning had gone into the band's unscheduled appearance. By now, Jimmy McGeachy was a student at Anniesland College and regularly went to see bands like The Police play the Apollo. But he never dreamt that one day he would be up on the stage in his kilt cranking out the familiar drum beat to McCartney's biggest hit. He said: 'They did the show and we watched from the upper back area. Then, before the encore, because no one knew what was happening, we had to go out on to the street. We came through a side door to the back of the stage and then up the stairs at the front. And then we just came up from underneath the stage. You just walked out and saw this massive bank of smiling faces. And everybody was swaying. It was a great buzz. Paul had a huge smile on his face and he just kept saying, "Wave guys, enjoy the moment." It really was fantastic, a real Scottish moment.'

8. Mull of Kintyre

The desolate beaches seem to stretch for miles, creating a golden carpet from one end of the peninsula to the other. Gazing down from above are soaring hills and miles of heather-clad moorland. Along the shoreline, old smugglers' caves can still be found. Eerily quiet, it resembles some kind of castaway's Shangri-La. Only the crashing sound of riptides rolling in from the mighty Atlantic disturbs the splendid feeling of isolation. The swirling wind bites into your face as you stroll along the coastline. And, if you're lucky, you really will see the ghostly mist rolling in from the sea just as described in the lyrical portrait painted by Paul McCartney's famous lilting song.

• • •

The Mull of Kintyre, a lonely archipelago on Scotland's Argyll coast just 30 miles from Ireland, is achingly beautiful. Derived from the Gaelic 'cinn' and 'tir', its ancient meaning is 'head of the land'. At the heart of this timeless and unspoilt area is Machrihanish Bay, 11 miles to the south of Campbeltown, which is as far from the madding crowd as you could possibly hope to get. Especially if you are someone who has lived a life of unsurpassed fame as a ruling member of pop music's aristocracy.

Unquestionably, the Mull would have been frozen forever in its splendid isolation had it not been for the former Beatle's decision to make a local rundown farmhouse his refuge from the goldfish bowl of Beatlemania. Not only did he immortalise the area in the eponymous song that became Britain's biggest-selling hit single, the Mull of Kintyre also rescued McCartney from slipping off the ladder of fame. In short, the Mull of Kintyre saved Paul McCartney at a time when his professional career was at its lowest ebb and was key to a number of life-changing decisions.

In 1966, The Beatles were at the 'toppermost of the poppermost'. *Revolver*, their seventh studio album, had been released to universal acclaim. *Sgt. Pepper's Lonely Hearts Club Band*, the apex of their recording career, was already taking shape in McCartney's mind. Creatively, he was on a winning streak. Songs like 'Eleanor Rigby', 'For No One', 'Here, There and Everywhere', 'Paperback Writer' and 'Got to Get You into My Life' proved there was no danger of McCartney's drive slowing down. Embryonic versions of 'Penny Lane', 'Fixing a Hole' and 'She's Leaving

Home', songs that would become part of the fabric of 1967's epochal Summer of Love, were already at an advanced stage.

McCartney was right at the heart of the swinging sixties. His house in London's Cavendish Avenue, a stone's throw from The Beatles' studio in Abbey Road, was often the scene for late-night parties involving a veritable who's who of showbiz. At other times, with actress girlfriend Jane Asher, he was a familiar face at first-night theatre shows, film premieres and gallery openings. In stark contrast, he would then mix things up by attending avant-garde concerts by the likes of German composer Karlheinz Stockhausen and John Cage. And, as the only Beatle bachelor, he was a regular figure at favourite showbiz haunts such as the Ad Lib and Scotch of St James where the rich and famous could relax all night after grafting all day in the studio. Restaurants reserved the best table in the house for Mr McCartney and Miss Jane. Moreso than John, George or Ringo, Paul McCartney was a prince of the city. And he revelled in the chance to soak up as many strands of culture as he could, to become a sponge for new ideas.

This was also the year that his accountant informed him – almost by the by – that he was officially a millionaire. He was just 24. But the memo from Geoffrey Maitland Smith of Thornton Baker was tempered with a note of caution. At that time, Britain's Labour Government, under Harold Wilson, was squeezing the country's nouveau riche with a top tax rate of 90p in the pound dropping into the treasury's barren coffers. So, as a means of sheltering some of his cash from Wilson's stingy grasp, McCartney's financial people suggested he invest in property. Among the schedules they sent him, there was one that pricked his interest. At first glance, the images of High Park Farm on the Mull of Kintyre were less than impressive. Years of neglect had taken their toll on the three-bedroom farmhouse. The grounds were overgrown with weeds and the only distinguishing feature about the living accommodation was the hole in the roof that needed fixing.

The asking price was £35,000 and the seller was a local farmer named Brown, who was incredulous when the buyer of his humble homestead was finally revealed. McCartney has never made explicit his reasons for plumping for a near-derelict bolthole; perhaps it was never clear in his own mind. Whatever the reason, for an unashamed urbanite at the epicentre of a cultural revolution, it was a highly unusual move and very much one that went against type. But it was the promptings of actress girlfriend Jane Asher that appear to have convinced McCartney, not known for his big spending habits, to become a Scottish landowner.

The deal was inked on 17 June 1966, the same day as McCartney was putting the final touches to 'Here, There and Everywhere' for *Revolver*.

Paul turned his back on city life and fled to High Park Farm to escape the pressures of The Beatles' split.

Occasionally breaking into a mock Scottish accent, a delighted Macca told the *NME*: 'It's just a wee, small place up at the tip of Scotland and I plan to make the occasional trip there for a wee spell of solitude. It's not too bad – 200 acres and a farmhouse as well. I can't tell you how much it was but it was worth every penny as far as I am concerned.'

But while the missives may have been completed on this date, another 18 months would pass before Paul, with Jane in tow during the cold winter of their relationship, took his first hesitant look round the farm.

Mr Brown and his wife Janet had lived at the farm since 1947 and were regarded as mainstays of the local community. Mrs Brown said at the time: 'Our farm has been up for sale for a while now but what a surprise my husband and I had when we saw the famous pair – Paul told me that it had always been his ambition to own a farm in Scotland.' That claim, no matter how sincerely meant at the time, was not borne out by McCartney's subsequent remarks in which the decision to forge a Celtic connection had more to do with the randomness of the property market than any grand plan. He could just as easily have bought a cottage in Sussex, which, of course, he eventually did.

But when he first turned into the single-track road leading to High Park, McCartney was instantly struck by the sense of solitude, his cheeks red from the raw winter breeze coming off the Atlantic, the first hint of winter around the corner. By the time they made this initial trip north in early December of 1967 McCartney needed to find a sanctuary, especially since filming *Magical Mystery Tour* had been more fraught than he bargained for. Accompanying them to Scotland was Alistair Taylor, The Beatles' gopher whose Mr Fix-It qualities were quickly called upon when all three first clapped eyes on High Park for real. It was little more than a broken-down shack.

Ever the optimist, though, McCartney was convinced of the benefits this pared-down lifestyle presented. Taylor was despatched into Campbeltown to track down some essentials, with two provisos from his employer ringing in his ear – keep it simple and keep it cheap. Taylor recalled: 'His orders were to make sure everything was second-hand except the beds. I got him a horrible little formica table and four formica chairs. We built our own sofa called the Sharpe's Express made out of potato boxes and a dirty old mattress we found in a barn. It was so far removed from his normal way of living but that is what Paul wanted. He wanted to live a simple life and at High Park he took that idea to the ultimate level. They were happy days.'

Happy indeed. The clear Scottish air seemed to cast a romantic spell on Paul and Jane. Their rollercoaster three-year affair had often come close to breaking point. That December, though, all the stars were in alignment as the couple returned from Scotland on 20 December and announced their engagement on Christmas Day. But there was to be no happy ever after for the celebrity couple of their day. Although Jane was instrumental in helping McCartney come to a decision, she only visited High Park a couple of times before her tempestuous relationship with her Beatle beau finally fizzled out. Ironically, then, it was the woman who became the first Mrs Paul McCartney who was quickest to realise the potential of High Park.

Linda Eastman, a ballsy New York photographer, had first met McCartney at the launch party for *Sgt. Pepper* in May 1967. McCartney was instantly attracted to the long-legged blonde divorcee. They exchanged phone numbers amid vague promises to keep in touch. Eventually, their slowburn transatlantic romance caught fire and McCartney became the last Beatle to give up his bachelor status on 12 March 1969 – five days before John Lennon married second wife Yoko Ono.

The material trappings of Paul's fame held little allure for Linda, the coltish epitome of the sixties free spirit. She came from a wealthy family from New York state, so was no stranger to affluence. Her father Lee was one of America's top lawyers. Paintings by Renoir and De Kooning hung in the family drawing room. But Linda had spurned the cosiness of the

American dream for homespun rustic reality. At heart, she yearned for a simple life of simple pleasures – and her down-to-earth attitude found a natural ally in Paul who was fast approaching a crossroads in his professional and private life.

McCartney took Linda on a voyage of discovery to his Scottish sanctuary. They drove up from London, stopping on the way to meet Paul's relatives in Liverpool. It was just the two of them and Heather, Linda's daughter from an impetuous first marriage. When they finally completed the long and winding road to the 200-acre farm – high up on the slope of a hill – Linda was instantly smitten. In the book *Many Years From Now*, Paul recalled how the farmhouse was virtually derelict, the rooms were crying out for a lick of paint and the wooden outbuildings were riddled with rat holes. Paul said: 'Linda just said we could do this place up. And I'd never thought of that. I thought it just stayed how you bought it. I just wasn't enterprising enough to actually think we could clean this place up. Linda really turned me onto it. I quite liked it before. I liked its isolation and I liked the privacy and the end-of-the-world remoteness compared to a city . . . We turned it into a great place and suddenly I began to love being there. The children loved it, too – we could walk, seemingly forever, and they could run free.'

In those early days, however, no one could have predicted just how big a part the farm would play in the lives of the McCartneys. The months after they got married were hardly the stuff of Mills and Boon. Pregnant with their first child, Mary, Linda had to run the gauntlet of fans who felt she had snatched away the last of the Fab Four. Bad enough that she had ensnared him through a shotgun marriage, they felt, but she was American into the bargain. At the same time, Paul was facing the biggest crisis of his career. Beset by bitter business wrangles and ripped apart by artistic differences, The Beatles as a band were facing the last rites. Maverick American businessman Allen Klein, a foul-mouthed New Yorker who had a reputation for squeezing big bucks out of record companies for his clients, had been brought in by John, George and Ringo to sort out their rapidly unravelling finances. McCartney wanted nothing to do with him, a decision that put him at odds with his bandmates.

In the studio, too, McCartney found himself equally ostracised. When John Lennon, now fully ensconced with Yoko and in the vice-like grip of a debilitating heroin habit, announced at a meeting that he 'wanted a divorce' and was quitting The Beatles, the game was up. For McCartney, the one member of the band who had worked tirelessly to keep The Beatles afloat since the death of their mentor Brian Epstein two years earlier, it was a crushing blow. The circle of friendship that had bound the band together for more than a decade was finally broken.

Wracked by uncertainty – and with his self-confidence crashing through the floor – McCartney turned his back on the bright lights of London. With Linda and Heather in tow, he packed as much as he could into his car and headed north to the one place he could go where no one would bother him. At High Park, he could simply tend the sheep, walk among the hills and shut out a world that seemed to have turned against him.

The locals at Campbeltown had at first expressed natural curiosity when McCartney's private venture had become public property. After all, it wasn't every Scottish town that boasted a Beatle in their midst, even if it was Linda who mostly ventured into town for provisions. By now, though, everyone respected his privacy and he could wander through the streets unmolested. Local councillor Alastair McKinlay said: 'Most people were happy to give him some space. Of course, it would be almost impossible to hide the fact you recognised him, but I don't know anyone who ever gave him hassle. And over time, he loosened up a little and you could have a conversation with him about family, kids, that sort of thing. When he first came here his children were very young, which is something a lot of people forget. But he must have liked being here because he kept coming back and we were always pleased to see him. He was never Mr Showbiz, just very ordinary.'

The close of the sixties was truly a time of change for McCartney. Although the band was imploding, he was about to become a father for the first time. And for all the growing distance between him and the other three Beatles, McCartney couldn't escape the feeling that his world was closing in. Normally, he would only stay a short time at the farm. But now the days stretched into weeks. His absence from the London social scene had not gone unnoticed. In those far-off days, though, there was no such thing as mobile phones, email or internet. To all intents and purposes, Paul McCartney, always the most accessible Beatle, had stepped off the showbiz express.

Inside, he was falling apart. Not quite close to walking off a cliff but certainly peering perilously over the edge. Recalling the days of The Beatles' nuclear winter, he declared: 'I was going through a hard period. I exhibited all the classic symptoms of the unemployed, the redundant man . . . If I did get up, I'd have a drink. Straight out of bed. I've never been like that. I sort of went a little crazy for a few weeks.' He elaborated on his pernicious feelings of redundancy in *Melody Maker*. 'Immediately after the break-up of The Beatles, I felt, what am I going to do? I needed at least a month to think. I went into a period of what everyone called being a recluse, a hermit in isolation. All sorts of little snide articles appeared saying "He's sitting up in Scotland looking into his mirror, admiring his

OFF THE BEATLE TRACK 20 –
BUNGALOW BILL BOUGHT JOHN'S VILLA

Bill Martin is the only Scottish songwriter to have one of his songs on a record by a Beatle – and it earned him FOUR PENCE in old money pre decimalisation when he threatened to sue EMI. George Harrison's 1971 album *All Things Must Pass*, the first proper Beatle solo record to be released after the band split, was a triple set and sold ten million copies. The third slice of vinyl contained a couple of fun studio jams that included a throwaway called 'It's Johnny's Birthday' in celebration of Lennon's 30th birthday. But the song was sung to the tune of 'Congratulations', Britain's 1968 entry to the Eurovision Song contest sung by Cliff Richard that was co-written by Bill Martin. He said: 'I listened to it and asked for the recording presses to be stopped. By my threatening to sue EMI I got four pence in old money. It was a great compliment to me that when John Lennon walked into the studio George Harrison started singing "It's Johnny's Birthday" to the tune of "Congratulations" which was a song I had co-written. But George said "leave it on (the album), I like Bill". So in essence I do have a tune on a record by one of The Beatles. But Govan-born Bill's connection to the mercurial Lennon goes much further than a shared interest in pop music . . . for the Scottish songwriter bought John's mock-Tudor house in Weybridge. John purchased 27-room Kenwood on 15 July 1964 – the first proper home he shared with wife Cynthia and two-year-old son Julian – at the height of Beatlemania for £20,000. He told me: 'I saw Kenwood was for sale and I bought it through a liquidator. Lennon told me he had spent another £30,000 on top of what he paid for it. He said some pop star will have to buy it. Well I bought it for a B-side and it recently sold for £6.8m. All the Lennon songs from '64 to '69 were written there.'

Bill first came into contact with Lennon and McCartney when their paths crossed in the early sixties at the offices of music publisher Dick James. Bill also got a toehold on the Merseybeat boom when one of his songs, Kiss Me Now, was recorded by Brian Epstein protégé Tommy Quickly. Bill, the only Scottish songwriter with four number one singles on his CV, told me: 'From a songwriter's perspective, they were unbelievable. When The Beatles came along everyone thought they could write songs. And it is very hard to write a hit song. I could write a song in five minutes with anyone on the phone but to write a hit song is very difficult. And they were the best at that. They were the only pop band to take their audience with them from "She Loves You" through to "Sergeant Pepper". That was the amazing thing. I always say Elvis changed the musical world, but The Beatles changed the whole world. They were a different class.'

image." It was not at all true. I was just planting trees. I was just getting normal again and giving myself time to think.'

Seclusion for Paul came easier than he thought. He spent his time taking long walks, exploring the hills with Linda, tidying up the farm, renovating the house and installing a makeshift mini studio (which he christened Rude Studios) in one of the outbuildings. Yet even in the wilds of Scotland, McCartney remained an unwitting prisoner of his own fame, still unable to shake off the spectre of his ever-present past.

In America, Detroit DJ Russ Gibb claimed to have uncovered evidence that Paul McCartney had been killed in a car crash in London in 1966. His death had been hushed up by the other Beatles to preserve the myth and avoid a worldwide outpouring of grief by fans. So they replaced him with a lookalike. But clues about Paul's apparent demise – it was claimed – had been planted in subsequent albums like *Sgt. Pepper*, the 'White Album' and *Abbey Road*. The fact that this Paul clone could knock off such McCartney-esque melodies like 'Fool on the Hill', 'Hey Jude', 'Back in the USSR' and 'Penny Lane' seems to have not mattered a jot. Of course, it was utter nonsense. But that didn't stop the rumour being picked up by every media organisation in the world. When the Apple office rang McCartney to tell him he was dead, he told them to play along with it. 'Nothing sells better than death,' he said. It was only when two hacks from *Life* magazine tracked him down to the farm in Scotland that he said reports of his death were, in fact, greatly exaggerated. 'If I was dead, I'd be the last to know,' he quipped.

As the swinging sixties were replaced by the cynical seventies, the change of decade did nothing to improve the mood within The Beatles' camp. No one, it seemed, was prepared to give peace a chance. McCartney remained entrenched in his Scottish retreat and slowly came to the realisation that an impasse had been reached. All that remained was the question of who would be the one to formally break the legal link that bound the Fab Four together. That was the dilemma McCartney's mind wrestled with one day in April as he went for a walk among the heather with his lawyer brother-in-law John Eastman. The cold wind only added to the chill factor in McCartney's bones as he realised he had just one course of action left to him. As he stared out over the Mull of Kintyre, Paul McCartney took the life-changing decision to take John Lennon, George Harrison and Ringo Starr to court to break up their partnership – and signal the end of The Beatles as a working band.

Paul recalled: 'John saw the position we were in and he sympathised. We'd have these meetings on top of hills in Scotland, we'd go for long walks. I remember when we actually decided we had to go and file suit. We were standing on this big hill which overlooked a loch – it was quite a nice day, a bit chilly – and we'd been searching our souls. Was there any other way? And we eventually said, "Oh, we've got to do it." The only alternative was seven years with the partnership – going through those same channels for seven years.' Decision made, McCartney then set in motion the litigation that broke up The Beatles – and forever branded him as the bad guy in the eyes of the press, even though John, always the leader of the band, was the first Beatle to quit.

McCartney remained at Kintyre, insulated from the media frenzy. He was in the middle of putting the finishing touches to his first solo album, *McCartney*, a deliberately lo-fi and homespun record. Many of the tracks had, in fact, been written at High Park, his new-found contentment with Linda and the beauty of the Mull providing him with both inspiration and a muse. Basic tracks for the likes of the magnificent 'Maybe I'm Amazed', 'Lovely Linda' and 'Every Night' (a song about battling depression), were laid down at the primitive four-track mini studio set up in one of the converted barns.

Gradually, with Linda's unflinching support, McCartney put the genie back into the bottle of Scotch and hauled himself out of his funk. Instead of going into rehab, he used Scotland as an environmental detox to get his life back, to breathe in fresh air. Slowly, the creative juices and the self-belief coalesced. And the crisis eventually passed. McCartney has always been quick to give his late wife the credit for pulling him back from the brink in those days spent in Scotland. He said: 'She gave me confidence. She said: "You're great, you're OK." We liked doing very simple and down-to-earth things. During the time we spent up there I did a lot of sheep-shearing. I helped with the shearing and mowing the fields – and went horse-riding. That was the biggest thing. Linda taught me to horse-ride. Through nature in Scotland, through riding and through her support, I did manage to get it back together.'

The couple revelled in their new-found bucolic freedom. For the first time since he was a teenager, large chunks of Paul's time were his own. On one occasion, with Linda now having given birth to their first child Mary, they decided on a whim to visit the Shetland Isles. On a visit to Scrabster, they chartered a boat called the *Enterprise* for £30 from local fisherman John Dunnet to take them to Orkney. The plan then was to get a plane from Kirkwall to Sumburgh.

Paul said at the time: 'We try never to organise our lives very much. We do things on the spur of the moment. We were in Scotland and we decided to take a trip to the Shetland Islands. So we piled in the Land Rover with the two kids, our English sheepdog, Martha, and a whole pile of stuff in the back with Mary's potty on the top. On the second day we get up to a little port called Scrabster at the top of Scotland.

'When we tried to get on the big car ferry, we got in the queue but were two cars too late – missed it. So, don't despair. Okay, make the best of it. We really didn't want to go on that big liner, a mass-produced thing. So we thought, let's beat the liner. But we gave that up – it became a bit difficult with airplanes and such. Let's try to get a ride in one of the little fishing boats, and how much should we offer?

'So the romantic idea was that they'd rather have a salmon or a bottle of Scotch than the £30. I went to a bunch of boats but they weren't going to the Orkney Islands. So I went on this one and I went to this trapdoor sort of thing, and they were sleeping down below – the smell of sleep is coming up through the door. At first the skipper said no, and then I said there was thirty quid in it for him, and they say they'll take us. It was a fantastic little boat called the *Enterprise* and the captain named George, he's wearing a beautiful Shetland sweater.

'We brought all our stuff aboard and it was low tide, so we had to lower Martha in a big fishing net and a little crowd gathers and we wave our farewells. As we steam out, the skipper gives us some beer, and Linda, trying to be one of the boys, takes a swig and passes it to me. Well, you shouldn't drink before a rough crossing to the Orkneys. The little one, Mary, throws up all over the wife, as usual. That was it. I was already feeling sick. I sort of gallantly walked to the front of the boat, hanging onto the mast. The skipper comes up and we're having light talk, light chit-chat. and I don't want it. So he gets the idea and points to the fishing baskets and says, "Do it in there!" So we were all sick, but we ended up in the Orkney Islands, and we took a plane to Shetland. It was great.'

• • •

By 1971, McCartney, in a professional sense at least, was officially a former Beatle, having won the court case that formally ended their partnership. His first solo album may not have changed the world, but its rural charm delighted Paul. The record's rootsy folkiness had its heart in Scotland, and Paul was determined to maintain the mood on his next album. This time, though, rather than a DIY effort where he played all the instruments himself, he began recruiting the members of a new band.

Auditions took place at Rude Studios for the sessions that became *Ram*. First on board was former Moody Blue Denny Laine, followed by drummer Denny Seiwell. Laine's career had taken him into McCartney's path several times in the sixties, not least when The Moody Blues were lower down the bill during a Beatles tour that also took in Glasgow and Edinburgh. Things went so well that within a few days, basic backing tracks for songs such as 'Back Seat of My Car' and 'Too Many People' were quickly laid down.

McCartney has always found his songwriting clicked easily into gear during his holidays in Scotland. In the past, classic Beatle songs such as 'The Long and Winding Road' had taken shape in Kintyre. Paul said: 'I just sat down at my piano in Scotland, started playing and came up with that song, imagining it was going to be done by someone like Ray Charles. I have always found inspiration in the calm beauty of Scotland and again it proved the place where I found inspiration.'

Inspiration, though, was one thing. Temptation was another. Paul and Linda had never made any secret of the fact they smoked dope. And the sheer remoteness of High Park meant they could indulge their private habit round night-time campfire singalongs as the sun set over the peninsula. Isolated from the rest of the world, perhaps they thought they were untouchable. But the scales of justice tipped against the McCartneys on 19 September 1972, the day local police constable Norman McPhee decided to carry out a chance check on High Farm, knowing that its famous occupants were currently not in residence.

The visit was not sparked by any notion of star-gazing, just good old-fashioned duty. He first checked that all the doors and windows were secure. Satisfied that the property was wind and watertight with no sign of any unexpected rubber-neckers out to bother a Beatle, PC McPhee was just about to leave when he decided to have a quick peek at the green-house.

Some 11 days earlier, the young PC had completed a drugs ID course in Glasgow and now knew that grass wasn't just something that grew out of the ground. So when he rubbed the greenhouse window, his policeman's instincts were jolted by the sight of the strange-looking plants that, according to one writer, were 'completely clogging' the outbuilding. McPhee instantly put his new-found knowledge to good use and, after checking with a drugs manual, reported back to his superiors. Even a hick from the sticks could put strange, exotic-looking plants and pop star together and come up with dope.

The next day, McCartney found himself staring at a rap sheet charging him with three counts of growing and possessing marijuana. This latest bust had come just a month after Swedish police intercepted a package that had been delivered to the band's Gothenburg hotel. Sliced open, out fell seven ounces of prime Peruvian flake. Banged to rights, McCartney was fined about £500 and virtually frog-marched out of the country. But High Farm was the last place he expected to get nicked. He was the third Beatle to get his collar felt for dope offences on UK soil – John Lennon and George Harrison had already earned criminal records as a result of high-profile raids by the Met's drug squad in 1969. Now, three years later, Paul faced the very real prospect of his reputation coming under the microscope of the Scottish judiciary and his Campbeltown retreat coming under siege by a ravenous Scottish press pack, themselves high on the whiff of a Beatle drugs bust.

Through his London lawyers, McCartney signalled he would be pleading not guilty, claiming a fan had sent him the seeds, which he then, in all innocence, had planted in his greenhouse. In financial terms, a conviction would not have amounted to a hill of Beatle beans. But its effects would be felt all over the world. As Lennon subsequently discovered, any trace of a criminal stain on your reputation can make visa applications, especially for entry to America and the Far East, particularly tricky.

So, potentially, the stakes were high when Paul and Linda stepped off their private jet at Machrihanish airport to face a sort of high noon in the little Argyll town on Friday, 8 March 1973. Campbeltown was already in the grip of a media frenzy as newspapers and camera crews descended on the town's sheriff court, the sight of a former Beatle in the dock on drugs charges making headlines all over the globe.

A few months earlier, Glasgow lawyer Len Murray had taken a call from a London-based legal firm asking if he would represent one of their clients, a musician, in an upcoming case. The name of the client was kept secret but Murray, who agreed to take the job, had already guessed his identity. Murray was one half of a two-member McCartney defence team. While he acted as the solicitor, Junior Counsel was advocate John McCluskey, who later became Lord McCluskey, one of the most distinguished legal figures of his generation and Solicitor General for Scotland from 1974 to 1979.

In the prosecution corner was Ian Stewart, one of the last part-time fiscals to serve the crown in Scotland and a man who was in the long afternoon of a legal career that had, by virtue of his location, been largely anonymous. Most of the cases he prosecuted were for breach of the peace, road traffic offences and the occasional sheep rustling. Nothing, then, prepared him for the media circus pitched outside the sheriff court.

Murray, already a streetwise solicitor who had learned his trade in the tough courts of Glasgow, felt nothing but sympathy for his legal adversary. 'I felt desperately sorry for him, I really did. The world had ignored him for his whole career, some 40 years, and then the circus came to town with this one case. Campbeltown wasn't quite the centre of the criminal universe. And the one time that the spotlight was shone on him it turned out to be a real cause célèbre. It was the second item in the BBC and ITV news that night. I think there was a bombing in Birmingham or something that was the main item. But the press coverage was really quite considerable.'

Len Murray was part of the two-man defence team that represented Paul during his court hearing in Campbeltown for drugs offences.

The night before the case was due to be heard, Murray and McCluskey went over the charges and quickly picked holes in the prosecution case. 'John and I met up with Ian Stewart the night before. We said to Ian that there were flaws in two of the charges. Our attitude was that if this went to debate it would not show the Crown in a good light and they would take a wee bit of a pasting. We said to Ian we won't make a fuss about it. Why don't we simply plead to possession? He really had no alternative because he knew that if we went to debate, two of the charges would be chucked out. So he said he would accept pleas of not guilty to two of the charges and guilty to possession.'

The next morning, the two Scottish lawyers shook hands with their famous client for the first time as he walked down the steps of his jet onto the runway and into Murray's Jaguar for the short journey into the centre of town. They quickly briefed him on what he could expect and brought him up to speed on the fact that he would only be pleading guilty to one charge of knowingly cultivating five cannabis plants, the other two allegations now languishing in the fiscal's bin.

Neither man cared a monkey's for McCartney's fame; the only thing that mattered to them was a result. Murray said: 'The fact that he was Paul McCartney honestly didn't faze me. I had been round the block and had had my arse kicked up and down the courts of Scotland. I was quite lucky in that I did represent a lot of folk whose names were quite well known. The fact that he was the biggest didn't particularly have any effect. I was there to represent him in court so the lawyer–client relationship was firmly in place right at the start.

'When we picked him up he did not know that two charges would be thrown out. That development came as a wee bit of a surprise to him but I don't think he was taken aback by it. It was really the least of the charges that he pled to. I drove him in to court and throughout it all he acted absolutely properly. He didn't chuck his weight about. We got on very well.'

On the bench that day was Sheriff Donald J. McDiarmid, a no-nonsense lawman who seemed unamused at his court being hijacked by members of the fourth estate, not to mention most of the town's legal fraternity. In truth, the venerable sheriff probably knew little of McCartney, coming from a generation that preceded The Beatles by some 25 years.

Ian Stewart laid bare the bones of the prosecution case and urged his lordship to take into account's McCartney's grand financial standing if he was thinking of imposing a fine. John McCluskey then rose to begin his attempt to mitigate his client's crime, telling the court the former Beatle had had a long-standing interest in all things horticultural. The undertone of that suggestion would, ordinarily, have provoked a nudge, nudge, wink, wink response from those in the courtroom – among them of course Linda – with more than a passing knowledge of McCartney's passion for grass. However, no one was prepared to risk McDiarmid's wrath so all giggles were stifled through pursed lips.

McCluskey went on to say: 'He frequently received gifts of various kinds from fans and among these were some seeds. Those which were planted and grown in the greenhouse were a gift from a fan and received through the post. They were grown absolutely openly in an ordinary greenhouse and could be seen easily from the outside. The point is that there was no attempt to conceal them as there could have been by white-washing the windows or putting in frosted glass.'

The advocate's advocacy appeared to have done the trick. Sheriff McDiarmid, anxious for the circus clowns to vacate his turf, hit McCartney with a £100 fine. In the end, the whole thing was over in just 25 minutes. McCartney, soberly dressed, held his hands up to possession and left the court £100 lighter in pocket. Somewhat cheekily, perhaps, McCluskey and Murray asked if the multi-millionaire Mr McCartney might be given time to pay. Three months, agreed McDiarmid, to sniggers from the public benches.

Right away, McCartney was ushered into a side room where he hugged his wife and gave a brief news conference, his few words of relief having been rehearsed during the plane journey from London. He said: 'I was planning on writing a few songs in jail. It would have been all right as long as I had a guitar.' As for his love of all things hemp: 'You have to be careful, I look on it like prohibition in the old days . . . I think the law should be changed – make it like the law of homosexuality with consenting adults in private. I don't think cannabis is as dangerous as drink,' said Paul, adding quickly that hard drugs was an altogether different matter.

'There was an element of relief on his part, which may be stating the obvious' said Len Murray, who was impressed by McCartney's common sense chutzpah. 'He was content just to sit there and take a slap. He expressed his gratitude and he acted the perfect gentleman throughout, exactly the way you want a client to conduct himself.'

Len Murray never again crossed paths with McCartney in a long and distinguished career that saw him embroiled in some of the most contro-versial cases ever to become before the Scottish Courts. But he did retain one souvenir when the musician autographed three pictures for him, dedicating one each to Len's sons. 'I wasn't a Beatles fan but my sons were 14, 12 and 10 and they were fans so that was a nice touch. At the end of the day we shook hands, he got back on the plane and John McCluskey

Free as a bird. Paul and Linda leave Campbeltown Sheriff Court after being fined £100 for growing cannabis at the farm.

and I headed back to Glasgow. It was a good job and it was done properly with no problems. John and I were quite delighted with the outcome. We got away lightly and it's not every day that you get instructions from a Beatle. I must say that by the time he left I was a fan of his.'

Inevitably, the case attracted massive domestic press coverage, although it was bumped off the front pages of UK newspapers by an IRA bomb blitz at the Old Bailey in London. So news that a pop star, no matter his celebrity status, had been fined £100 for growing cannabis in his own greenhouse on one of the most remote corners of the UK, paled somewhat by comparison.

It merited scant attention on the other side of the Atlantic but the *Glasgow Herald*'s distinguished journalist Murray Ritchie speculated that the ripples from McCartney's conviction would easily spread to America. As a UK national with a criminal conviction against his name, the musician, then 30 years old, could find that Uncle Sam would no longer throw open his arms in welcome to an ex-Beatle – such were the strict guidelines surrounding visa applications. McCartney would not need to look far for proof of such hurdles; John Lennon's 1969 drugs conviction was stamped loud and clear on his passport, ideal grounds to boot him out of the land of the free for good. So while Lennon was fighting to stay in America, Ritchie reasoned that his old bandmate, until now without a blemish on his character, would soon find it equally as tough to even set foot in the States. He backed up his line by quoting John McCluskey's own words to Sheriff McDiarmid. In his article he wrote:

'Paul McCartney, formerly of The Beatles, may be banned from entering the United States, where he has extensive business interests, because of a £100 fine imposed on him yesterday at Campbeltown Sheriff Court.

'Mr John McCluskey, QC, said McCartney, who had no previous convictions, was unlikely to be allowed into the United States because of this conviction.

'"We understand the immigration authorities in the US will refuse admission to a person who has a conviction even though it is of a technical nature." Mr McCluskey said later that the US ban could last for two years, although the authorities had the power to waive it if they felt such action was justified in the light of circumstances in a particular case.

'Mr McCluskey submitted that the offence was technical and much less serious than possessing cannabis. The five plants could have produced an extremely small quantity of cannabis. He said McCartney was very well known and found extreme difficulty in finding privacy. He acquired High Park because of its remoteness. There was no access road. He was a man of considerable means but there was no question involved in this case of a public figure flouting a breach of the law. He was not even at the farm on the date in question. McCartney was a musician, in particular a composer, and had been honoured for this with the MBE.

'Sheriff McDiarmid told McCartney: "I take into account the fact that these seeds were given to you in a gift, but I have also to take into account that you are a public figure of considerable interest, particularly to young people and I must deal with you accordingly."'

On the other side of the newspaper spectrum, the *Daily Record*'s former Chief Reporter Gordon Airs played the court case with a straight bat. He simply reported the outcome of the 25-minute hearing unadorned:

'Millionaire ex-Beatle Paul McCartney, given 14 days by a Sheriff to pay a £100 drugs fine, sighed with relief yesterday.

'Minutes after standing in the dock at Campbeltown Sheriff Court on a charge of growing five cannabis plants in a greenhouse, he said: "I was worried. I was expecting to write my next songs in jail."

'Earlier, Paul had admitted cultivating the five cannabis plants in a greenhouse on one of his farms – High Park near Campbeltown.

'As he walked from the dock after being fined, his wife Linda, sitting in the tiny packed court, clapped her hands. Paul and Linda, wearing a black bowler hat, had just flown from London to the quiet fishing town in a specially-chartered jet. And after the 25-minute court case, they pushed their way through the fans to be driven back to the airport.

'Fiscal Ian Stewart told the court that Paul himself had created the greenhouse last May. In June he bought some pots and later the five plants were potted. Last September a crime prevention police officer spotted the plants during a routine check at the farm in Paul's absence and confirmed they were cannabis.

'Mr John McCluskey, QC for Paul, said: "My client has no option but to plead guilty. He frequently gets gifts from many fans and the seeds which were planted were a gift through the post."

'Sheriff Donald McDiarmid fined Paul £100 and, amid laughter, he granted Mr McCluskey's request for 14 days to pay.'

Whether in fact McCartney's first UK criminal conviction did hamper his movements abroad is unknown. He spent the next few weeks away from Campbeltown working in London on a TV special, recording tracks for Wings' third studio album, *Red Rose Speedway*, and also working on a track for Ringo Starr's classic and eponymous album, which also included major songwriting and musical contributions from John and George.

It is quite possible that during this time, diplomatic strings were being pulled behind the scenes to allow Wings and McCartney to fly off anywhere they wanted without the prospect of immigration officials ordering them onto the first plane back. After all, McCartney was a superb social networker, and his celebrity allowed him access to the corridors of power.

So it was that Campbeltown Sheriff Court and the prospect – however remote – of being banged up in Oban jail faded into the memory like Brigadoon when, just over a month later, the McCartneys jetted out from Heathrow to the Caribbean for three days. No questions were asked on their arrival. It was as if it had never happened.

•   •   •

Despite a bumpy take off, Wings, like the jet that left Machrahanish that March morning, were eventually taking flight. By the mid seventies, McCartney's ad-hoc garage band had emerged from the shadows of The Beatles to become one of the biggest groups in the world. While never eclipsing his previous achievements – how could he? – he was back on top. Albums like *Band on the Run, Venus and Mars* and *Wings at the Speed of Sound* had re-established his rock star credentials. Many of the songs from these albums first saw the light at High Park where Paul had the space and peace to shape the songs from rough-edged recordings at his home-made studio at the farm.

The wounds from The Beatles split were also beginning to heal. With his career restored, sightings of the McCartneys in and around

Mother nature's son. Paul, Linda and Martha, his beloved Old English Sheepdog, gaze out over the hills around the time The Beatles called it a day.

Campbeltown became less frequent. Loyalty, though, is one of McCartney's strongest suits. He has always been grateful for the fact that, by and large, the local community rarely gave their celebrity guest a second glance. Payback often came in the form of private donations to public causes in the Campbeltown community. And he continued to spend several weeks in summer at High Farm, becoming a familiar face at the town's local agricultural show for several years. An inveterate doodler – just like John Lennon – Paul frequently sent his former bandmates postcards depicting Campbeltown high street. But no one in the town could ever have imagined that McCartney's gratitude would ultimately bestow on them a gift of such major proportions.

The story of 'Mull of Kintyre' has been documented in the previous chapter from the point of view of the Campbeltown Pipe Band. McCartney's idea was to write an anthemic Scottish song in a modern context. He declared: 'It occurred to me that no great Scottish songs had been written for quite a while. I looked into it: all the bagpipe stuff was

Lovely Linda. Locals in Campbeltown were delighted when Paul commissioned this statue of his wife.

from the previous century and some of the popular folk songs were really old and, I noticed, written by Englishmen. I wondered if I could write one, too. I certainly loved Scotland enough. So, I came up with a song about where we were living, an area called Mull of Kintyre. It was a love song, really, about how I enjoy being there and imagining I was travelling away and wanting to get back to it.'

•   •   •

'Mull of Kintyre' proved to be the apex of McCartney's Celtic connection with Scotland, in a musical sense at least. Of course, he still laid down rough tracks at Rude Studios, mostly for his own amusement. Some of them eventually flowered into full-blown album tracks. Throughout much of the eighties, however, inconsistency dogged his musical output. It was only when he hooked up with fellow Liverpudlian Elvis Costello that the first green shoots of recovery were planted. The subsequent fruit of their collaboration provided the backbone to *Flowers in the Dirt*, his first album of the nineties and the first one recorded with a new band that also included Scottish musician Hamish Stuart.

In the months and years that followed, the family continued to commute to their Scottish bolthole, but the visits became more low-key and less frequent. Instead, most of their time was spent at their sprawling farmhouse in Sussex. Then, in 1993, McCartney's life suffered a jolt that was like an arrow through his heart. Linda had discovered a lump in her breast. Months of treatment followed and, at first, hopes were high that the cancer had been caught in time. A provisional all-clear turned into a false dawn. Tragically, Linda McCartney succumbed to that most ravaging of diseases on Friday, 17 April 1998, on the family ranch in Arizona surrounded by the great outdoors that was so redolent of Argyll. She was just 57.

As I reported on the front-page splash of the *Daily Record*, she died in Paul's arms, the man who had been her lover and best friend for 30 years. For the people of Campbeltown, the sense of loss ran deep. They mourned the passing of a community anchor, someone who had been a global champion for their little corner of the planet and a selfless and silent benefactor to a host of local good causes. In fact, she came to symbolise the family's Campbeltown connections more than Paul.

'There was a stunned shock,' said local vet Alastair Cousin, a frequent visitor to High Park to check on the McCartney's livestock. 'She was someone warmly associated with the community. She was a real outdoors person. She loved it here and it was here, of course, that she and the family converted to vegetarianism which was a cause célèbre with her. They had these lambs on the farm and they decided they could never contemplate eating them so that's how they reached their decision.'

McCartney knew that a little bit of his beloved wife would always rest in Scotland. So he delighted the local community by commissioning his cousin Kate Robbins to create a bronze statue of Linda that would be the centrepiece of a memorial garden. It was unveiled on 1 November, 2002, in the teeth of a howling gale and driving rain, watched by the couple's daughters Mary and Stella. Paul's absence – he was working in America at the time – invited adverse comment from cynical newspaper leader writers but did not detract from the heartfelt sentiment of the occasion. The local community preferred to think he would visit at a time of his own choosing, long after the media ghouls had left town. Instead, it was left to Stella and Mary to convey the family's thanks. In a statement they said: 'Scotland was one of mum's favourite places and it is wonderful to have a permanent statue to remind us of the great times we spent with her there. We would like to say thanks to the people of Campbeltown for honouring her in this way.'

Paul did eventually make his own personal pilgrimage back to the place his beloved wife had so taken to her heart. But a light had gone out and visits north became infrequent. Paul had married charity activist Heather Mills in 2002 and, not unnaturally, she felt uncomfortable in the homespun charm of the remote farm that still contained traces of another Mrs McCartney.

These days, the Mull of Kintyre has slipped back into geographical obscurity, although the local tourist board still tries to eke out its Beatle connection. Travel writers rarely miss a mention of the lilting tune and pockets of dedicated fans still follow the long and winding road that eventually takes you to Campbeltown. The initial interest may have long since subsided, but Alastair Cousin, who has known McCartney since his first visits with Linda in 1968, for one is convinced the haunting lament has been a huge boon to the area. 'They gave the area a sense of identity. We are a peninsula which is a bit off the beaten track. A lot of people even in this country had never heard of Kintyre or Campbeltown before Paul McCartney's involvement . . . I think we have as much to thank him for as he has to thank us.'

Today, High Park and several of its neighbouring farms, quietly purchased over time to increase the family's privacy, is run by its caretaker manager. Its owner now may be more of an absentee English landlord whose memory, according to the title of his last album, is almost full. But should the passage of time ever mist over that memory, all he has to do is get out his guitar, close his eyes and gently sing the words to a song that will instantly summon up images of 'the life and the times of the Mull of Kintyre' . . . no matter where he may be in the world.

Afterword

In cyberspace, no one can hear you scream. Which is just as well for John Lennon, Paul McCartney, George Harrison and Ringo Starr. Because at least on the world wide web, The Beatles are sheltered from the pandemonium that greeted every note, every guitar chord, every shake of the head and every song.

Type the words 'The Beatles' into Google and you discover there are more than 30,600,000 hits on the information superhighway. Elvis is languishing some six million entries behind The Fabs. And the Stones barely register half that astonishing total. Proof that even in today's internet-dominated age The Beatles still reign supreme. A band that, in name at least, is almost 50 years old . . . and yet forever young.

Echoes from the songs The Beatles wrote continue to trickle down through the generations. Of course, two of them are gone, part of a celestial super group. I'll never forget the day John died. I was 18 and working as a rookie reporter on a local newspaper in Livingston, West Lothian. I arrived at the office with the tears forming tramlines down my cheeks. It was a terrible, terrible day. When George died in 2001, I had already written his obituary for the Glasgow *Evening Times*. To those of us on the inside track of fandom who knew how ill he was, his death, though still awful, was not a surprise. But the tears, unashamedly, flowed again.

In 1979, I joined hundred of others outside the Glasgow Apollo clutching a flask and a sleeping bag to queue up for tickets to see Paul and Wings. I was 17 and fourth in the queue. My parents, John and Moira, knew how much it meant for me to see a real Beatle in the flesh. They were so cool about it.

This book has been a hugely enjoyable labour of love. How could it not be? Neville Moir, at Polygon, joked that I may end up hating the band when the final full stop had been applied to this project. An old hand at the publishing game, he knew the kind of stringent checks that would inevitably be required on a book of this nature, where the devil really is in the detail. In that respect, editor Seán Costello has done a hell of a job. His meticulous attention to detail has been awesome.

Just over 30 years since I bought my first Beatles album, my love affair with the Fab Four remains as strong as ever. Mad really. But, as Paul McCartney's cosmic sign-off on Abbey Road says, the love you take really is equal to the love you make. And that really is The End.

We love you, yeah, yeah, yeah. One fan in full voice at the Glasgow Odeon, 1964.

Photographs

The publishers acknowledge the following sources for granting permission for their copyright illustrations to be reproduced in this book.

Kenny Anderson 143; Associated Newspapers 121, 122; Pattie Boyd 211; George Burton 270; Campbeltown Courier 295; Frank Creighton 116; Fionna Duncan 257; Sam Emerson 220–221, 224–225; Johnny Gentle & Gavin Askew 35, 49; Getty Images, 207; Catherine Hamilton 23; Keystone Press 264; Stuart Lindsay 29; Jimmy McGeachy 298; Ken McNab 3, 7, 12; Mike Merritt 291; Tom Murray 201, 202; Newsquest 129, 135, 138, 153, 184, 209, 231, 240, 245. 258, 259, 263, 268, 284, 304, 313; May Pang 166; Reuters 190; John Ruggeri 69; Scottish Daily Record & Sunday Mail 4, 93, 94, 103, 105, 118, 146, 162–163, 172, 194, 208, 214, 228, 278, 283, 292, 308, 316, 319, 320; Scottish Television 78; Scotsman Publications 110, 113, 114,132, 232; Liz Short 148; Struan Stevenson 156; Al Stewart 287; Sir Jackie Stewart 275; Malcolm Strachan 159; The private collection of Pauline Sutcliffe, copyright © Astrid Kircherr; 50, 60–61; The Stuart Sutcliffe Estate 65; DC Thomson 96–97, 99; 100, 101; University of Dundee 171; Fraser Watson 252, 255; Wee County News 31, 77, 136; Andy White 237; Derek Yeaman 16, 20 Paul Young 81, 82–83, 84, 86–87, 174–175

Index